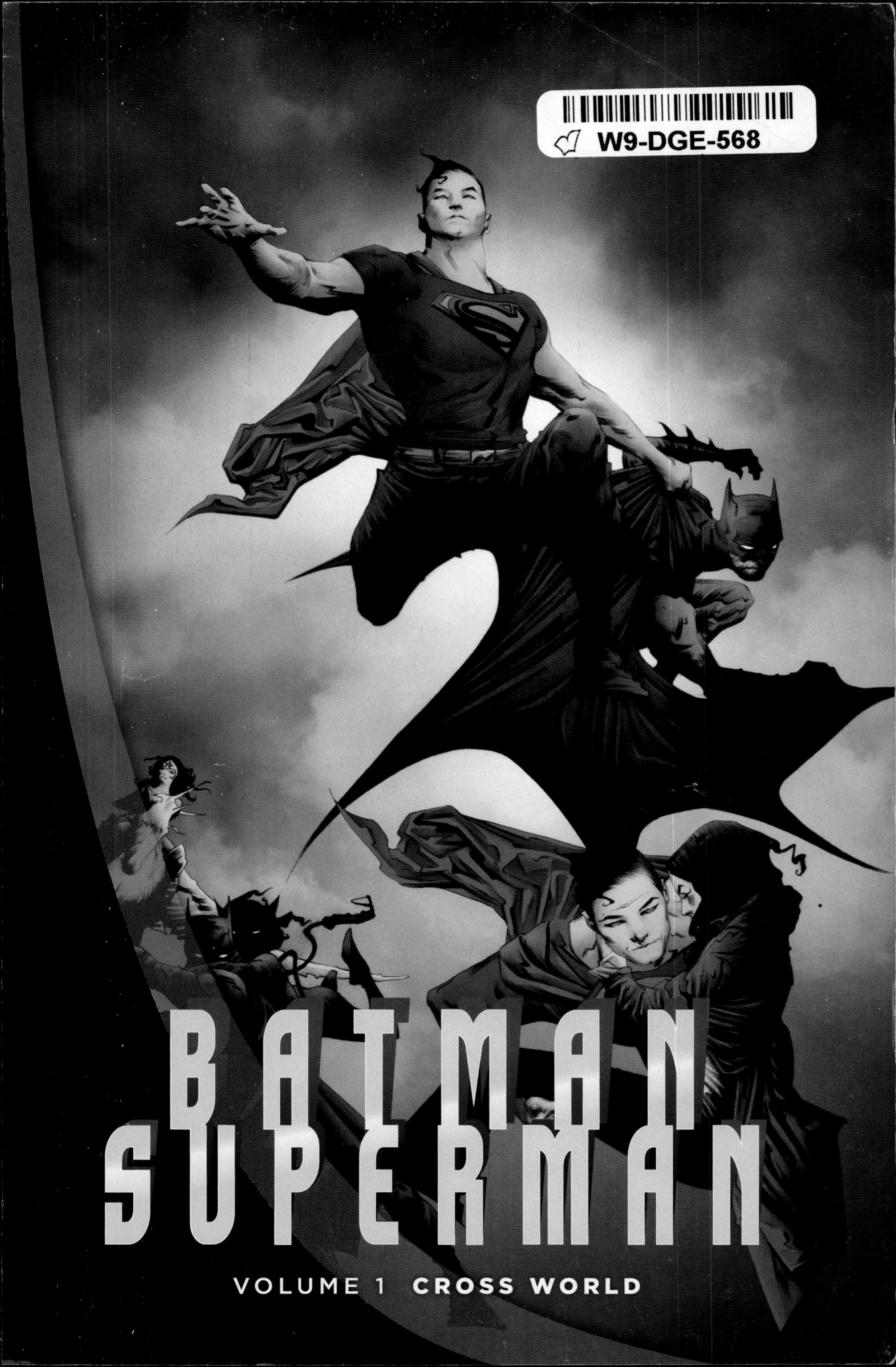

BATMAN SUPERMAN

VOLUME 1 **CROSS WORLD**

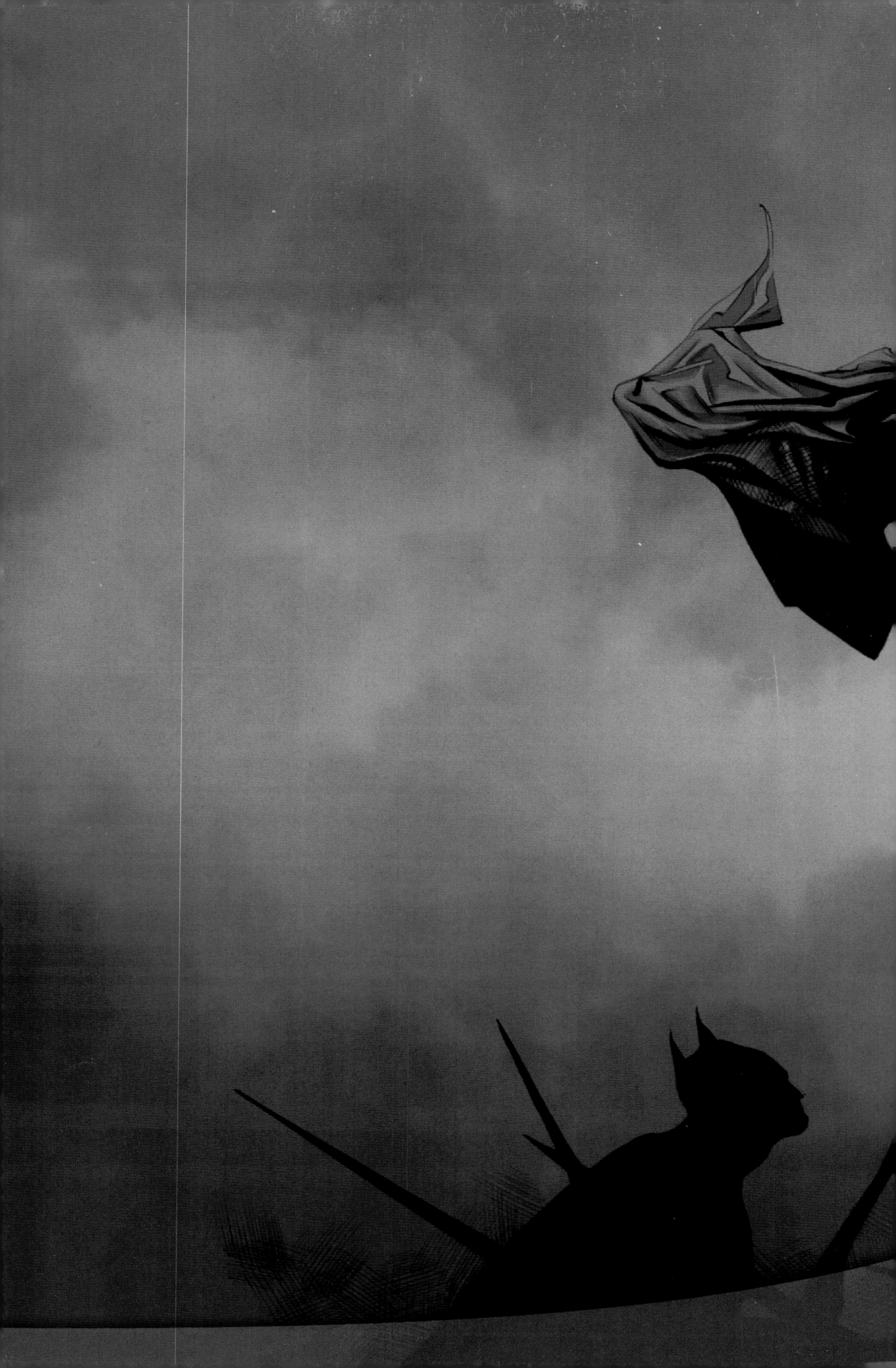

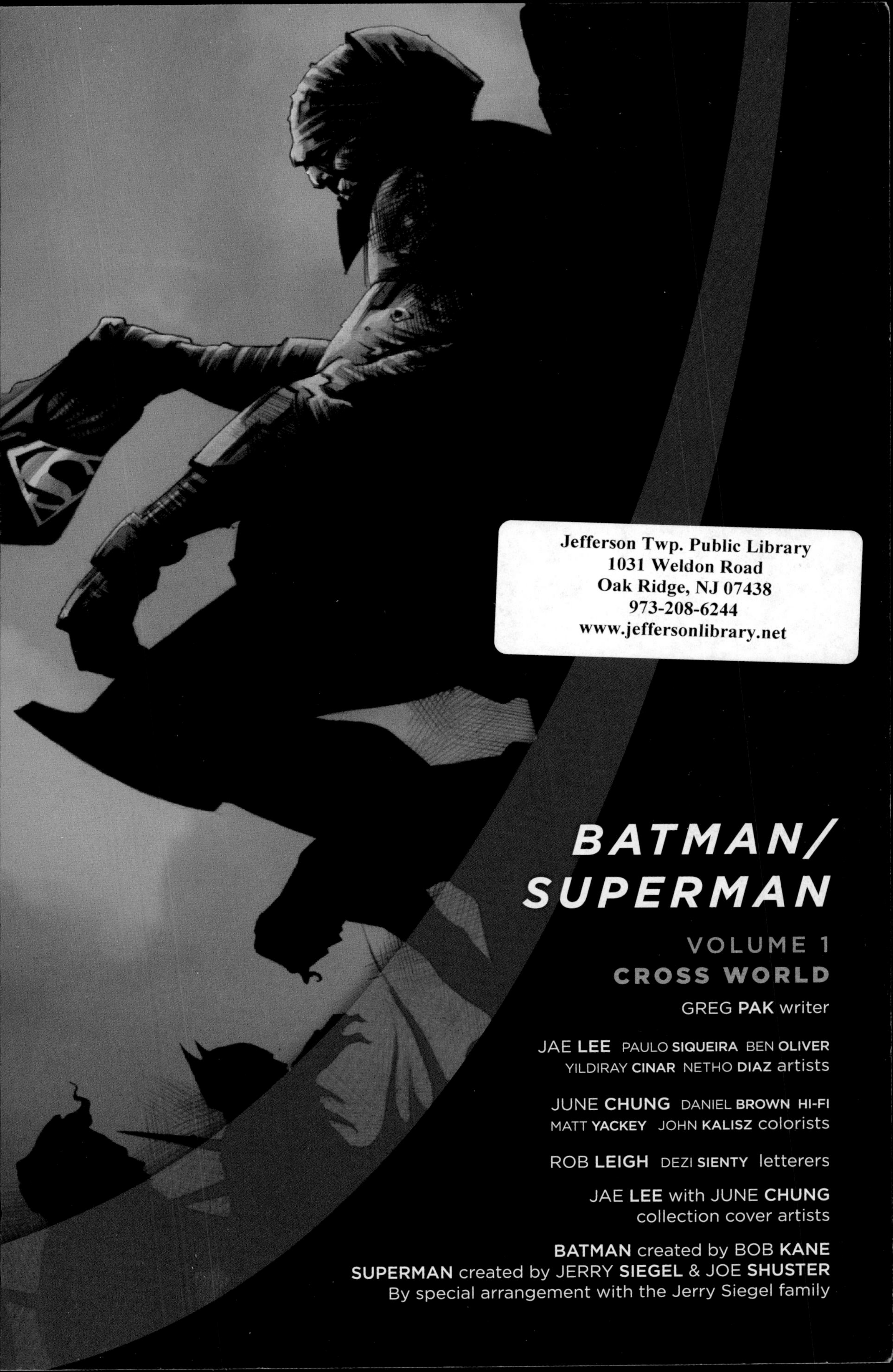

BATMAN/ SUPERMAN

VOLUME 1
CROSS WORLD

GREG **PAK** writer

JAE **LEE** PAULO **SIQUEIRA** BEN **OLIVER** YILDIRAY **CINAR** NETHO **DIAZ** artists

JUNE **CHUNG** DANIEL **BROWN** **HI-FI** MATT **YACKEY** JOHN **KALISZ** colorists

ROB **LEIGH** DEZI **SIENTY** letterers

JAE **LEE** with JUNE **CHUNG** collection cover artists

BATMAN created by BOB **KANE**
SUPERMAN created by JERRY **SIEGEL** & JOE **SHUSTER**
By special arrangement with the Jerry Siegel family

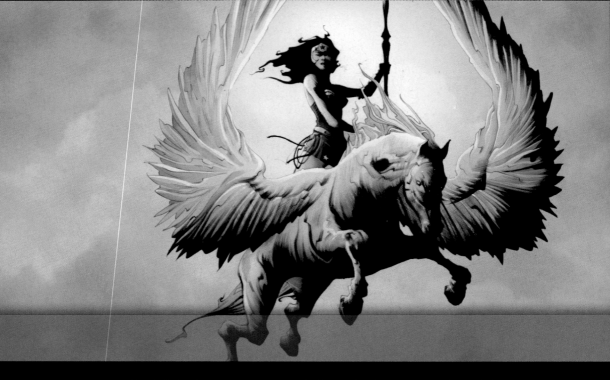

EDDIE BERGANZA Editor – Original Series RICKEY PURDIN Associate Editor – Original Series
ANTHONY MARQUES Assistant Editor – Original Series ROBIN WILDMAN Editor ROBBIN BROSTERMAN Design Director – Books
ROBBIE BIEDERMAN Publication Design

BOB HARAS Senior VP – Editor-in-Chief, DC Comics

DIANE NELSON President DAN DIDIO and JIM LEE Co-Publishers GEOFF JOHNS Chief Creative Officer
AMIT DESAI Senior VP – Marketing and Franchise Management
AMY GENKINS Senior VP – Business and Legal Affairs NAIRI GARDINER Senior VP – Finance
JEFF BOISON VP – Publishing Planning MARK CHIARELLO VP – Art Direction and Design
JOHN CUNNINGHAM VP – Marketing TERRI CUNNINGHAM VP – Editorial Administration
LARRY GANEM VP – Talent Relations and Services ALISON GILL Senior VP – Manufacturing and Operations
HANK KANALZ Senior VP – Vertigo and Integrated Publishing JAY KOGAN VP – Business and Legal Affairs, Publishing
JACK MAHAN VP – Business Affairs, Talent NICK NAPOLITANO VP – Manufacturing Administration SUE POHJA VP – Book Sales
FRED RUIZ VP – Manufacturing Operations COURTNEY SIMMONS Senior VP – Publicity BOB WAYNE Senior VP – Sales

BATMAN/SUPERMAN VOLUME 1: CROSS WORLD

DC Comics, 1700 Broadway, New York, NY 10019
A Warner Bros. Entertainment Company.
Printed by RR Donnelley, Salem, VA, USA. 10/10/14. First Printing..
ISBN: 978-1-4012-4934-2

Library of Congress Cataloging-in-Publication Data

Pak, Greg, author.
Batman/Superman. Volume 1, Cross World / Greg Pak ; illustrated by Jae Lee.
pages cm. — (The New 52!)
Batman created by Bob Kane.
Superman created by Jerry Siegel and Joe Shuster.
ISBN 978-1-4012-4934-2
1. Graphic novels. I. Lee, Jae, 1972- illustrator. II. Title. III. Title: Cross World.
PN6728.B36P34 2014
741.5'973—dc23
2014000327

SUSTAINABLE FORESTRY INITIATIVE
Certified Chain of Custody
20% Certified Forest Content,
80% Certified Sourcing
www.sfiprogram.org
SFI-01042

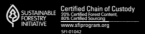

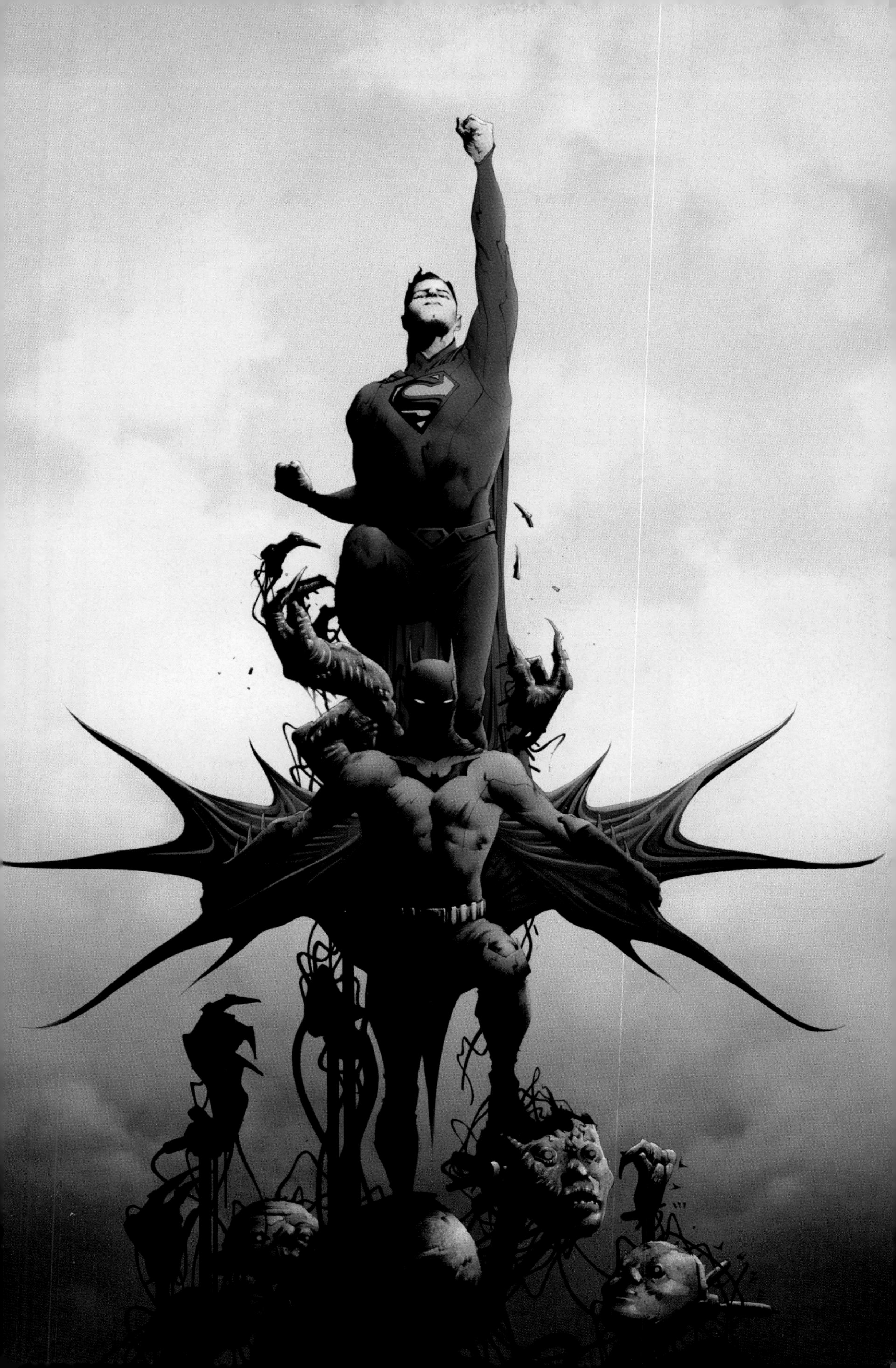

GREG PAK writer **JAE LEE BEN OLIVER** artists **JUNE CHUNG DANIEL BROWN** colorists cover by **JAE LEE** with **JUNE CHUNG**

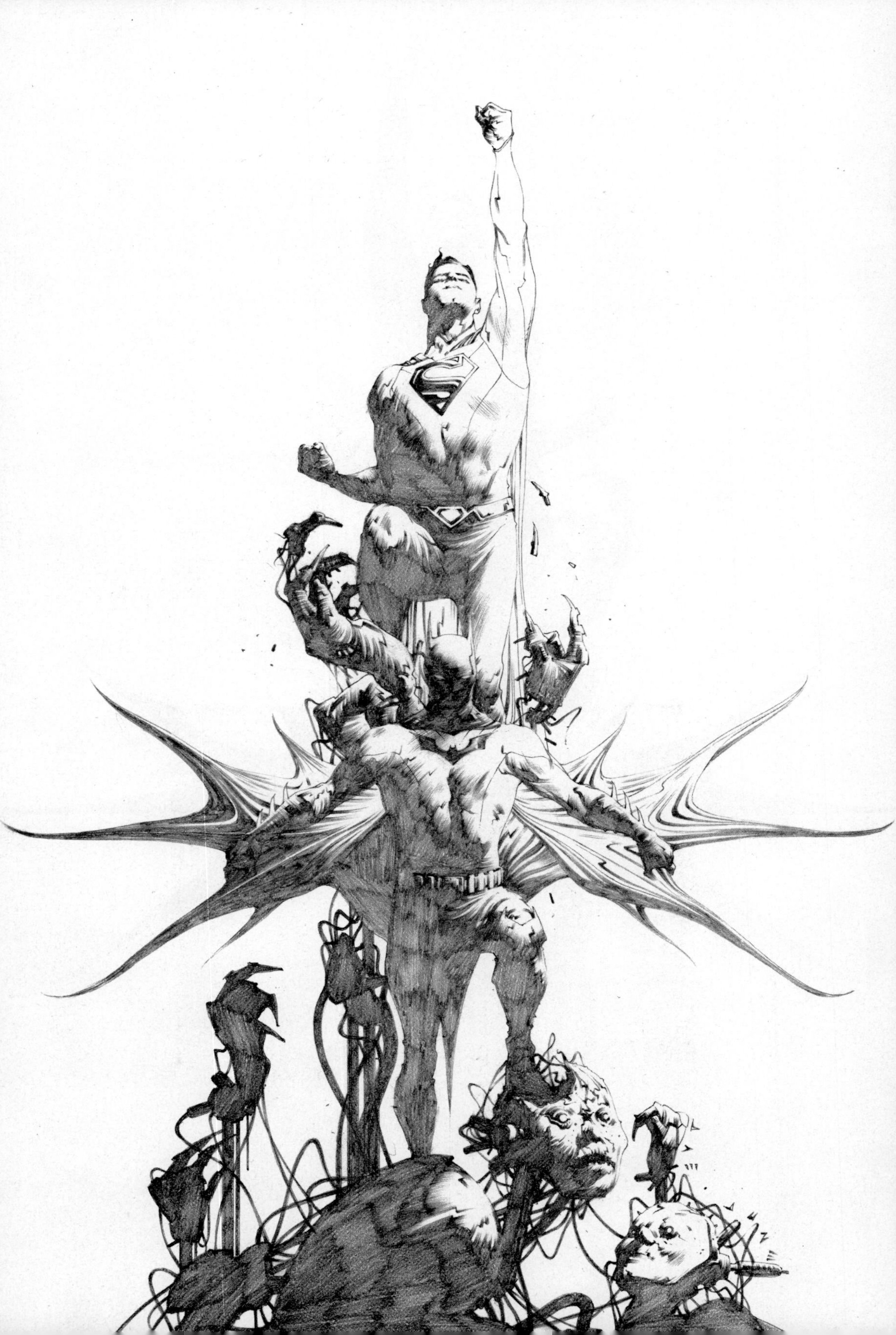

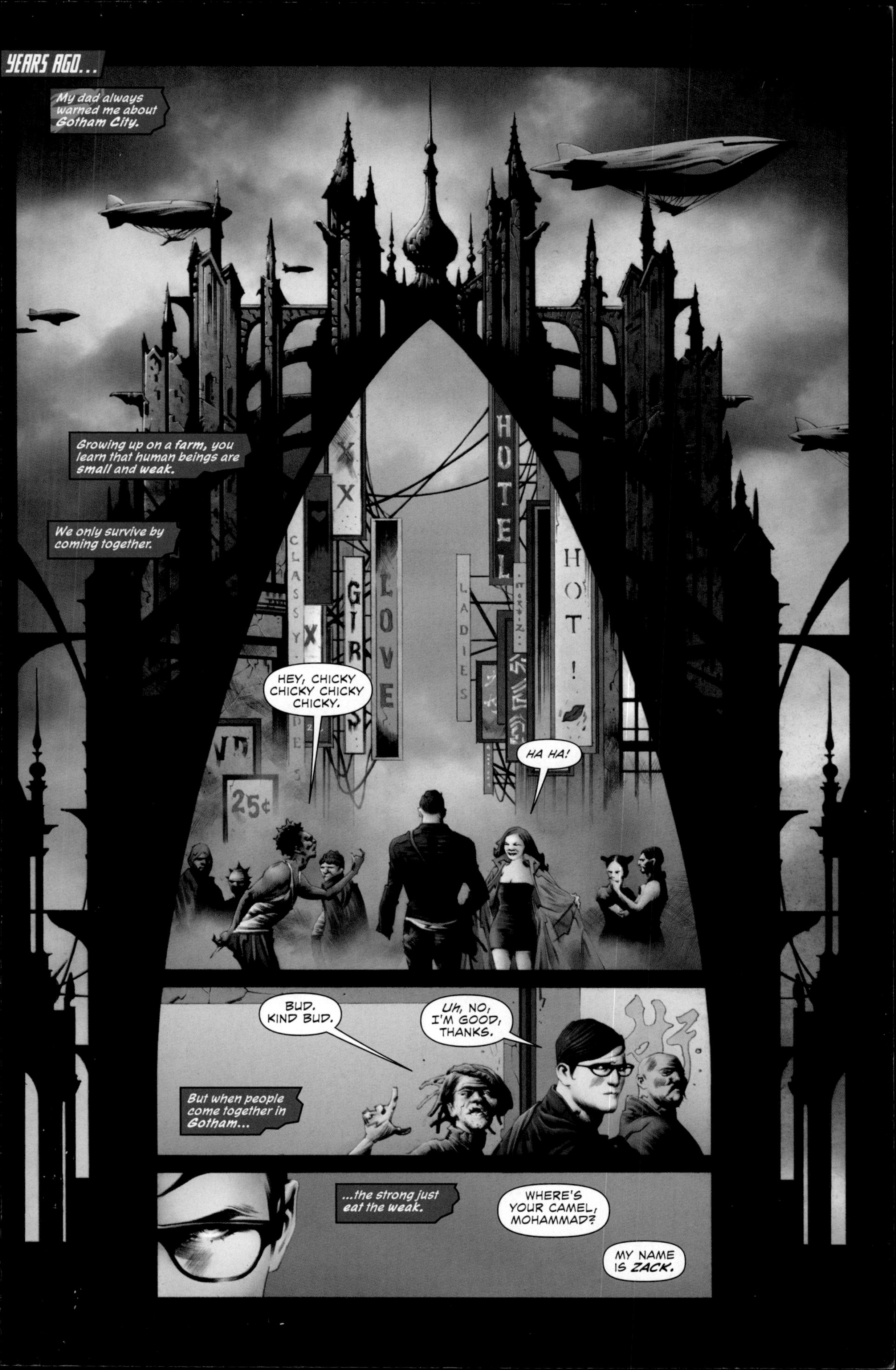
YEARS AGO...
My dad always warned me about Gotham City.
Growing up on a farm, you learn that human beings are small and weak.
We only survive by coming together.
HOTEL
LOVE
HOT!
LADIES
CLASSY
25¢
HEY, CHICKY CHICKY CHICKY CHICKY.
HA HA!
BUD. KIND BUD.
UH, NO, I'M GOOD, THANKS.
But when people come together in Gotham...
...the strong just eat the weak.
WHERE'S YOUR CAMEL, MOHAMMAD?
MY NAME IS ZACK.

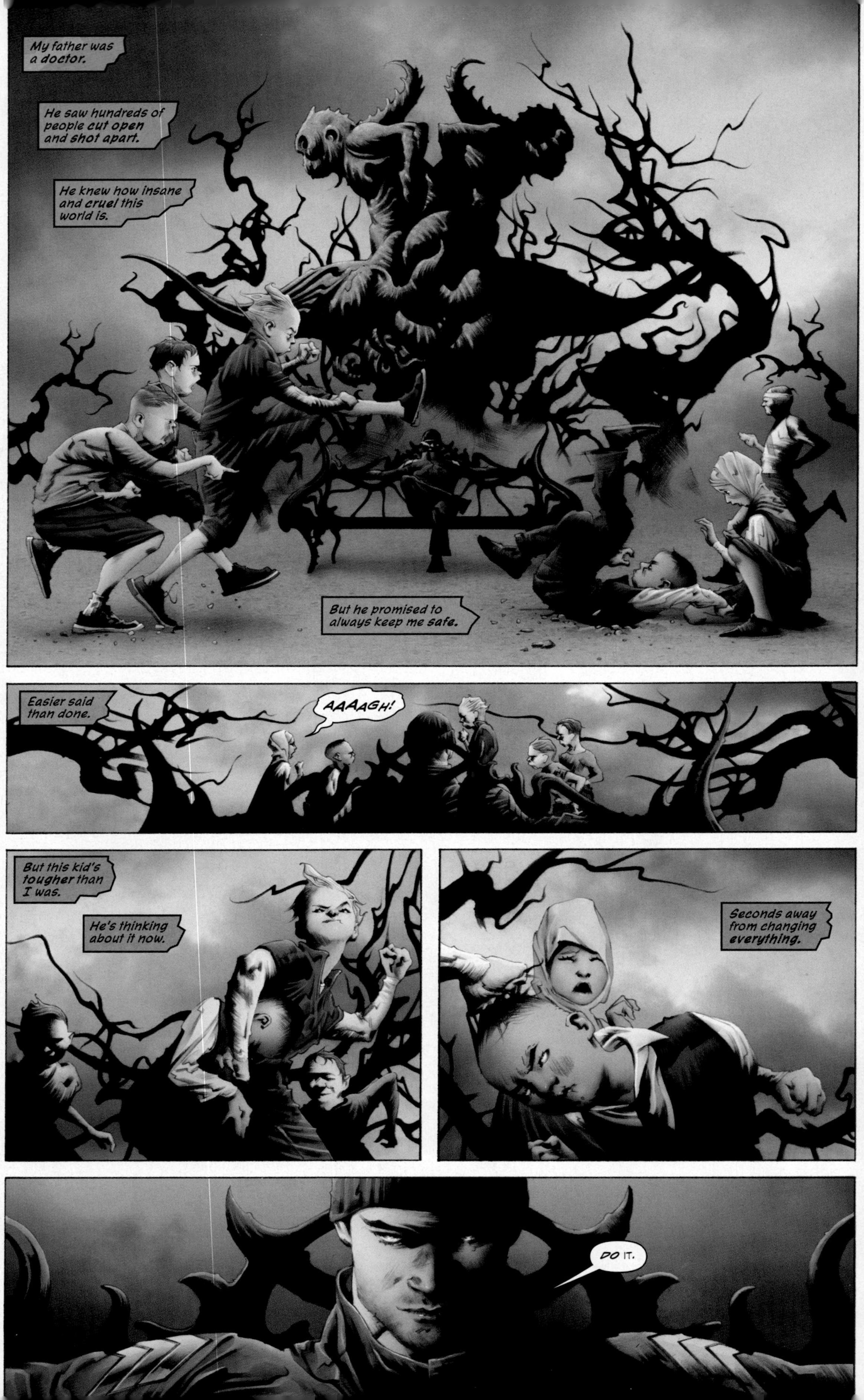
My father was a doctor.
He saw hundreds of people cut open and shot apart.
He knew how insane and cruel this world is.
But he promised to always keep me safe.
Easier said than done.
AAAAGH!
But this kid's tougher than I was.
He's thinking about it now.
Seconds away from changing everything.
DO IT.

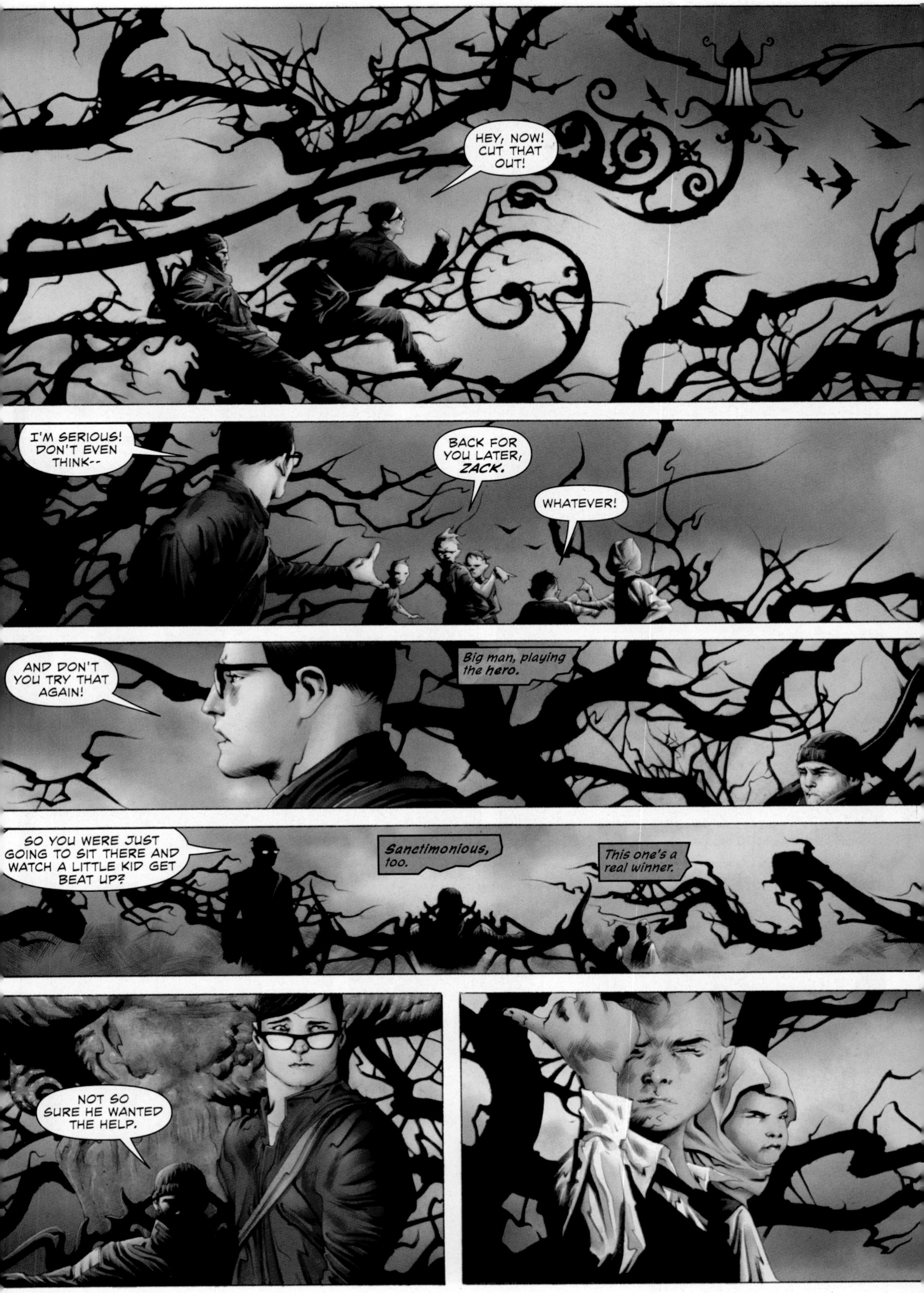
HEY, NOW! CUT THAT OUT!
I'M SERIOUS! DON'T EVEN THINK--
BACK FOR YOU LATER, ZACK.
WHATEVER!
AND DON'T YOU TRY THAT AGAIN!
Big man, playing the hero.
SO YOU WERE JUST GOING TO SIT THERE AND WATCH A LITTLE KID GET BEAT UP?
Sanctimonious, too.
This one's a real winner.
NOT SO SURE HE WANTED THE HELP.

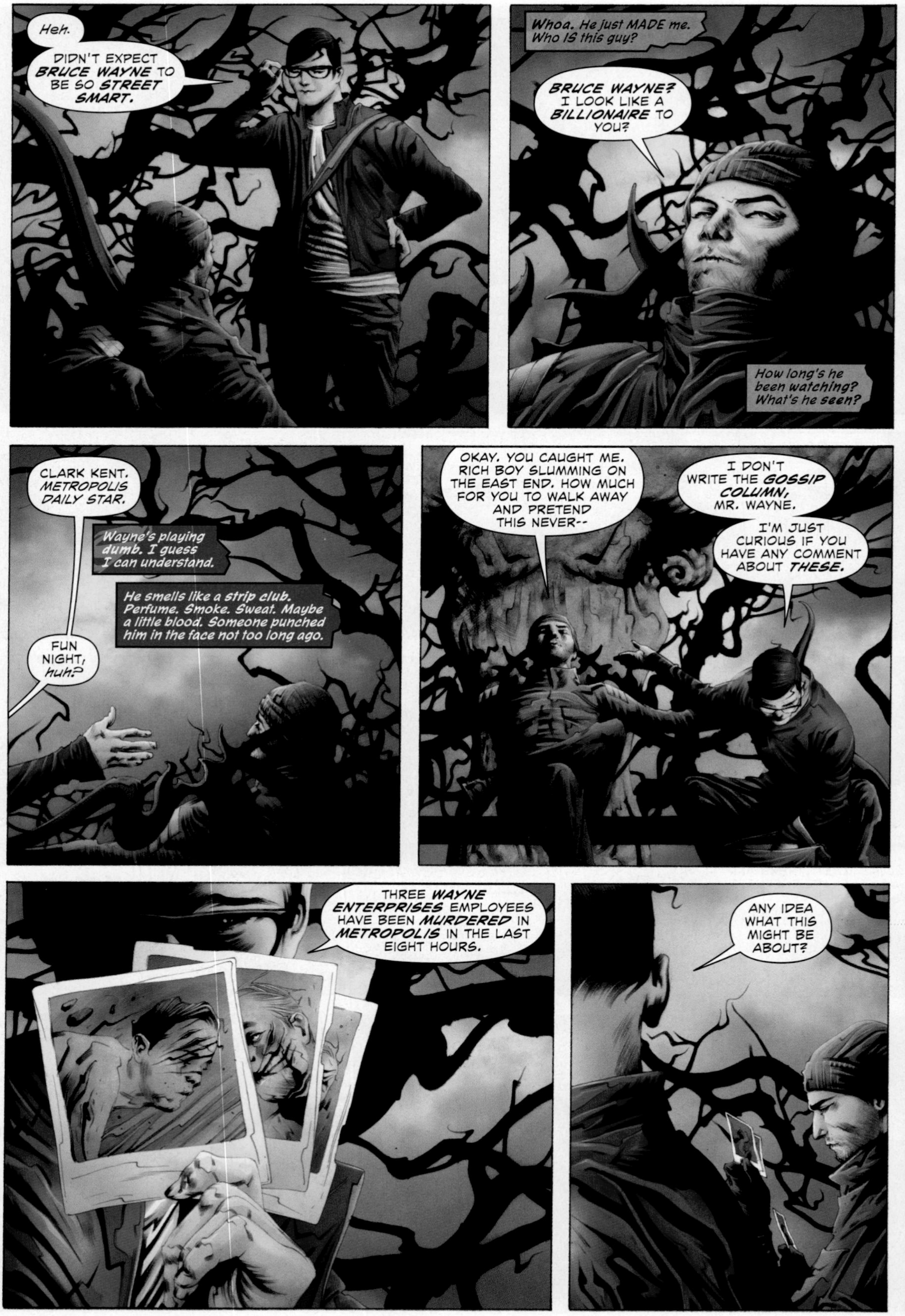
Heh.
DIDN'T EXPECT BRUCE WAYNE TO BE SO STREET SMART.
Whoa. He just MADE me. Who IS this guy?
BRUCE WAYNE? I LOOK LIKE A BILLIONAIRE TO YOU?
How long's he been watching? What's he seen?
CLARK KENT. METROPOLIS DAILY STAR.
Wayne's playing dumb. I guess I can understand.
He smells like a strip club. Perfume. Smoke. Sweat. Maybe a little blood. Someone punched him in the face not too long ago.
FUN NIGHT, huh?
OKAY. YOU CAUGHT ME. RICH BOY SLUMMING ON THE EAST END. HOW MUCH FOR YOU TO WALK AWAY AND PRETEND THIS NEVER--
I DON'T WRITE THE GOSSIP COLUMN, MR. WAYNE.
I'M JUST CURIOUS IF YOU HAVE ANY COMMENT ABOUT THESE.
THREE WAYNE ENTERPRISES EMPLOYEES HAVE BEEN MURDERED IN METROPOLIS IN THE LAST EIGHT HOURS.
ANY IDEA WHAT THIS MIGHT BE ABOUT?

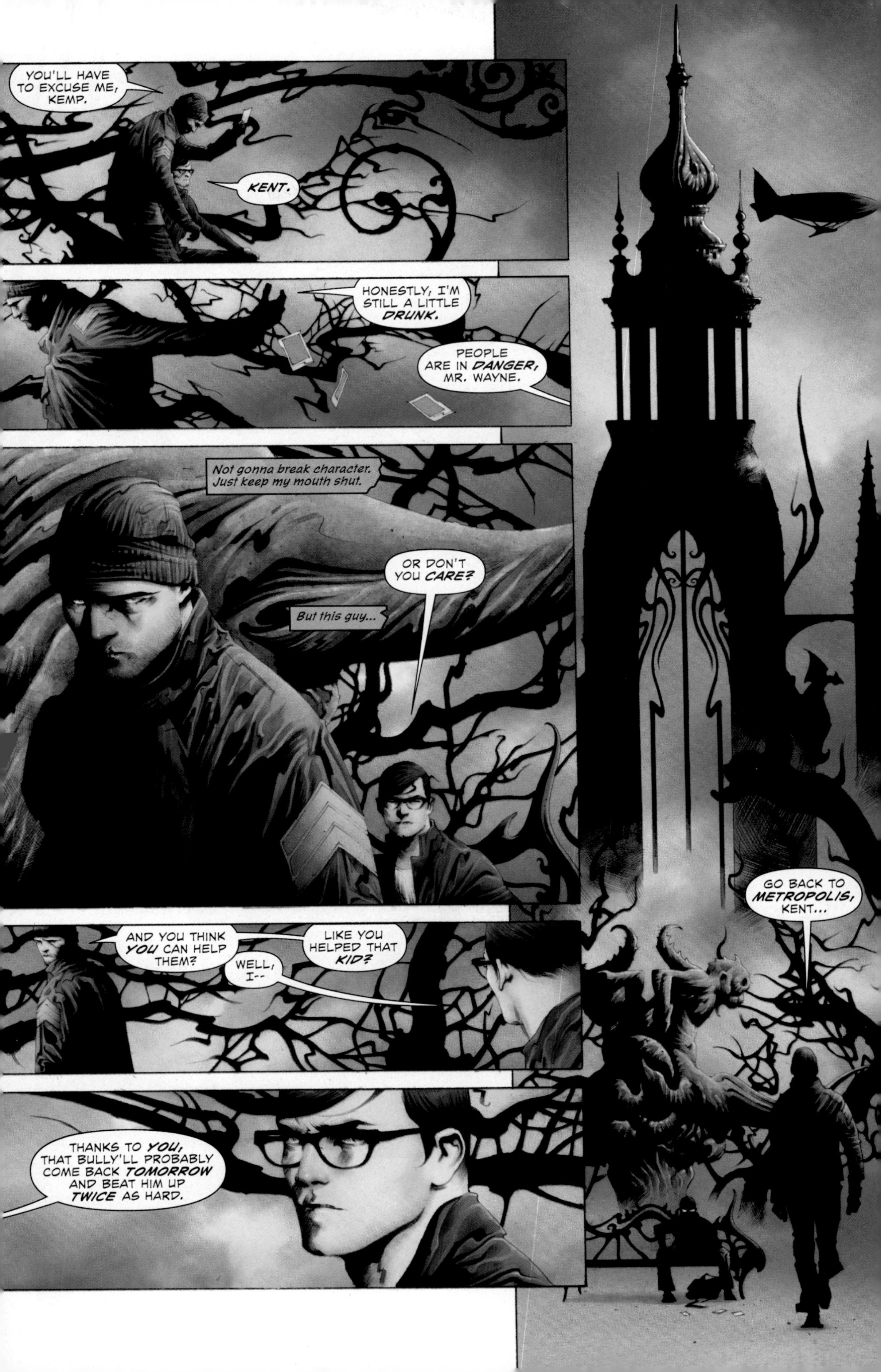

YOU'LL HAVE TO EXCUSE ME, KEMP.
KENT.
HONESTLY, I'M STILL A LITTLE DRUNK.
PEOPLE ARE IN DANGER, MR. WAYNE.
Not gonna break character. Just keep my mouth shut.
OR DON'T YOU CARE?
But this guy...
AND YOU THINK YOU CAN HELP THEM?
LIKE YOU HELPED THAT KID?
WELL, I--
THANKS TO YOU, THAT BULLY'LL PROBABLY COME BACK TOMORROW AND BEAT HIM UP TWICE AS HARD.
GO BACK TO METROPOLIS, KENT...

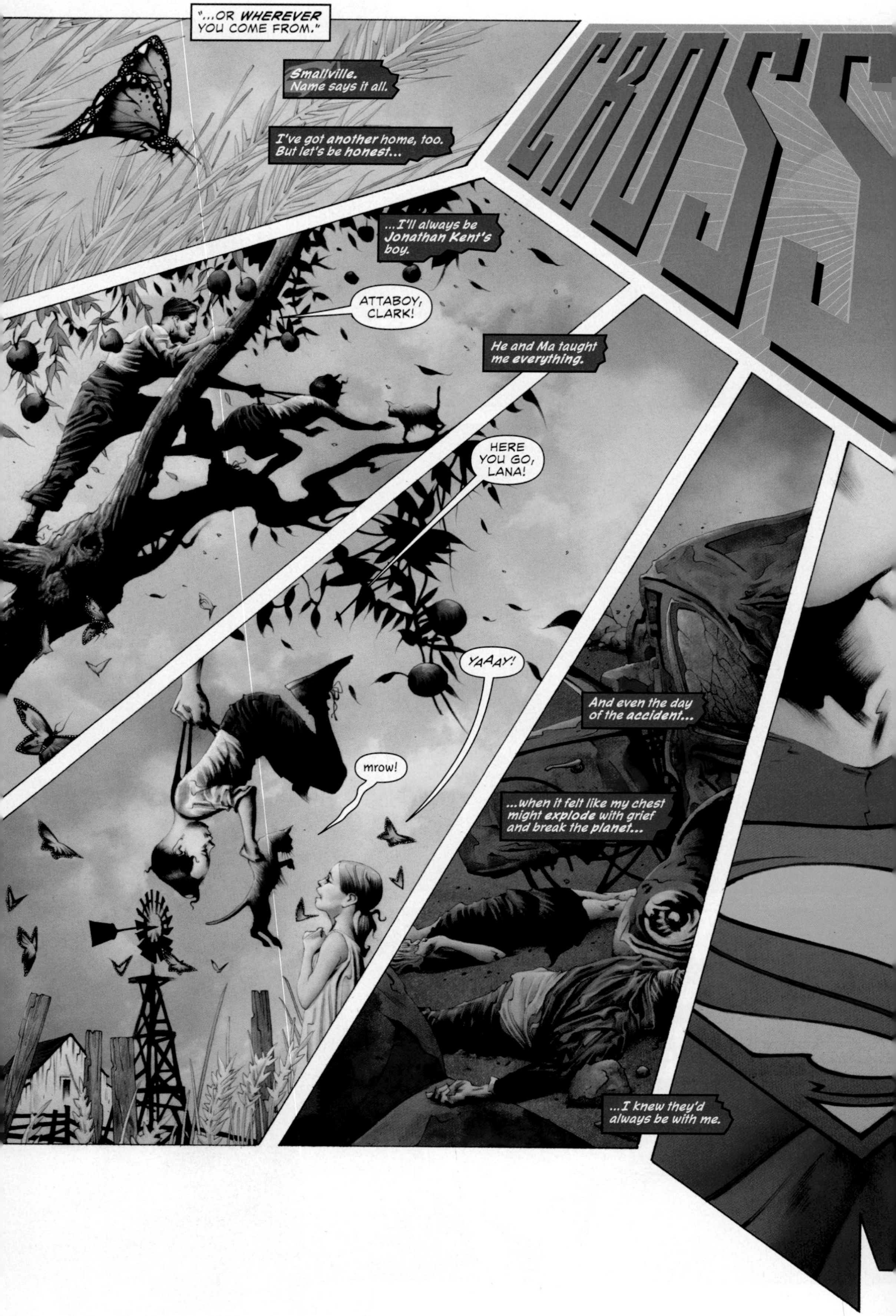
"...OR WHEREVER YOU COME FROM."
Smallville. Name says it all.
I've got another home, too. But let's be honest...
CROSS
...I'll always be Jonathan Kent's boy.
ATTABOY, CLARK!
He and Ma taught me everything.
HERE YOU GO, LANA!
YAAAY!
mrow!
And even the day of the accident...
...when it felt like my chest might explode with grief and break the planet...
...I knew they'd always be with me.

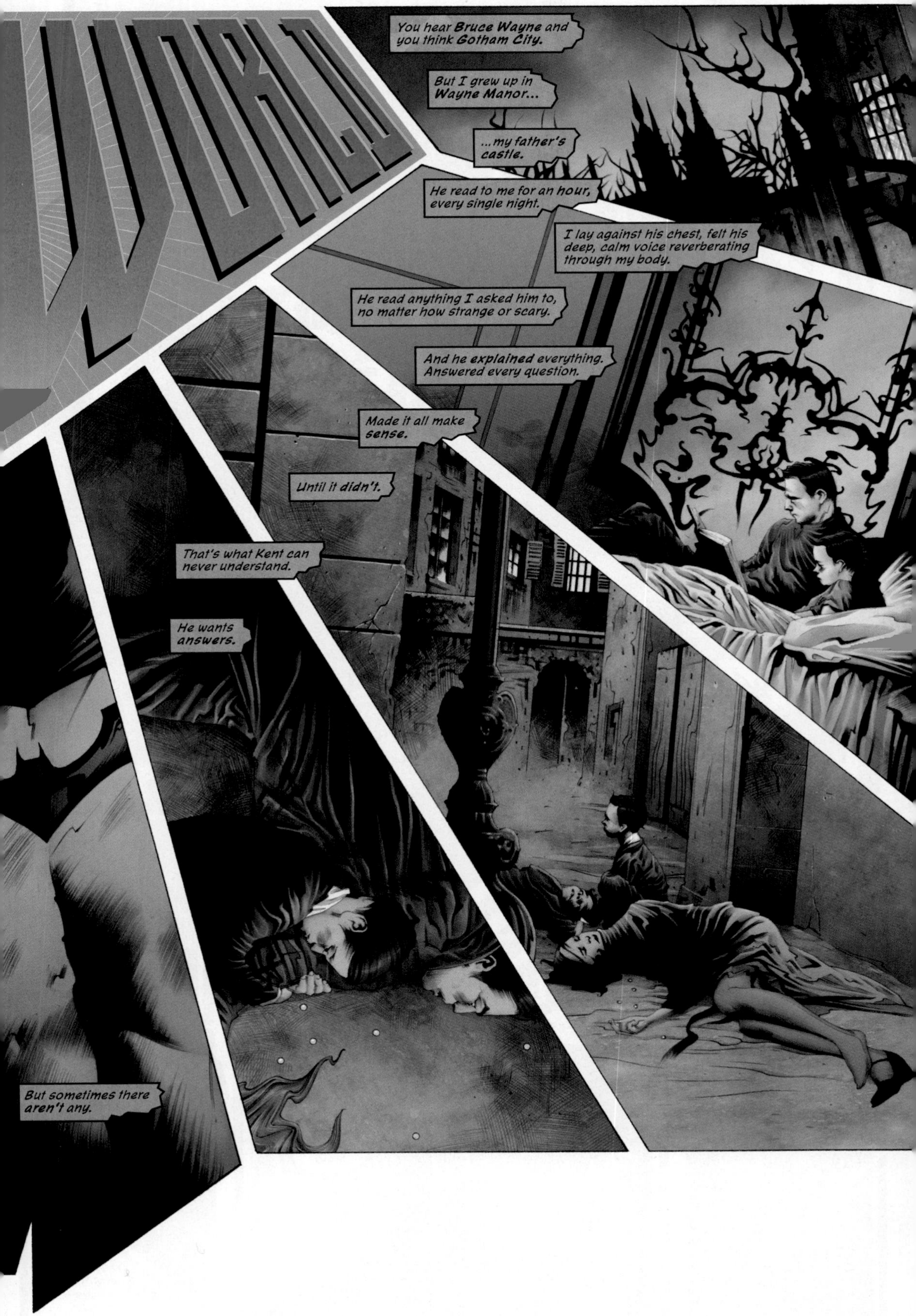
You hear Bruce Wayne and you think Gotham City.
But I grew up in Wayne Manor...
...my father's castle.
He read to me for an hour, every single night.
I lay against his chest, felt his deep, calm voice reverberating through my body.
He read anything I asked him to, no matter how strange or scary.
And he explained everything. Answered every question.
Made it all make sense.
Until it didn't.
That's what Kent can never understand.
He wants answers.
But sometimes there aren't any.

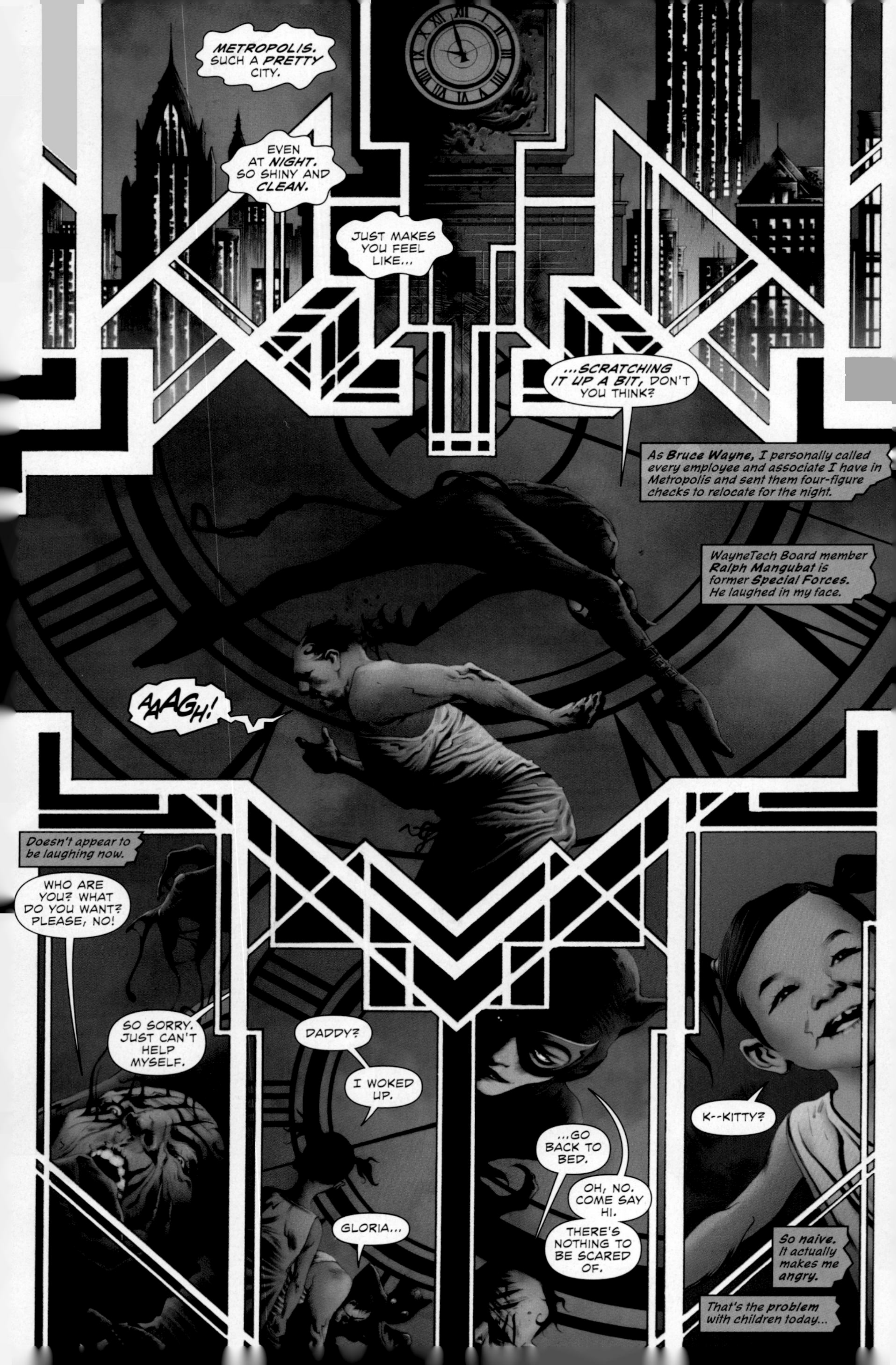
METROPOLIS. SUCH A PRETTY CITY.
EVEN AT NIGHT. SO SHINY AND CLEAN.
JUST MAKES YOU FEEL LIKE...
...SCRATCHING IT UP A BIT, DON'T YOU THINK?
As Bruce Wayne, I personally called every employee and associate I have in Metropolis and sent them four-figure checks to relocate for the night.
WayneTech Board member Ralph Mangubat is former Special Forces. He laughed in my face.
AAAGH!
Doesn't appear to be laughing now.
WHO ARE YOU? WHAT DO YOU WANT? PLEASE, NO!
SO SORRY. JUST CAN'T HELP MYSELF.
DADDY?
I WOKED UP.
GLORIA...
...GO BACK TO BED.
OH, NO. COME SAY HI.
THERE'S NOTHING TO BE SCARED OF.
K--KITTY?
So naive. It actually makes me angry.
That's the problem with children today...

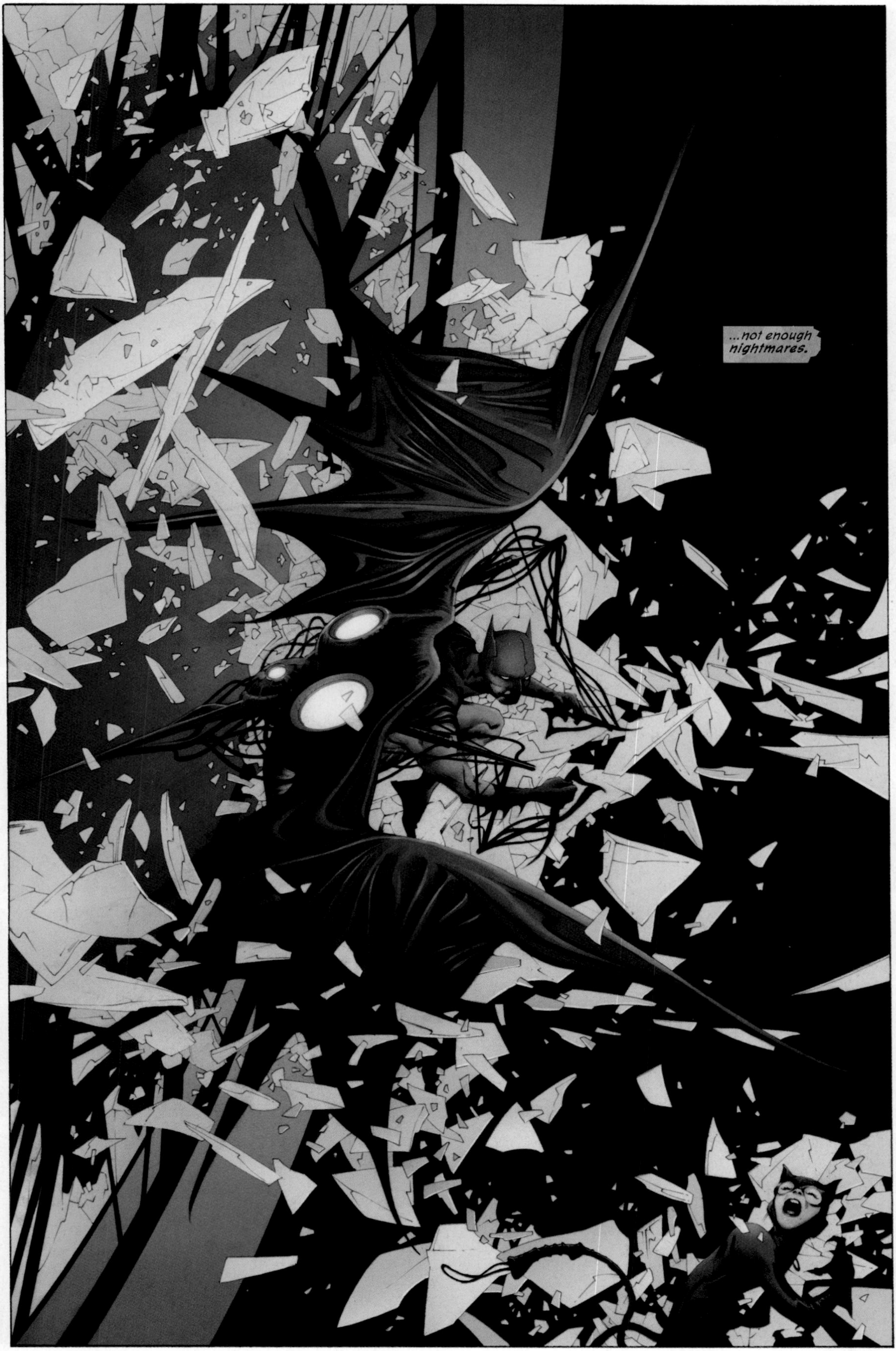
...not enough
nightmares.

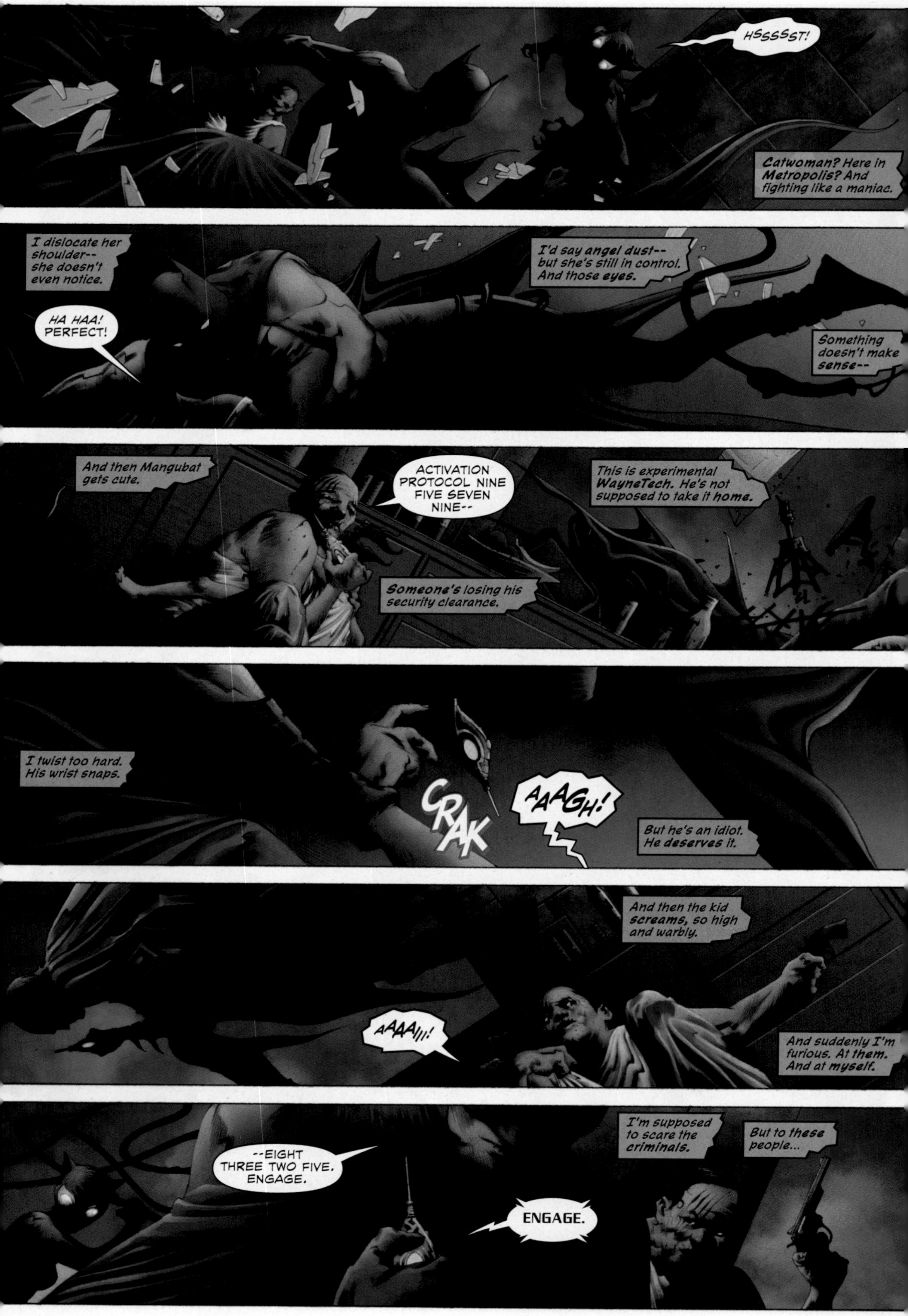
HSSSSST!
Catwoman? Here in Metropolis? And fighting like a maniac.
I dislocate her shoulder--she doesn't even notice.
HA HAA! PERFECT!
I'd say angel dust--but she's still in control. And those eyes.
Something doesn't make sense--
And then Mangubat gets cute.
ACTIVATION PROTOCOL NINE FIVE SEVEN NINE--
This is experimental WayneTech. He's not supposed to take it home.
Someone's losing his security clearance.
I twist too hard. His wrist snaps.
CRAK
AAAGH!
But he's an idiot. He deserves it.
And then the kid screams, so high and warbly.
AAAAIII!
And suddenly I'm furious. At them. And at myself.
--EIGHT THREE TWO FIVE. ENGAGE.
ENGAGE.
I'm supposed to scare the criminals.
But to these people...

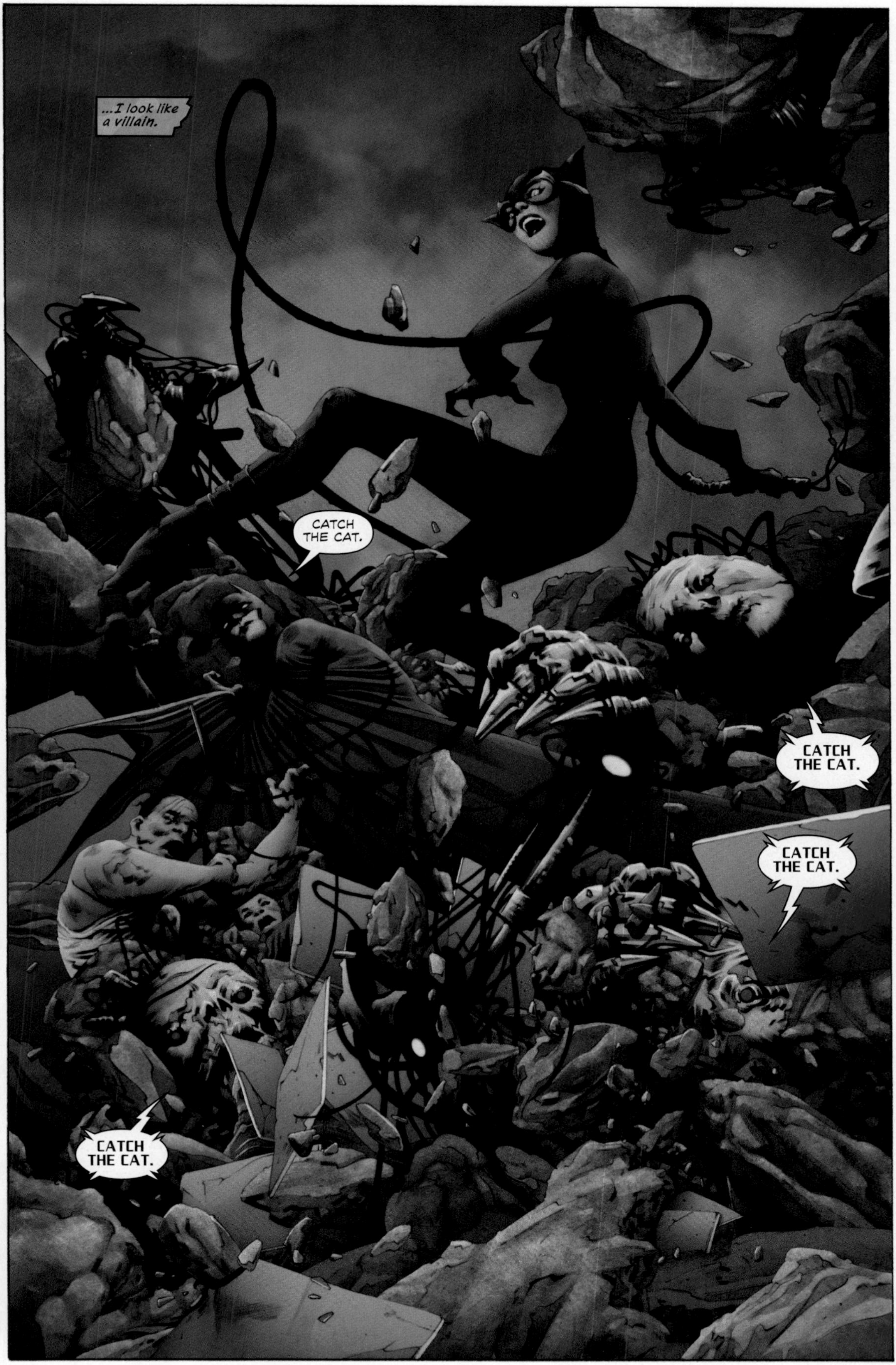
...I look like a villain.
CATCH THE CAT.
CATCH THE CAT.
CATCH THE CAT.
CATCH THE CAT.

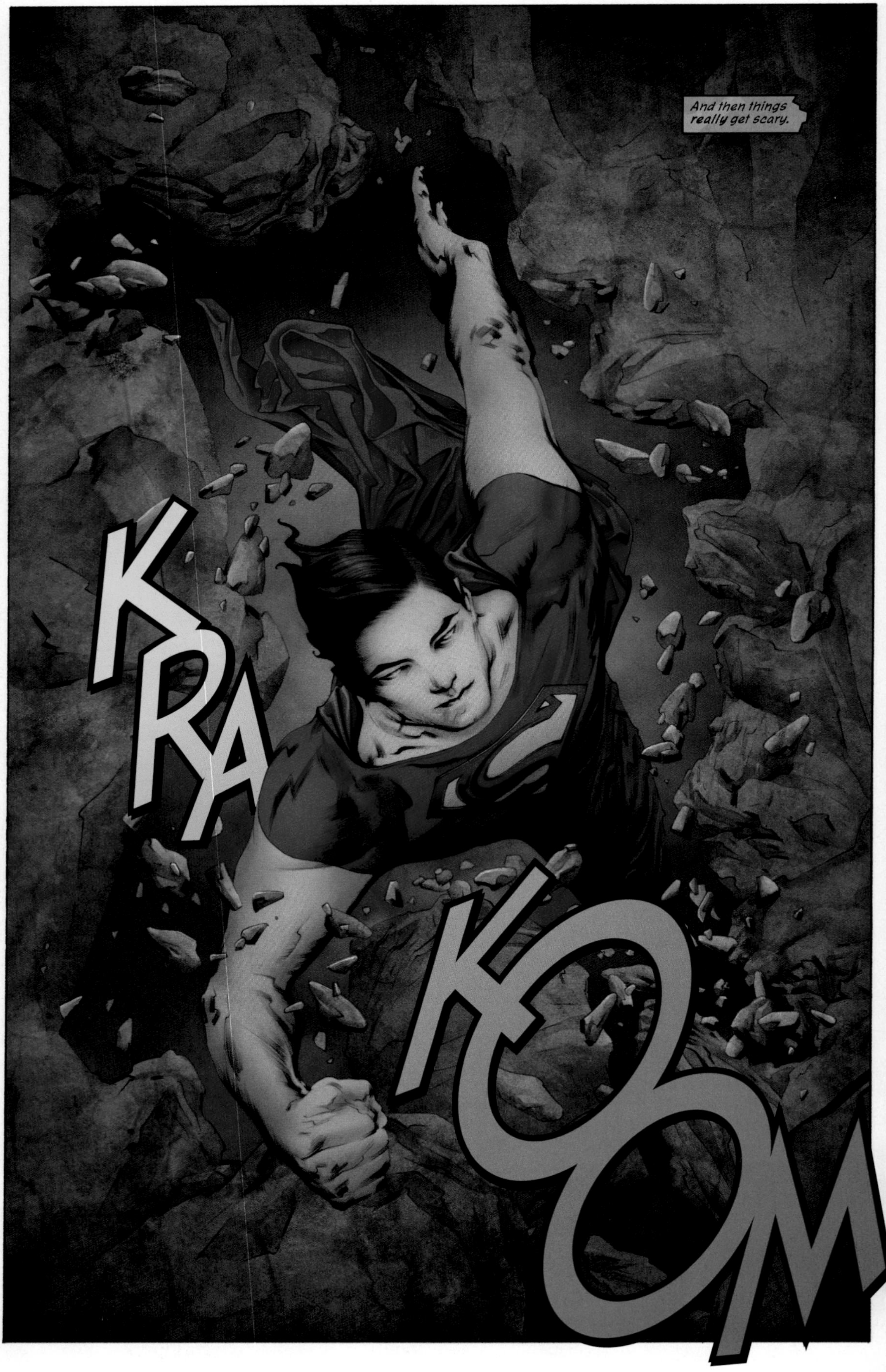
And then things really get scary.
KRA
KOOM

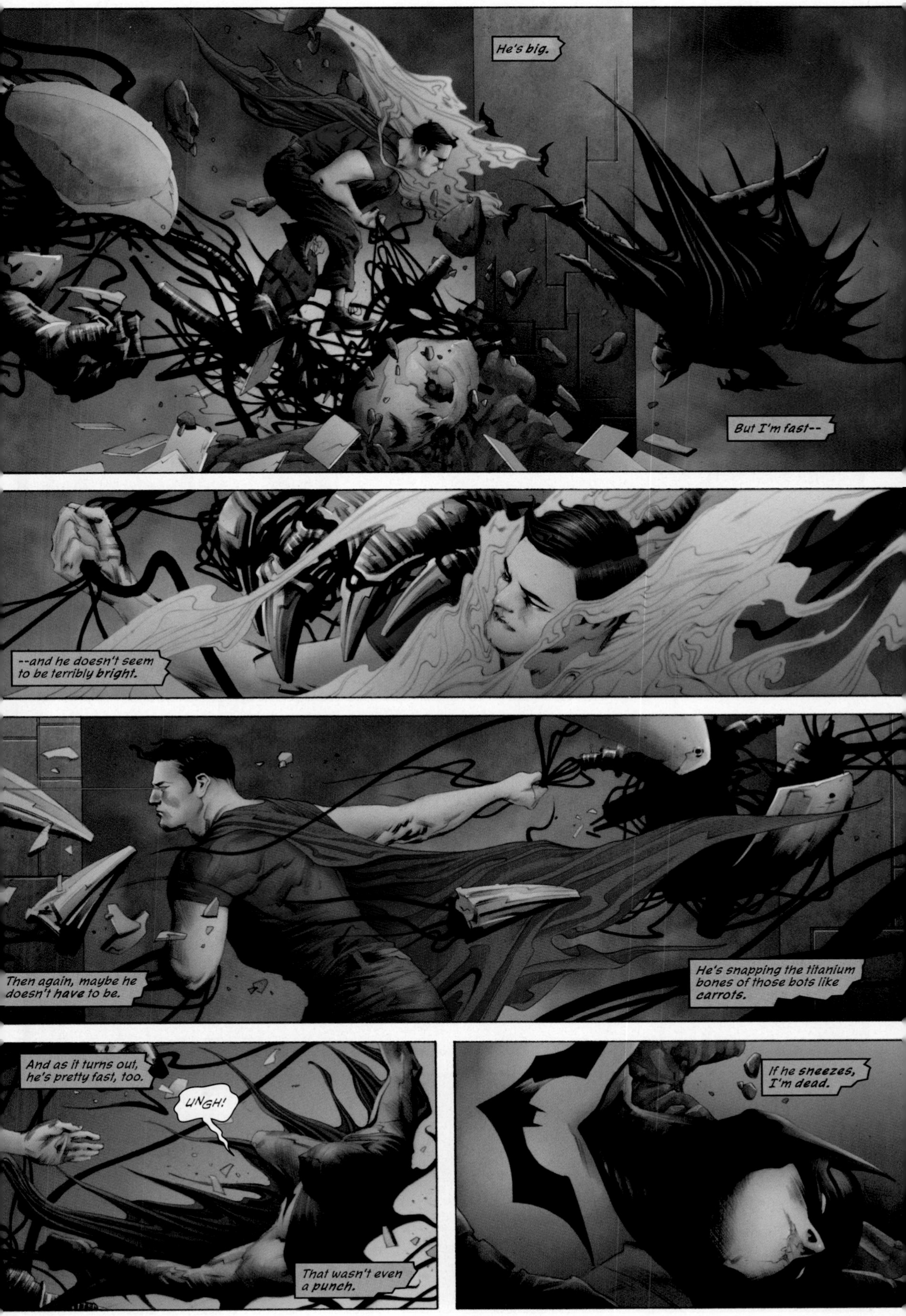
He's big.
But I'm fast--
--and he doesn't seem to be terribly bright.
Then again, maybe he doesn't have to be.
He's snapping the titanium bones of those bots like carrots.
And as it turns out, he's pretty fast, too.
UNGH!
That wasn't even a punch.
If he sneezes, I'm dead.

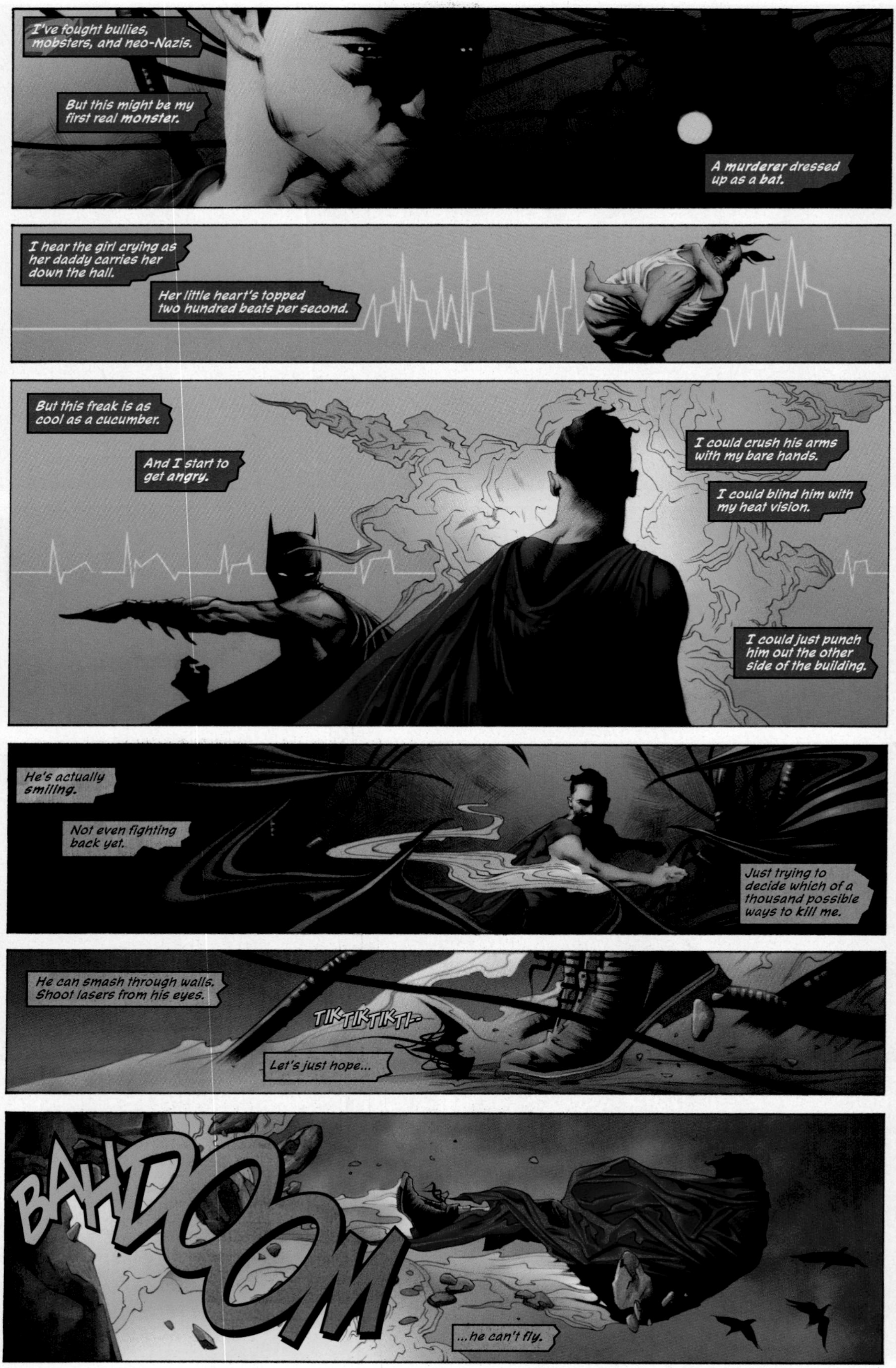

I've fought bullies, mobsters, and neo-Nazis.
But this might be my first real monster.
A murderer dressed up as a bat.
I hear the girl crying as her daddy carries her down the hall.
Her little heart's topped two hundred beats per second.
But this freak is as cool as a cucumber.
And I start to get angry.
I could crush his arms with my bare hands.
I could blind him with my heat vision.
I could just punch him out the other side of the building.
He's actually smiling.
Not even fighting back yet.
Just trying to decide which of a thousand possible ways to kill me.
He can smash through walls. Shoot lasers from his eyes.
TIKTIKTIKTI-
Let's just hope...
BAHDOOM
...he can't fly.

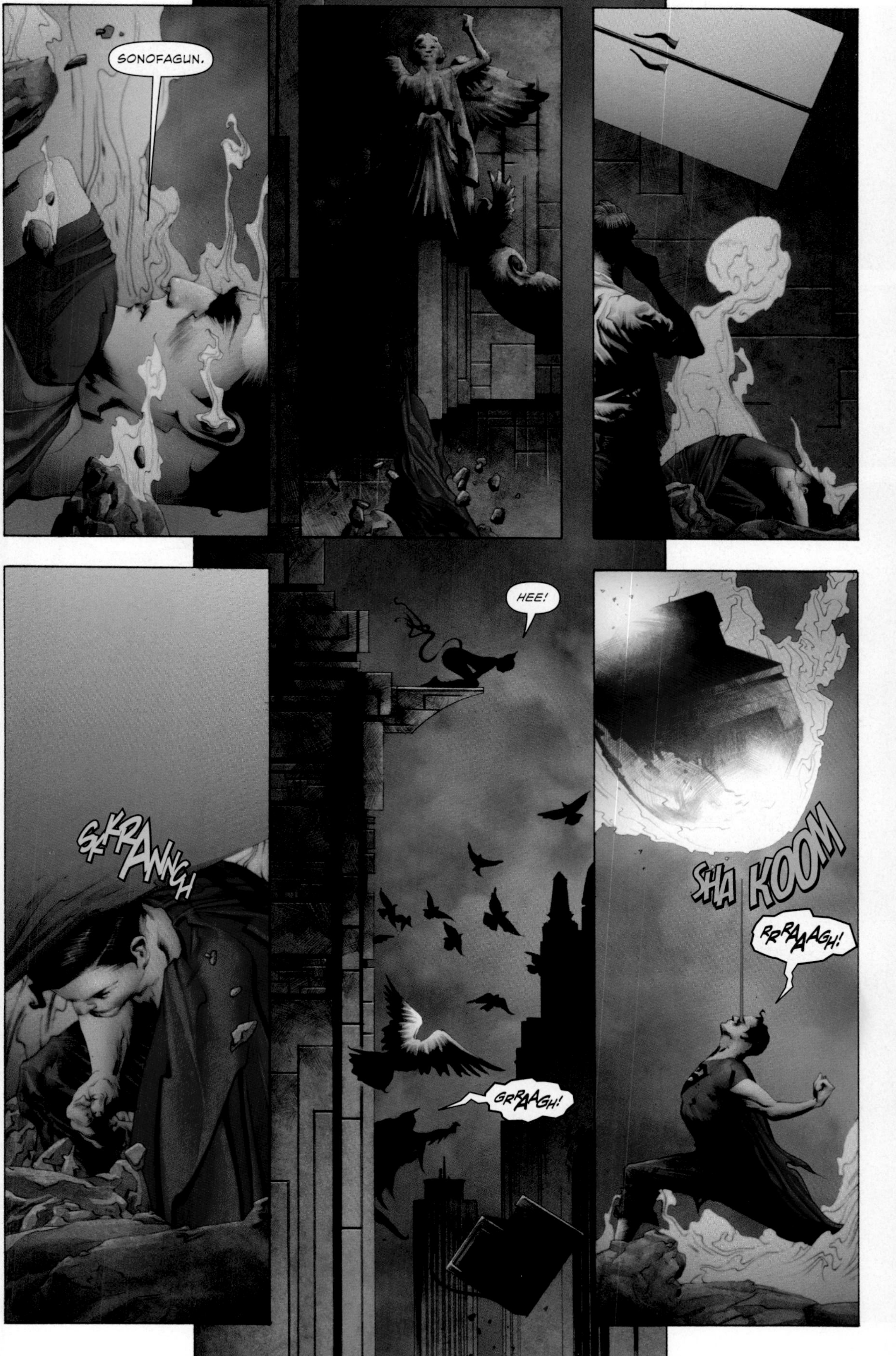
SONOFAGUN.
SKKRANNNCH
HEE!
GRRAAGH!
SHA KOOM
RRRAAAGH!

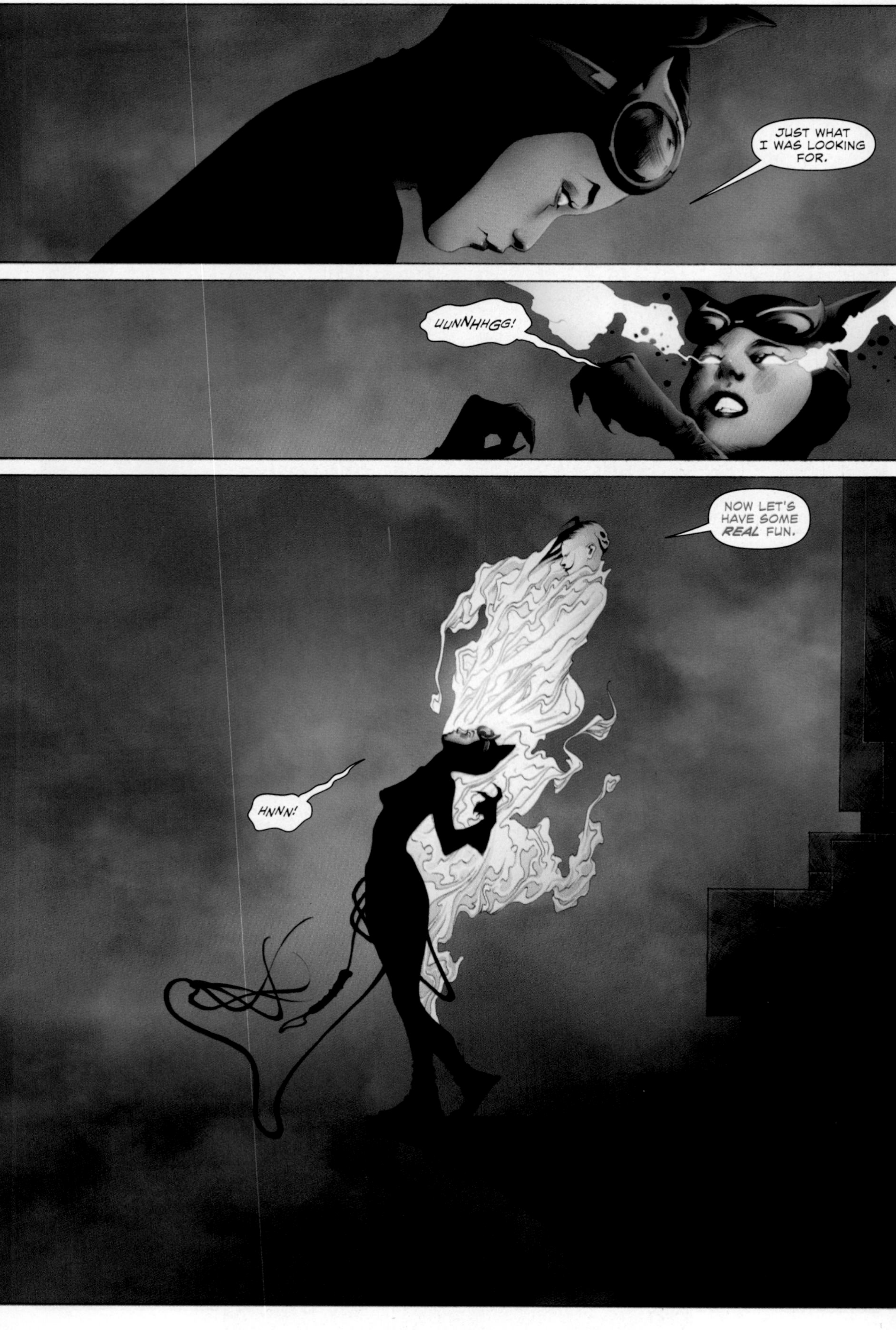
JUST WHAT I WAS LOOKING FOR.
UUNNHHGG!
NOW LET'S HAVE SOME REAL FUN.
HNNN!

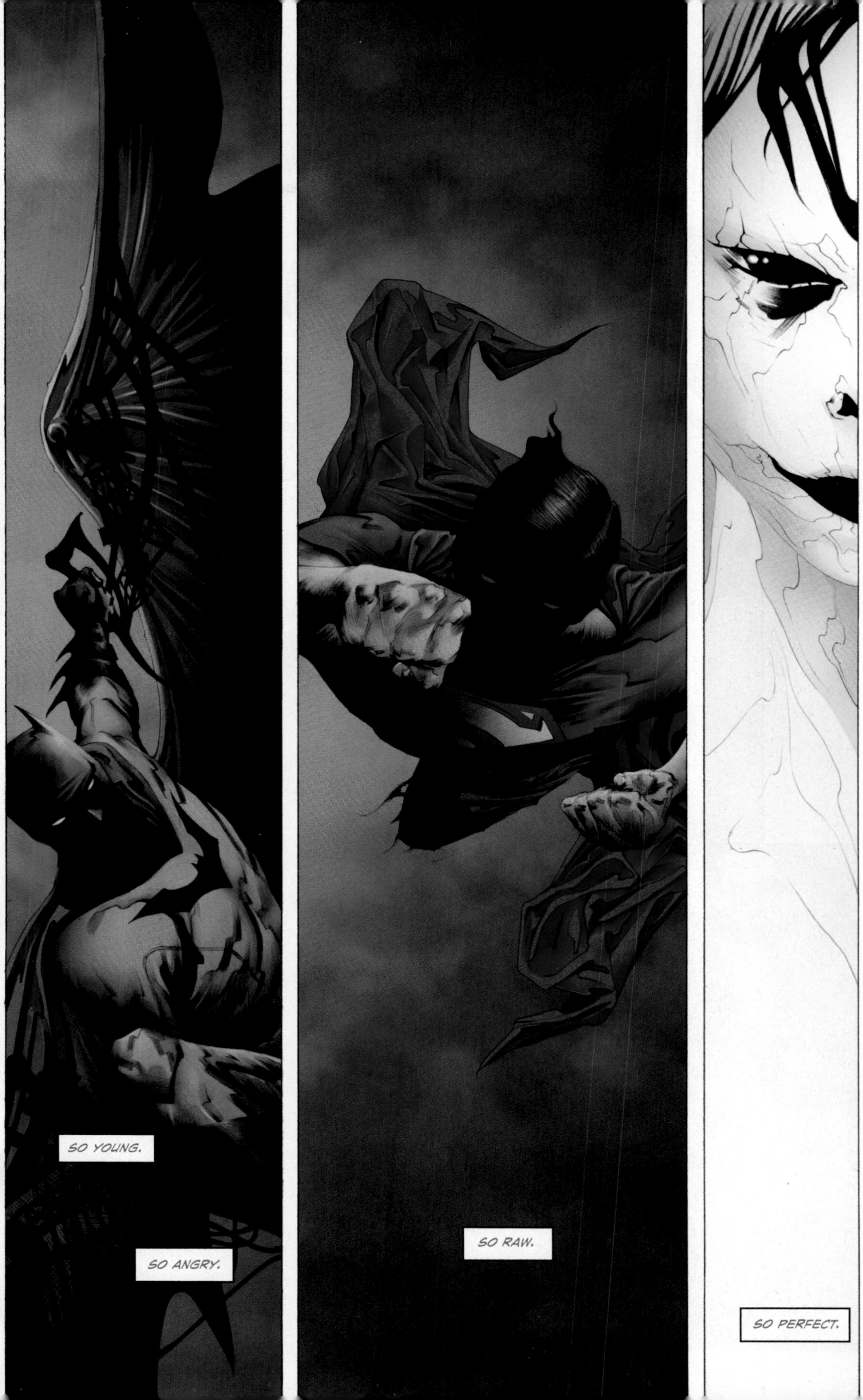
SO YOUNG.
SO ANGRY.
SO RAW.
SO PERFECT.

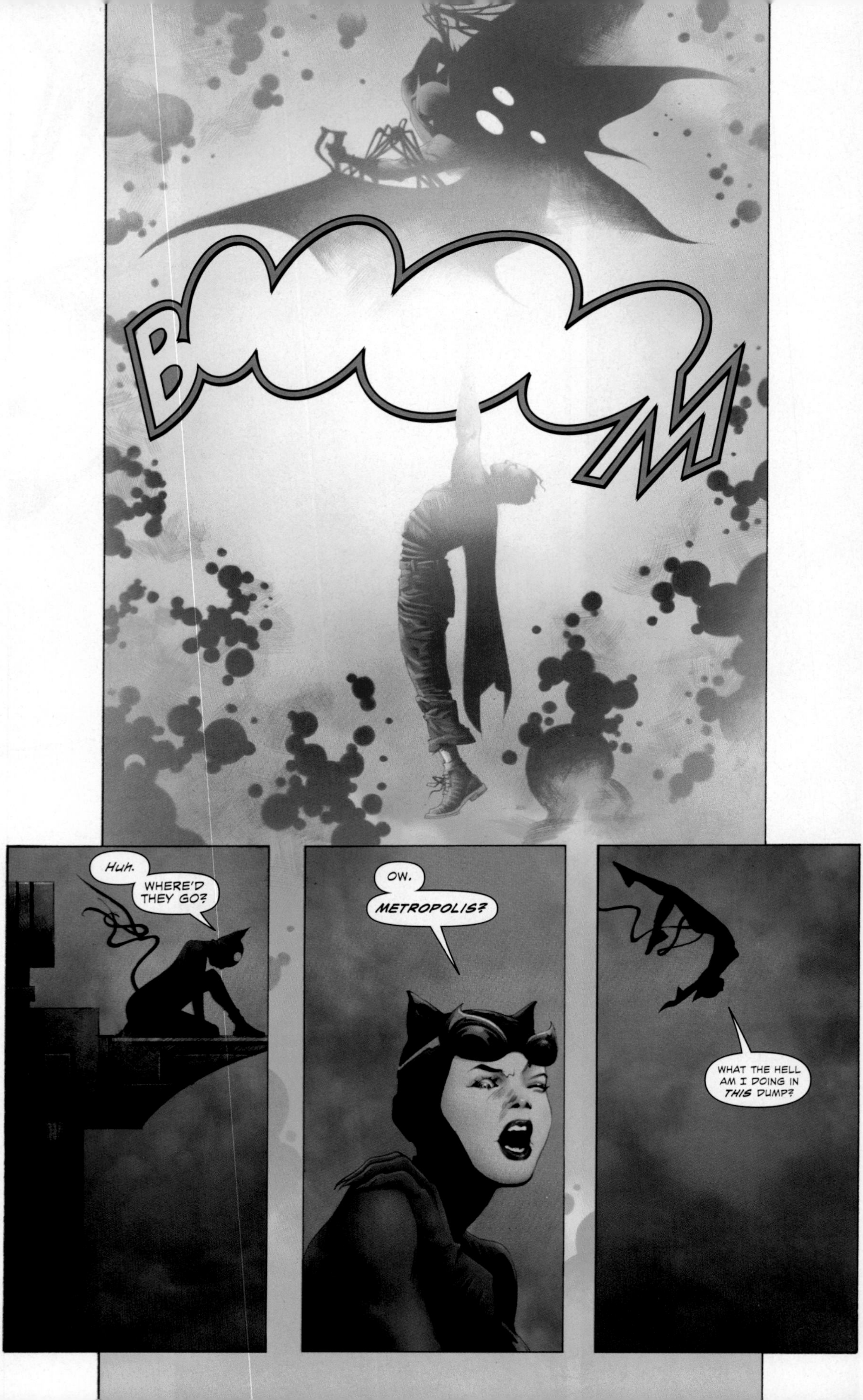
BOOOOM
Huh.
WHERE'D THEY GO?
OW.
METROPOLIS?
WHAT THE HELL AM I DOING IN THIS DUMP?

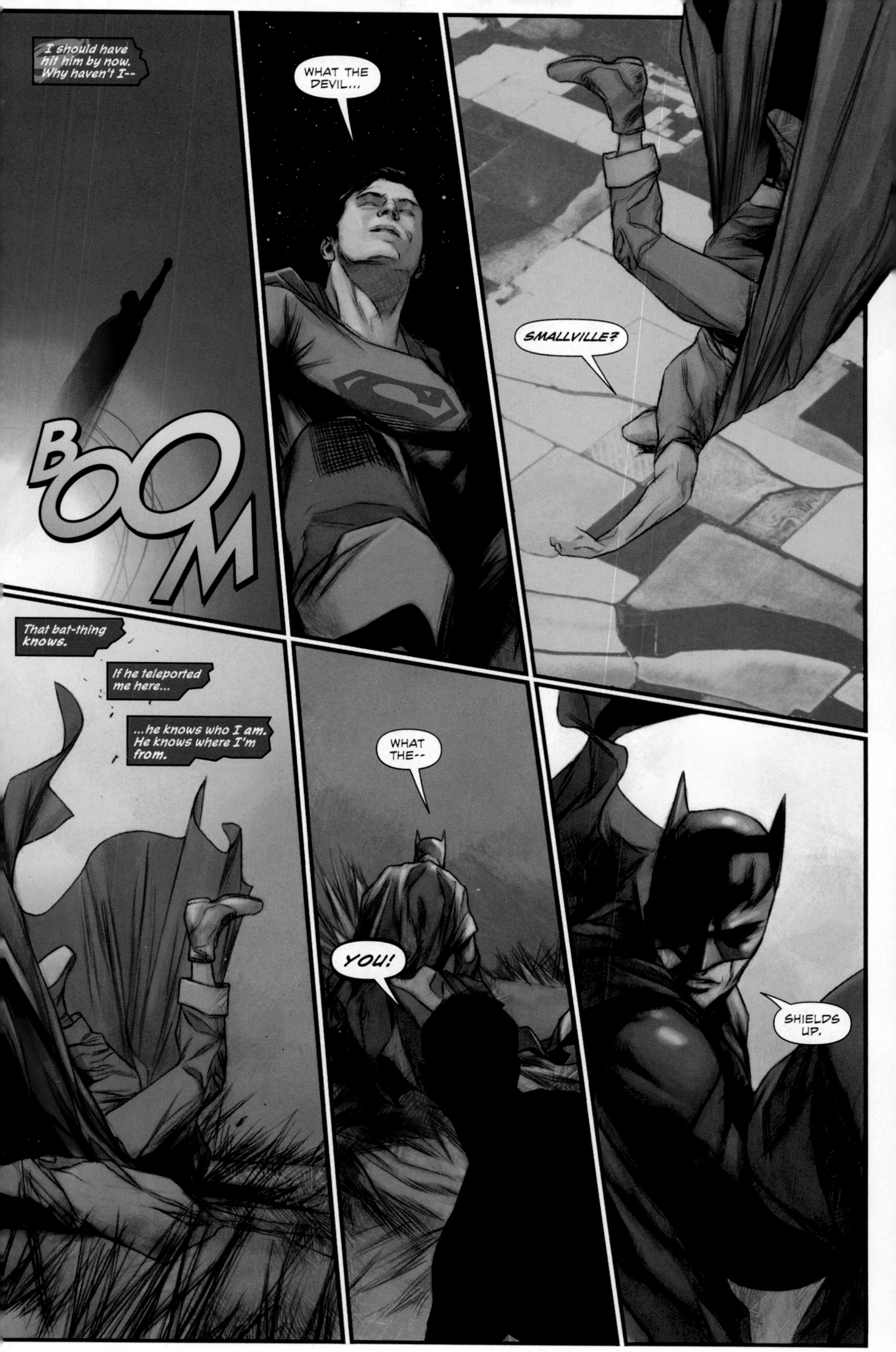
I should have hit him by now. Why haven't I--
BOOM
WHAT THE DEVIL...
SMALLVILLE?
That bat-thing knows.
If he teleported me here...
...he knows who I am. He knows where I'm from.
WHAT THE--
YOU!
SHIELDS UP.

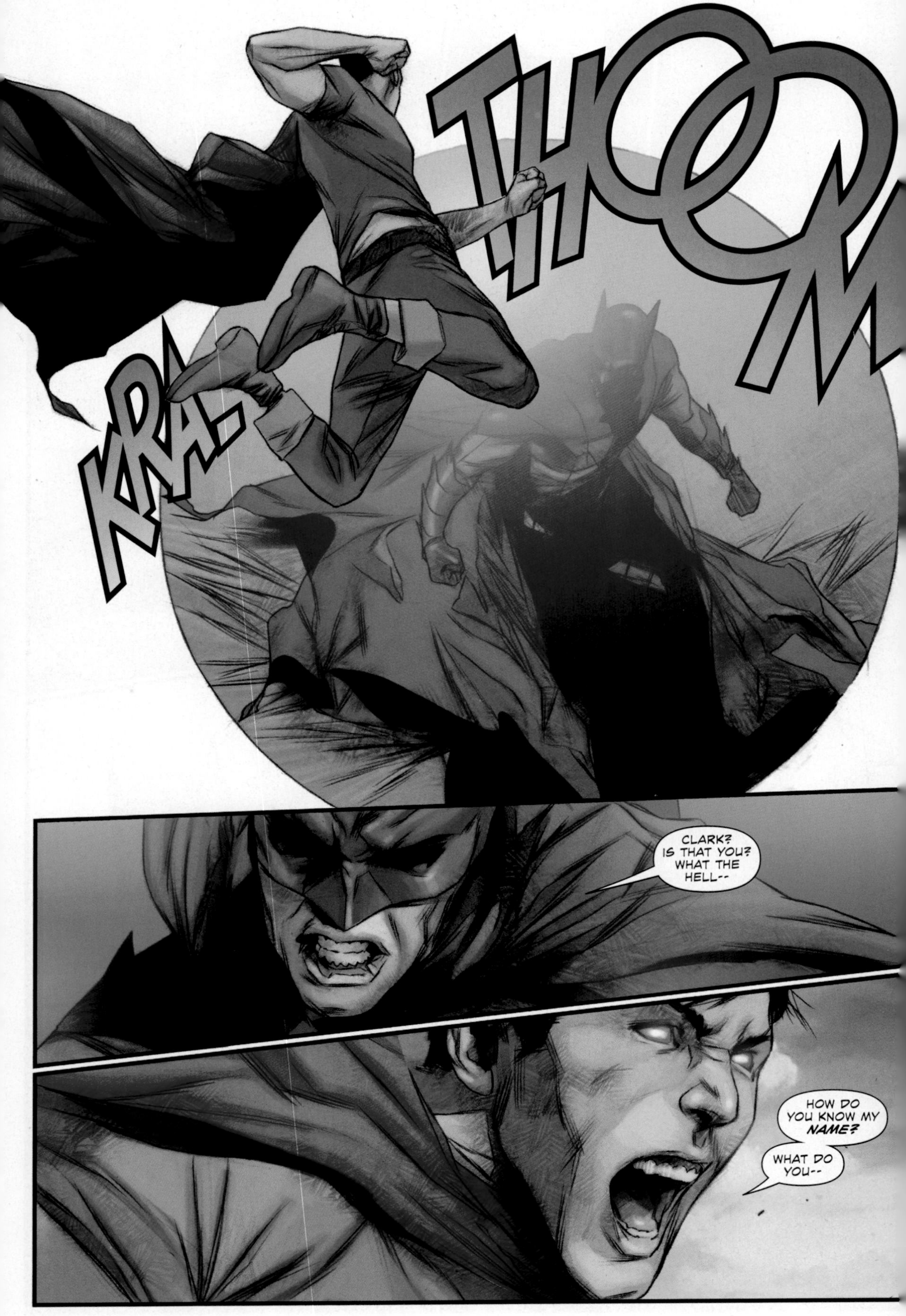
THOOM
KRA-
CLARK? IS THAT YOU? WHAT THE HELL--
HOW DO YOU KNOW MY NAME?
WHAT DO YOU--

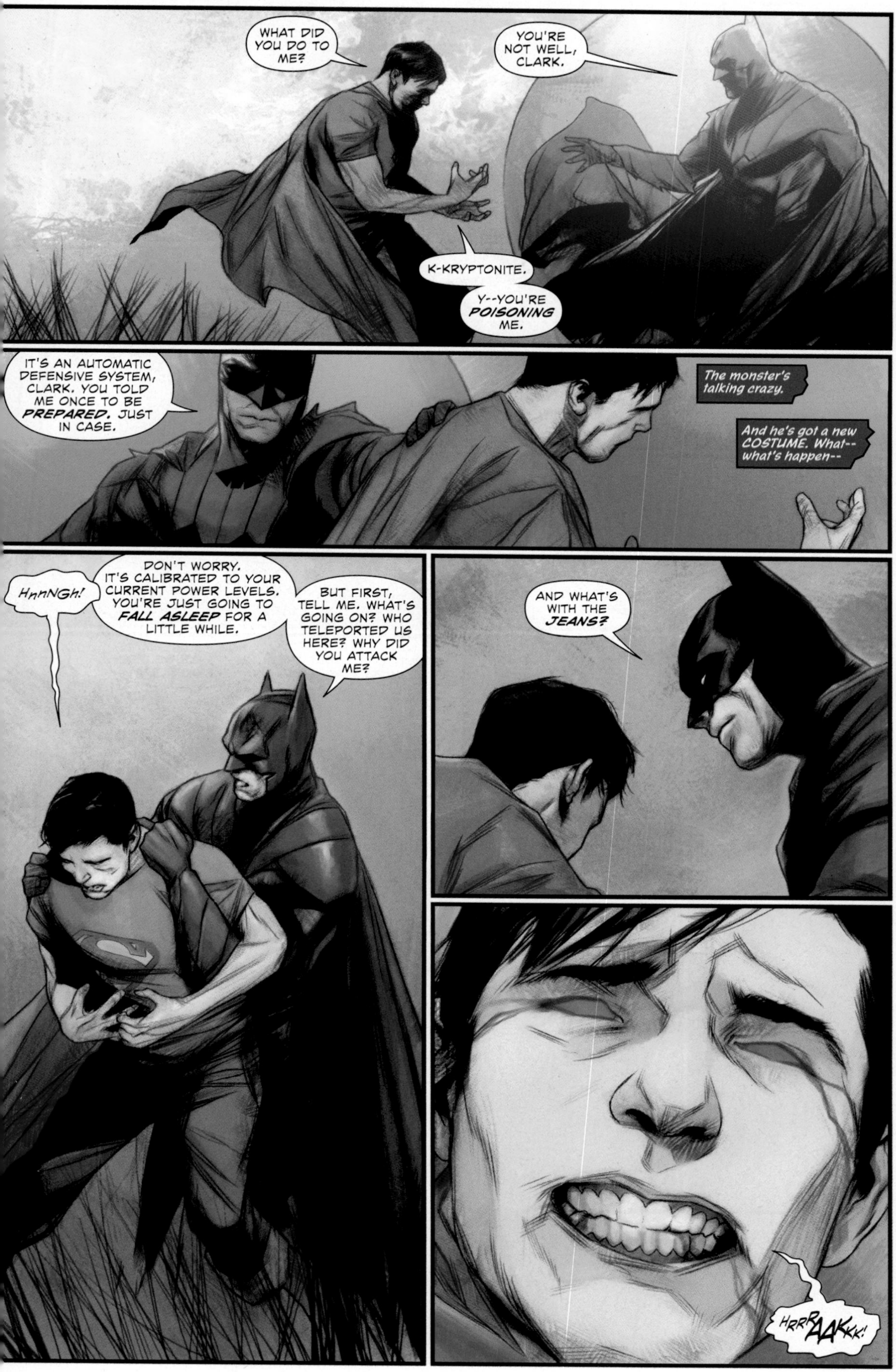
WHAT DID YOU DO TO ME?
YOU'RE NOT WELL, CLARK.
K-KRYPTONITE.
Y--YOU'RE POISONING ME.
IT'S AN AUTOMATIC DEFENSIVE SYSTEM, CLARK. YOU TOLD ME ONCE TO BE PREPARED. JUST IN CASE.
The monster's talking crazy.
And he's got a new COSTUME. What--what's happen--
HnnNGh!
DON'T WORRY. IT'S CALIBRATED TO YOUR CURRENT POWER LEVELS. YOU'RE JUST GOING TO FALL ASLEEP FOR A LITTLE WHILE.
BUT FIRST, TELL ME. WHAT'S GOING ON? WHO TELEPORTED US HERE? WHY DID YOU ATTACK ME?
AND WHAT'S WITH THE JEANS?
HRRRAAKKK!

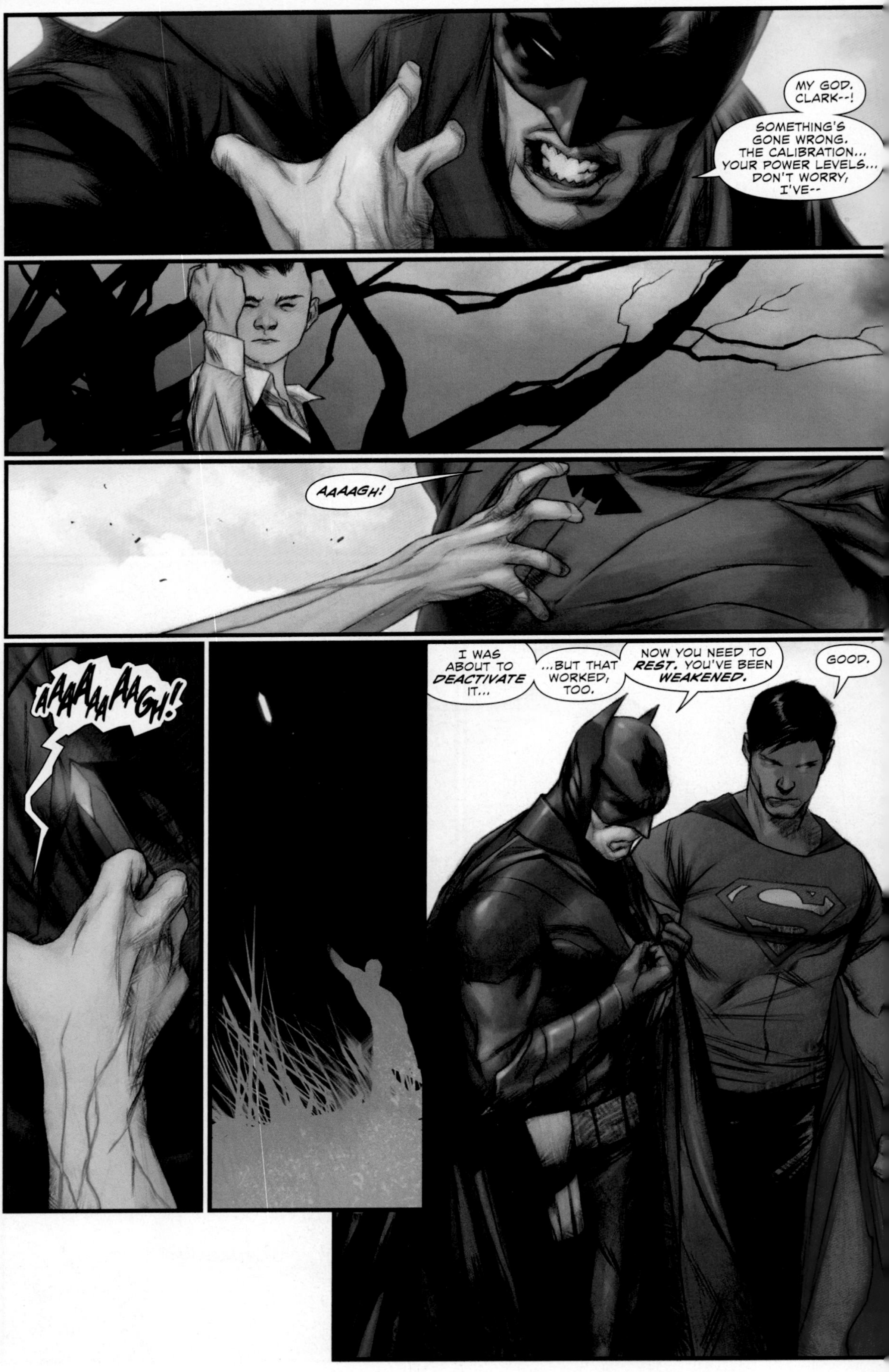
MY GOD. CLARK--!
SOMETHING'S GONE WRONG. THE CALIBRATION... YOUR POWER LEVELS... DON'T WORRY, I'VE--
AAAAGH!
AAAAAAAAAGH!
I WAS ABOUT TO DEACTIVATE IT...
...BUT THAT WORKED, TOO.
NOW YOU NEED TO REST. YOU'VE BEEN WEAKENED.
GOOD.

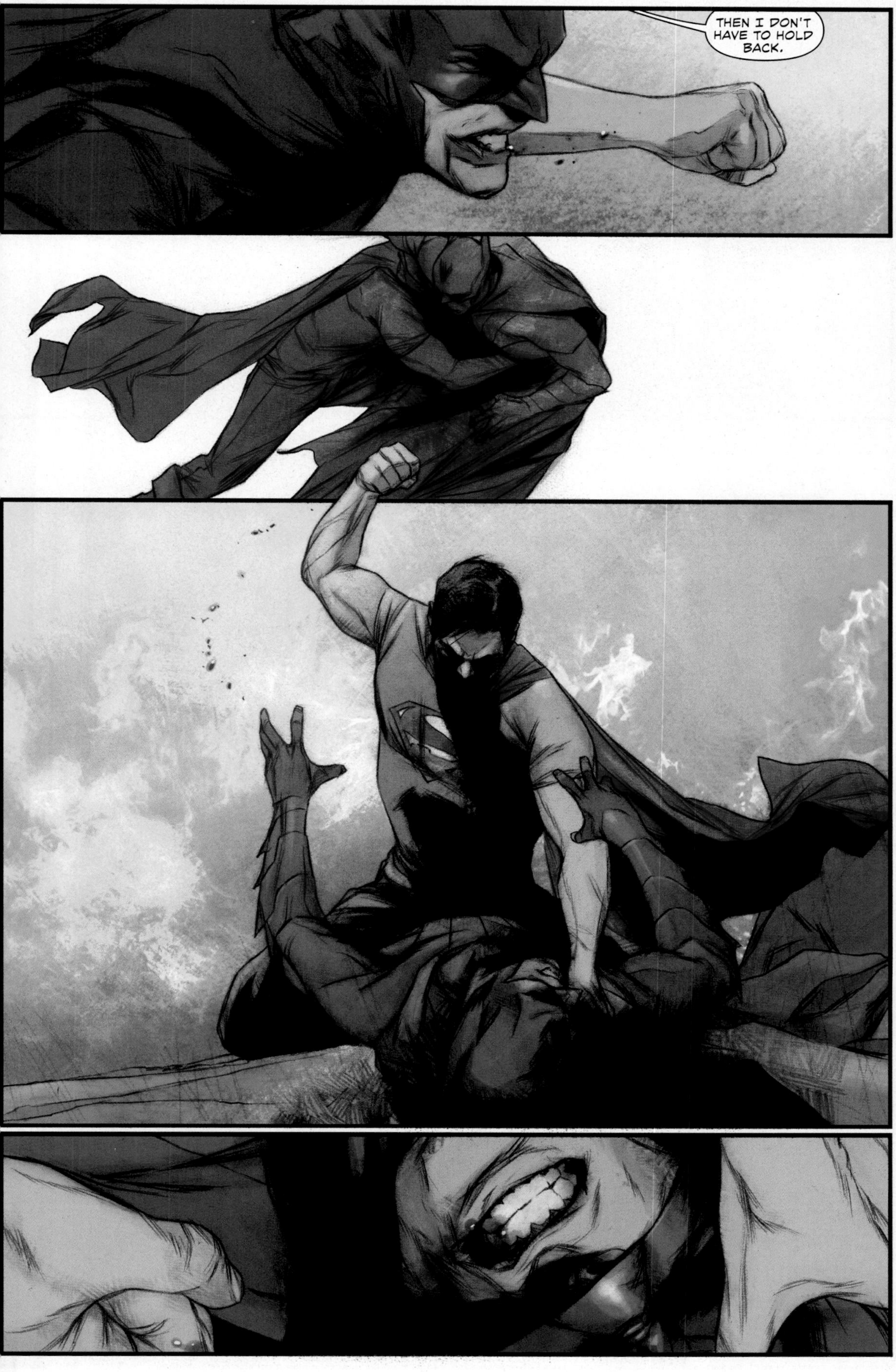
THEN I DON'T HAVE TO HOLD BACK.

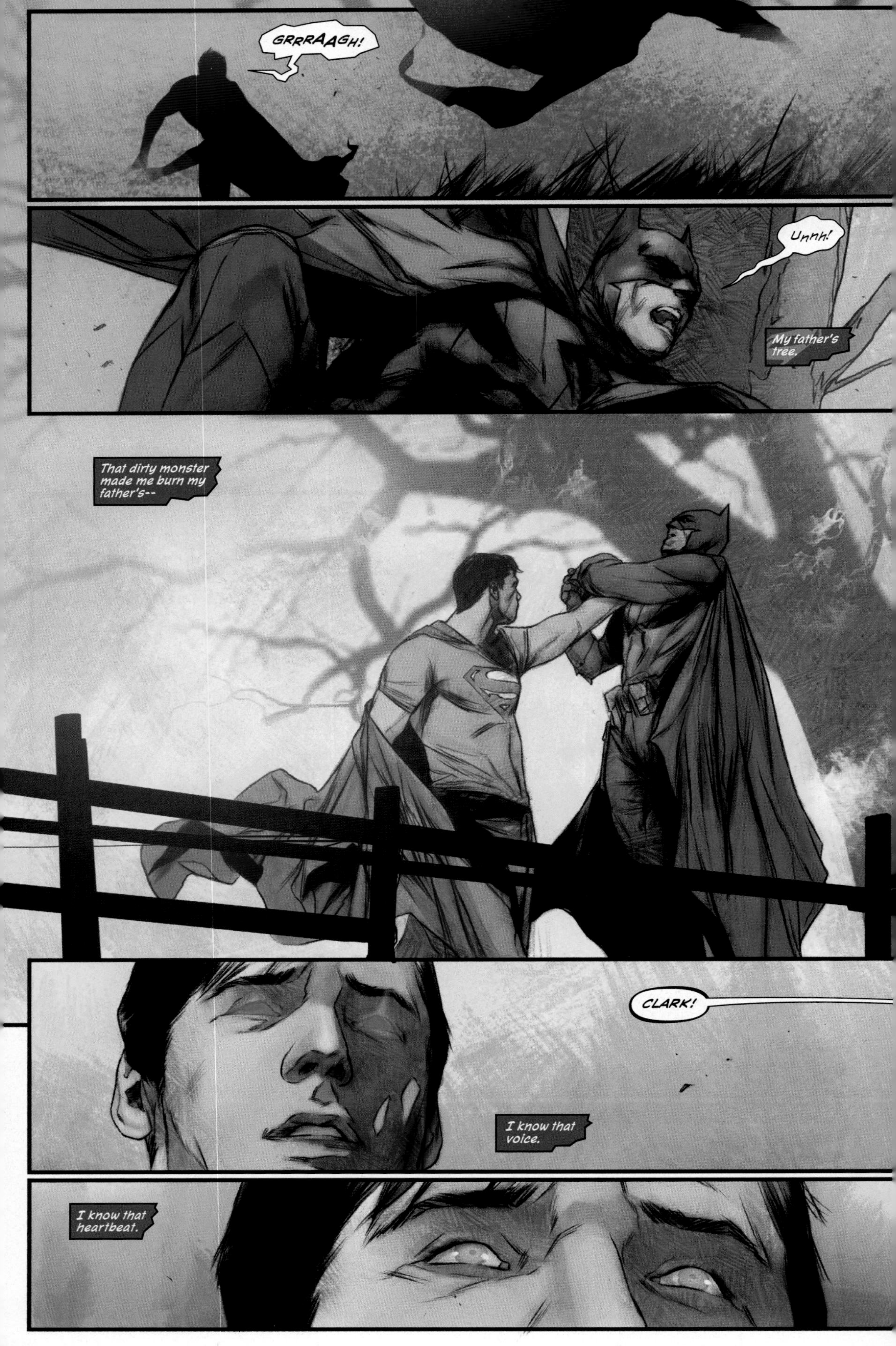
GRRRAAGH!
Unnh!
My father's tree.
That dirty monster made me burn my father's--
CLARK!
I know that voice.
I know that heartbeat.

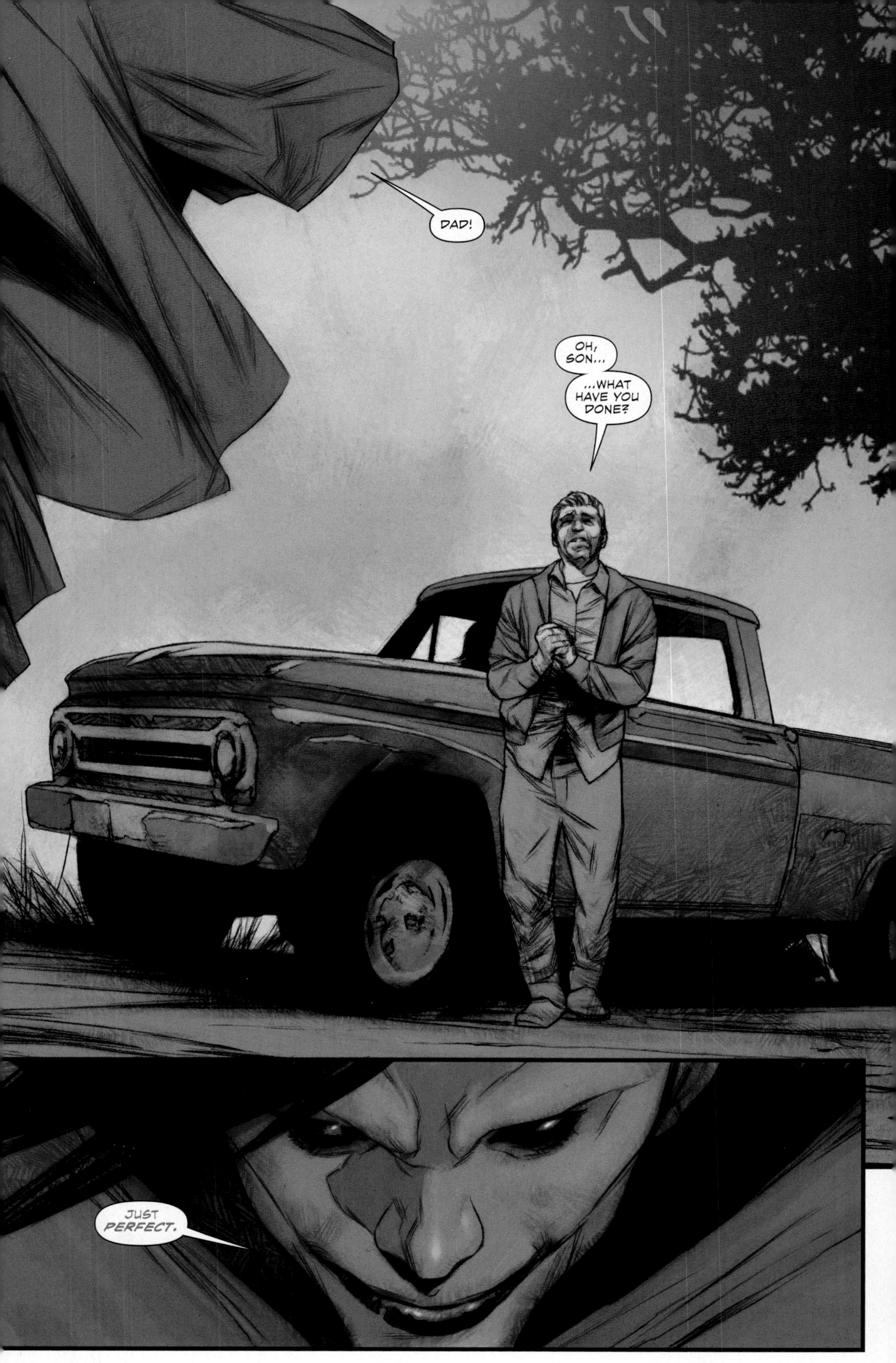
DAD!
OH, SON...
...WHAT HAVE YOU DONE?
JUST *PERFECT.*

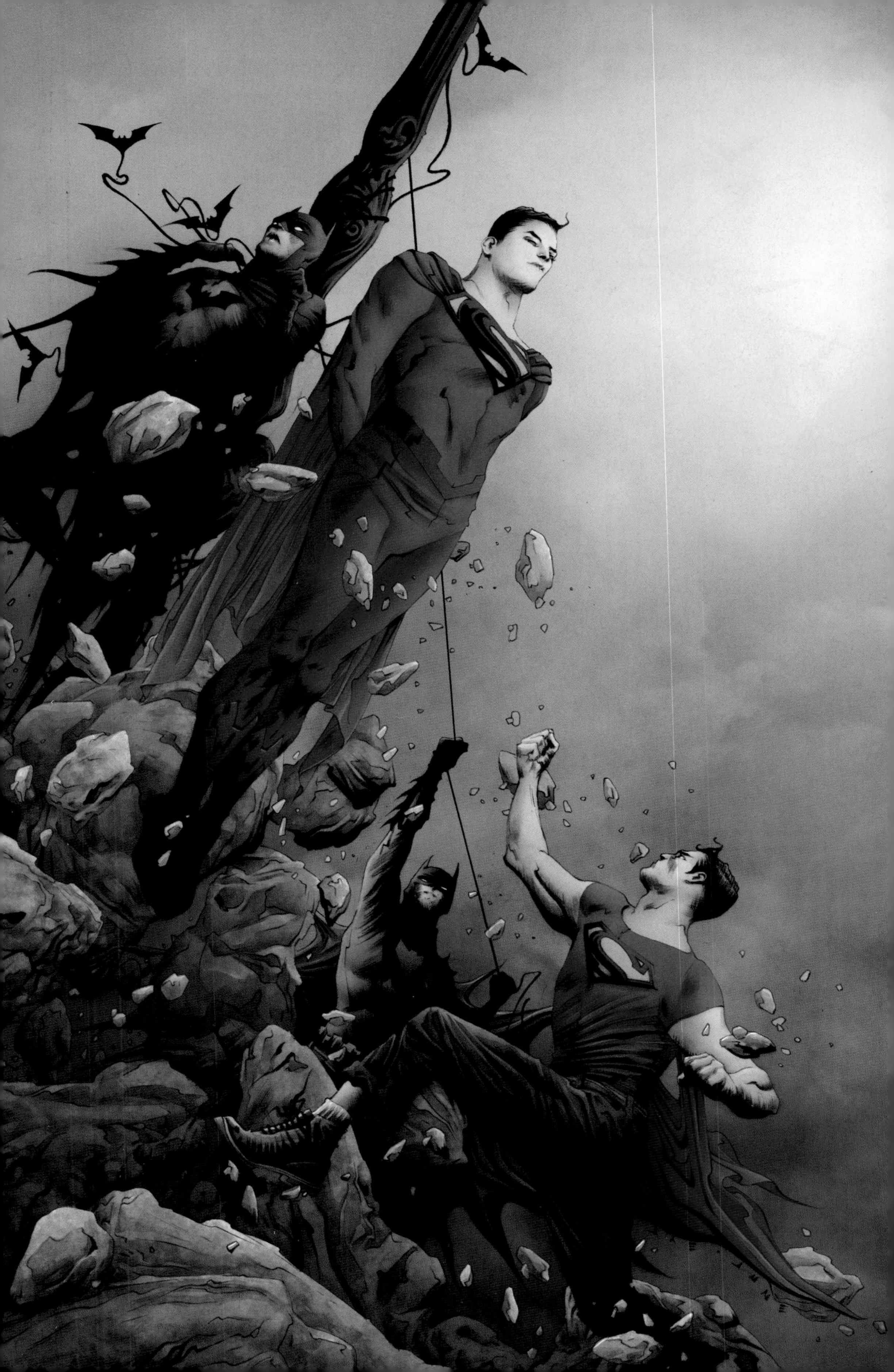

GREG PAK writer JAE LEE artist JUNE CHUNG colorist cover by JAE LEE with JUNE CHUNG

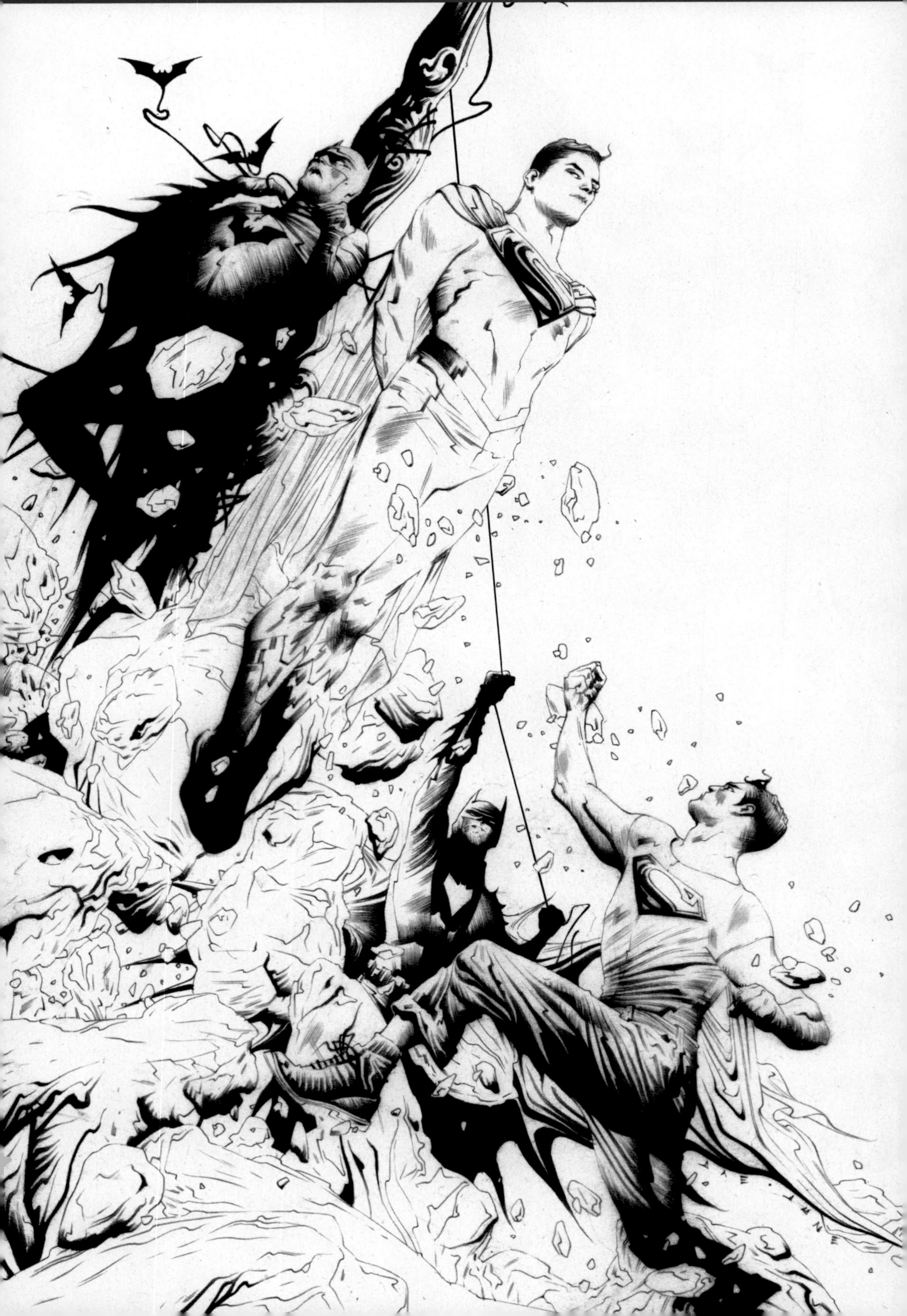

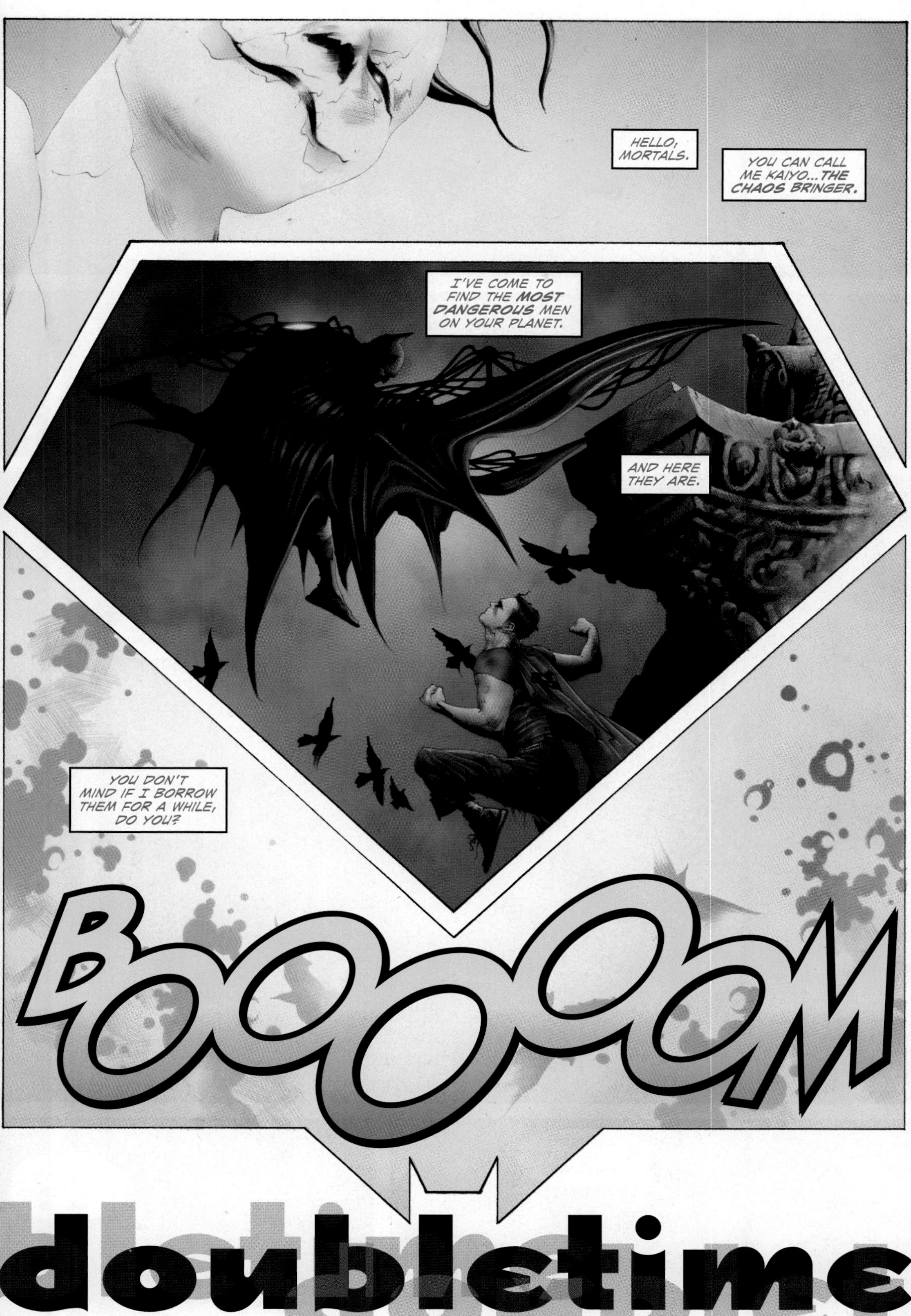
HELLO, MORTALS.
YOU CAN CALL ME KAIYO...THE CHAOS BRINGER.
I'VE COME TO FIND THE MOST DANGEROUS MEN ON YOUR PLANET.
AND HERE THEY ARE.
YOU DON'T MIND IF I BORROW THEM FOR A WHILE, DO YOU?
BOOOOOM

doubletime

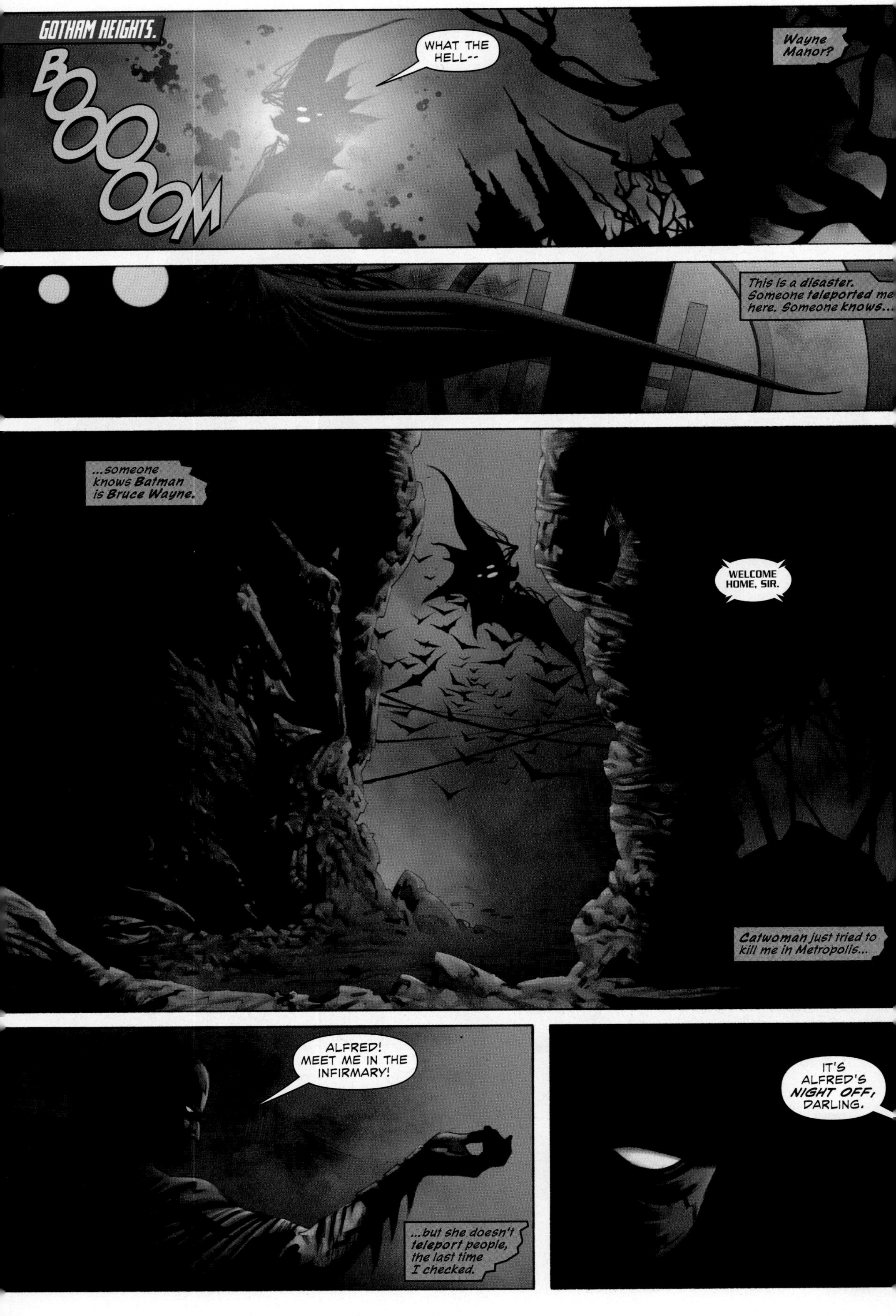
GOTHAM HEIGHTS.
BOOOOOM
WHAT THE HELL--
Wayne Manor?
This is a disaster. Someone teleported me here. Someone knows...
...someone knows Batman is Bruce Wayne.
WELCOME HOME, SIR.
Catwoman just tried to kill me in Metropolis...
ALFRED! MEET ME IN THE INFIRMARY!
...but she doesn't teleport people, the last time I checked.
IT'S ALFRED'S NIGHT OFF, DARLING.

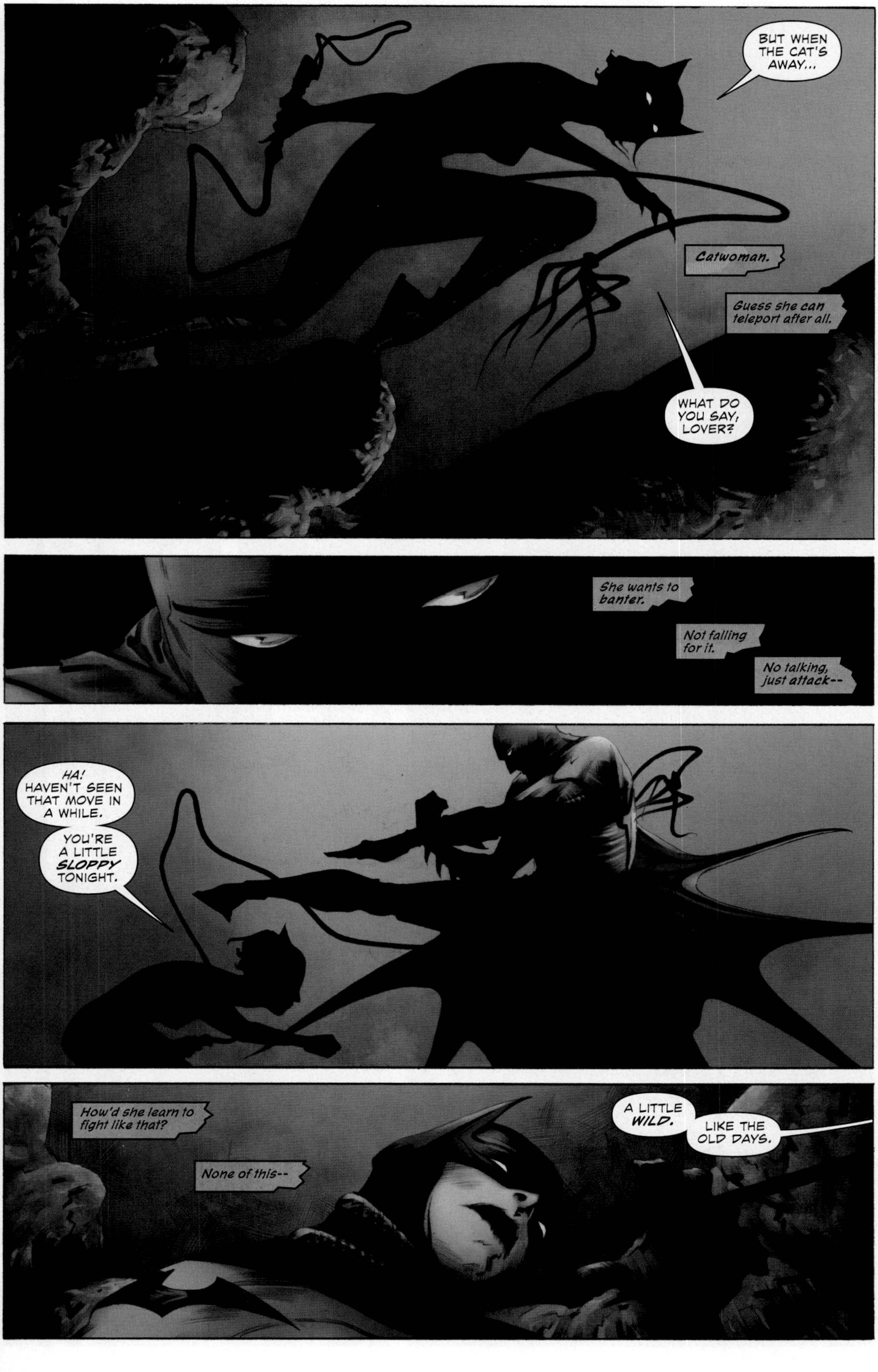
BUT WHEN THE CAT'S AWAY...
Catwoman.
Guess she can teleport after all.
WHAT DO YOU SAY, LOVER?
She wants to banter.
Not falling for it.
No talking, just attack--
HA! HAVEN'T SEEN THAT MOVE IN A WHILE.
YOU'RE A LITTLE SLOPPY TONIGHT.
How'd she learn to fight like that?
None of this--
A LITTLE WILD.
LIKE THE OLD DAYS.

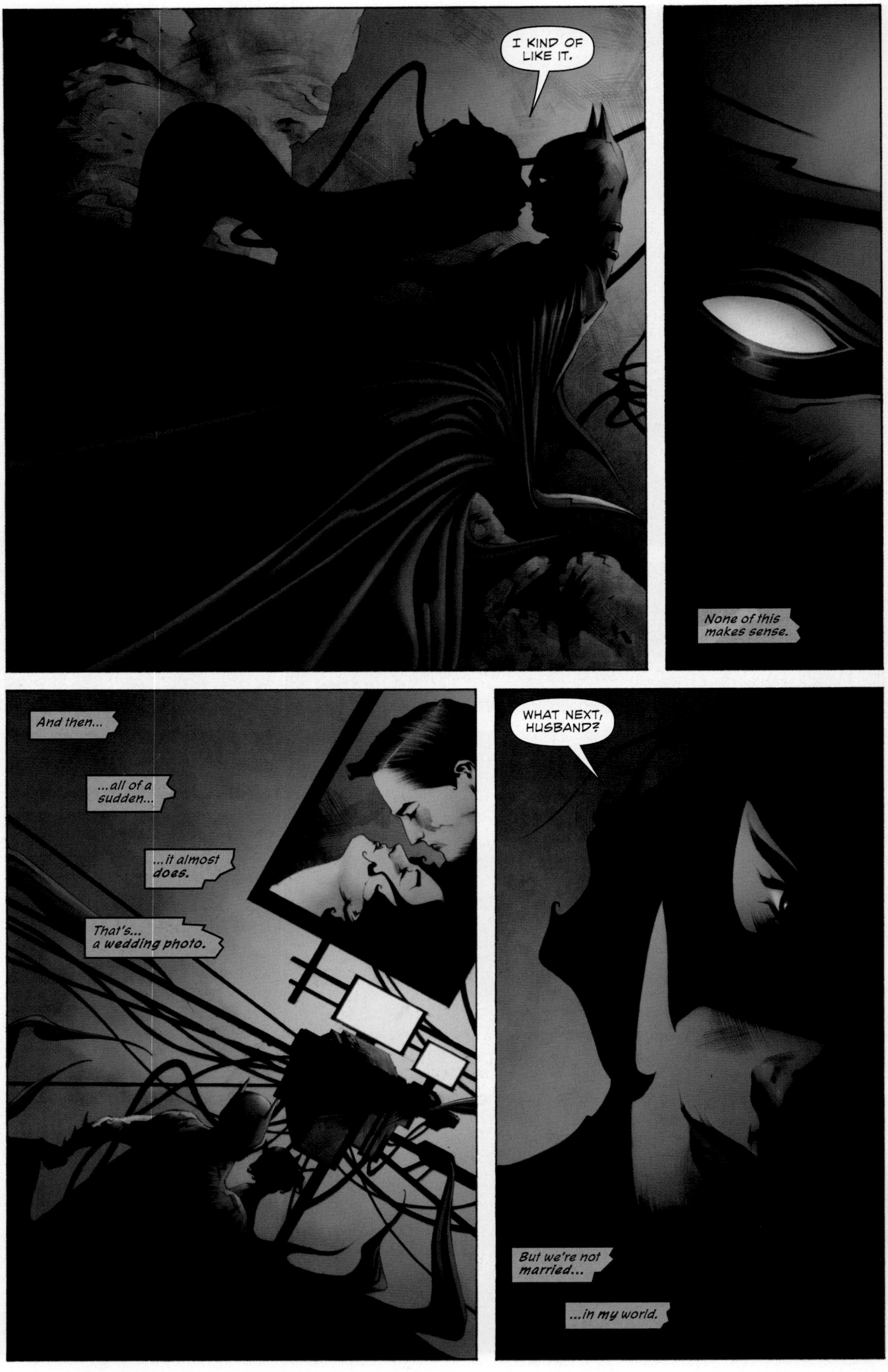
I KIND OF LIKE IT.
None of this makes sense.
And then...
...all of a sudden...
...it almost does.
That's... a wedding photo.
WHAT NEXT, HUSBAND?
But we're not married...
...in my world.

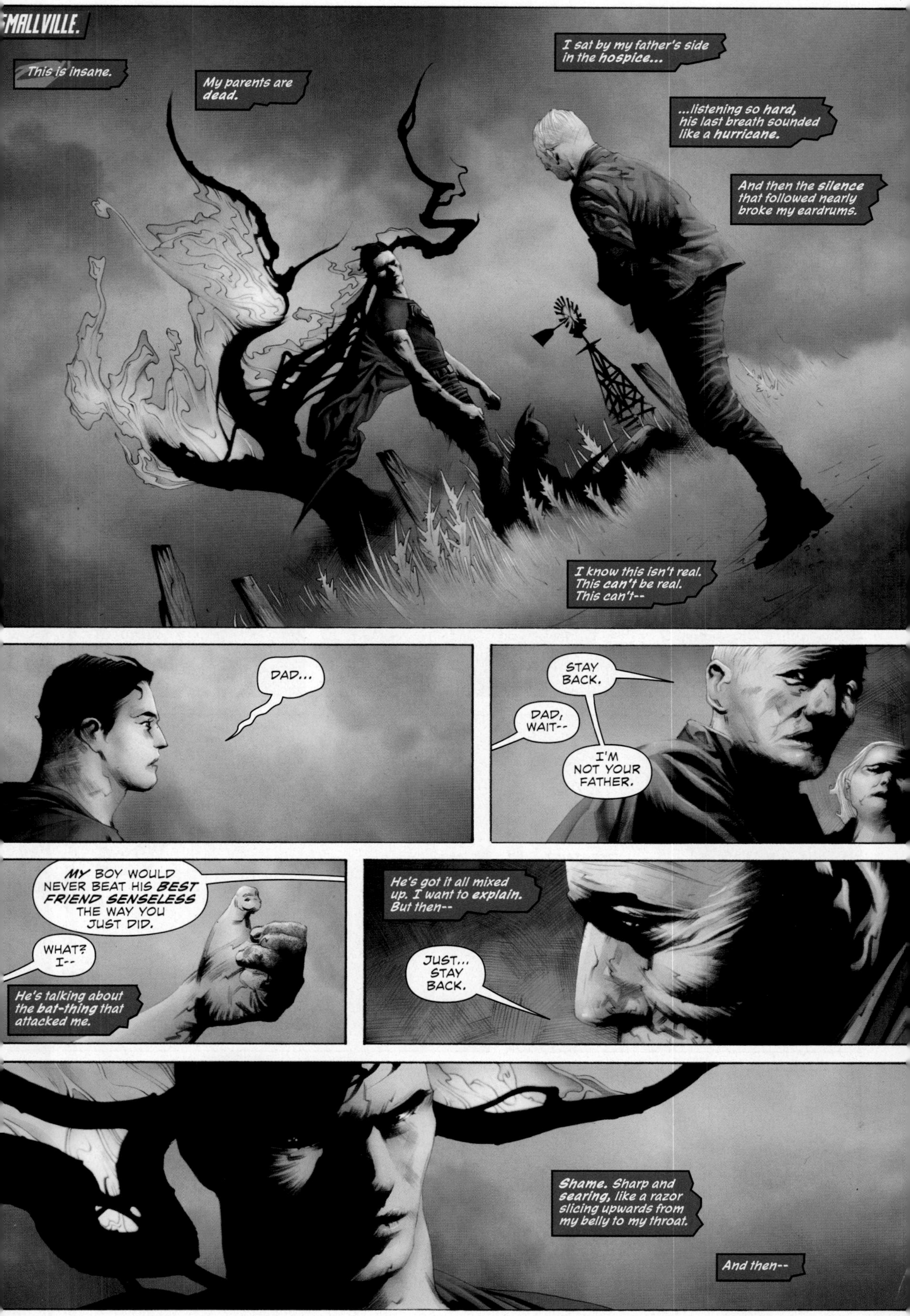
SMALLVILLE.
This is insane.
My parents are dead.
I sat by my father's side in the hospice...
...listening so hard, his last breath sounded like a hurricane.
And then the silence that followed nearly broke my eardrums.
I know this isn't real. This can't be real. This can't--
DAD...
STAY BACK.
DAD, WAIT--
I'M NOT YOUR FATHER.
MY BOY WOULD NEVER BEAT HIS BEST FRIEND SENSELESS THE WAY YOU JUST DID.
WHAT? I--
He's talking about the bat-thing that attacked me.
He's got it all mixed up. I want to explain. But then--
JUST... STAY BACK.
Shame. Sharp and searing, like a razor slicing upwards from my belly to my throat.
And then--

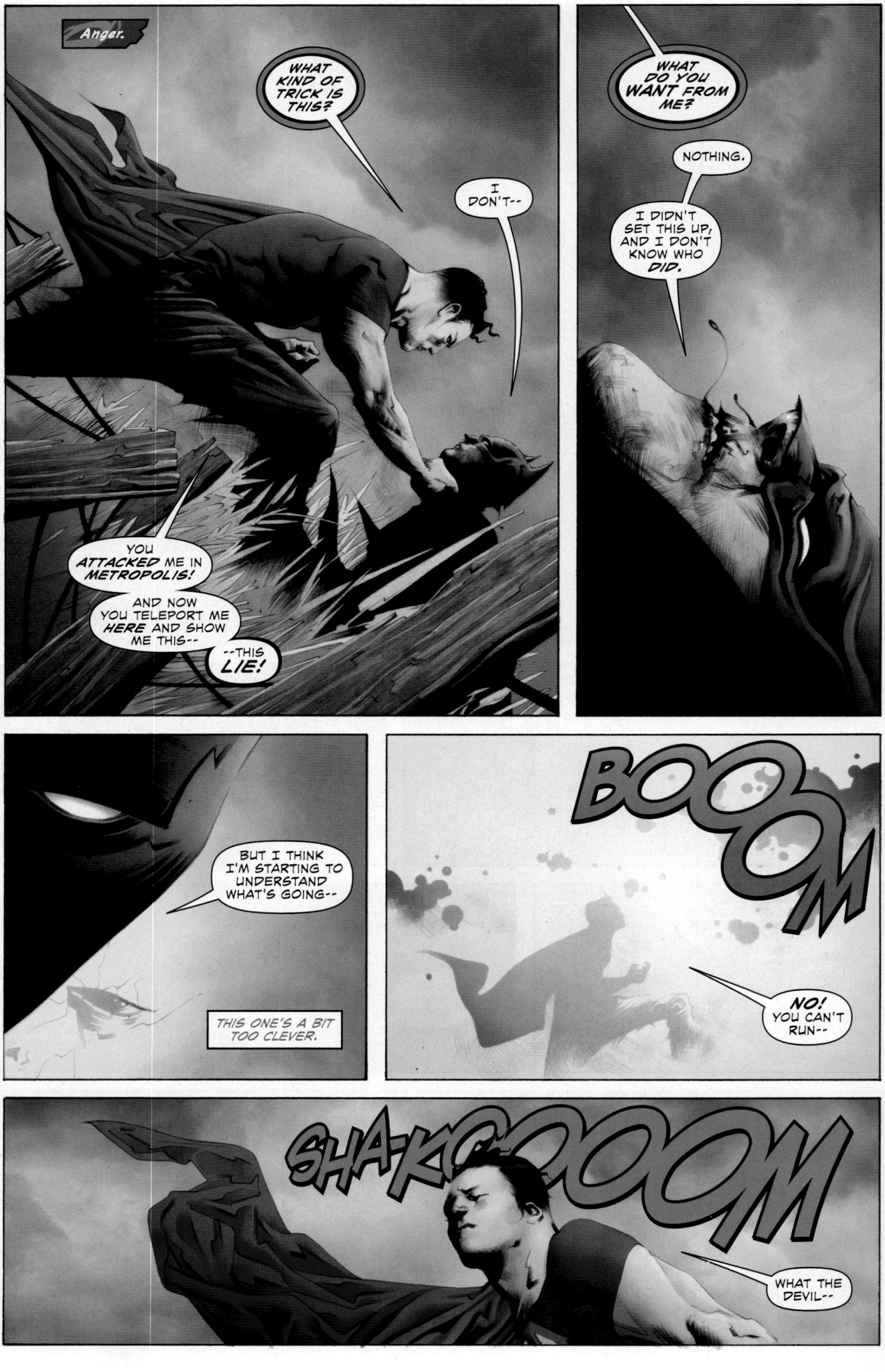
Anger.
WHAT KIND OF TRICK IS THIS?
I DON'T--
YOU ATTACKED ME IN METROPOLIS!
AND NOW YOU TELEPORT ME HERE AND SHOW ME THIS--
--THIS LIE!
WHAT DO YOU WANT FROM ME?
NOTHING.
I DIDN'T SET THIS UP, AND I DON'T KNOW WHO DID.
BUT I THINK I'M STARTING TO UNDERSTAND WHAT'S GOING--
THIS ONE'S A BIT TOO CLEVER.
BOOOOM
NO! YOU CAN'T RUN--
SHA-KOOOOM
WHAT THE DEVIL--

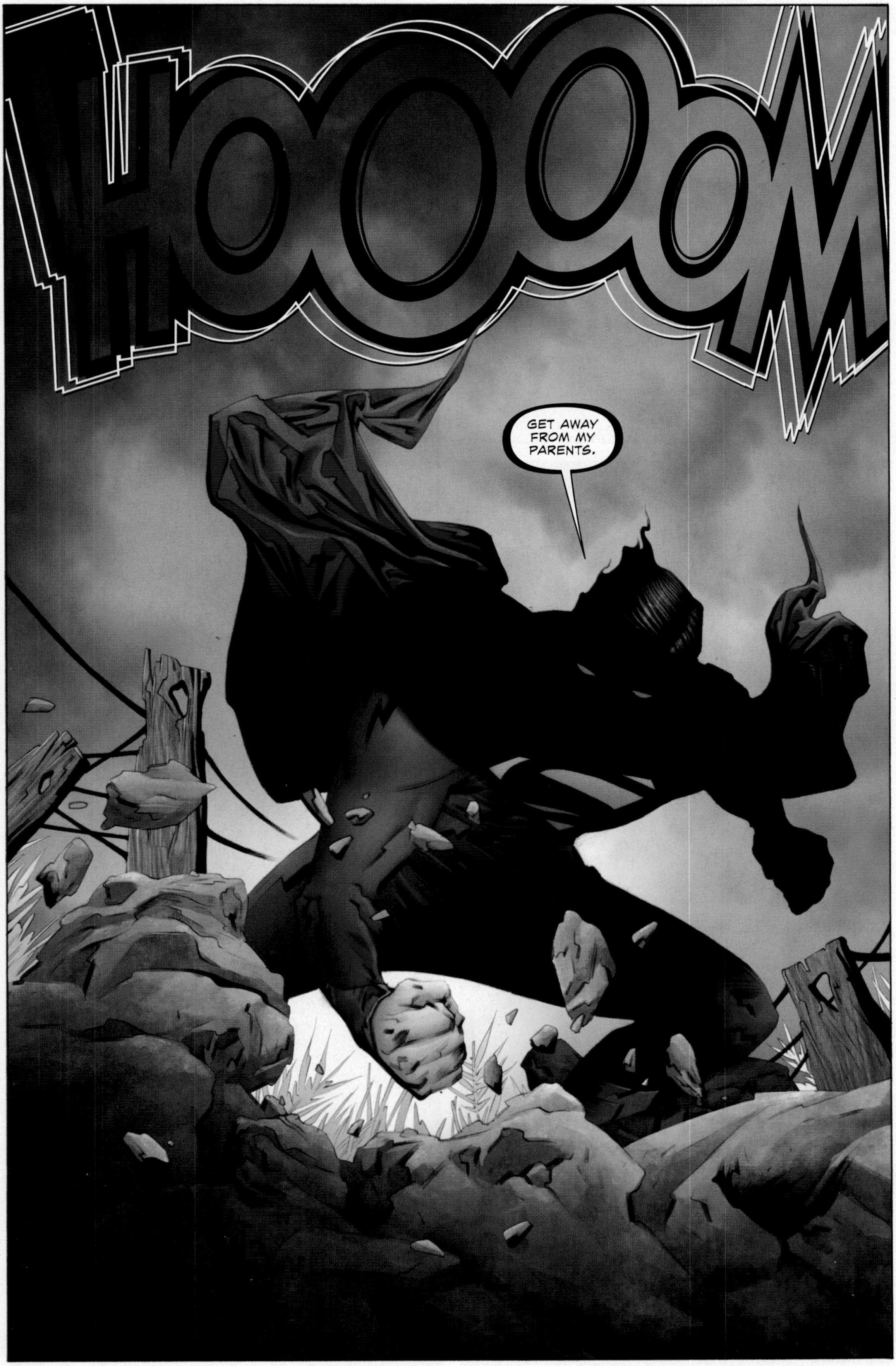

WHOOOOM
GET AWAY FROM MY PARENTS.

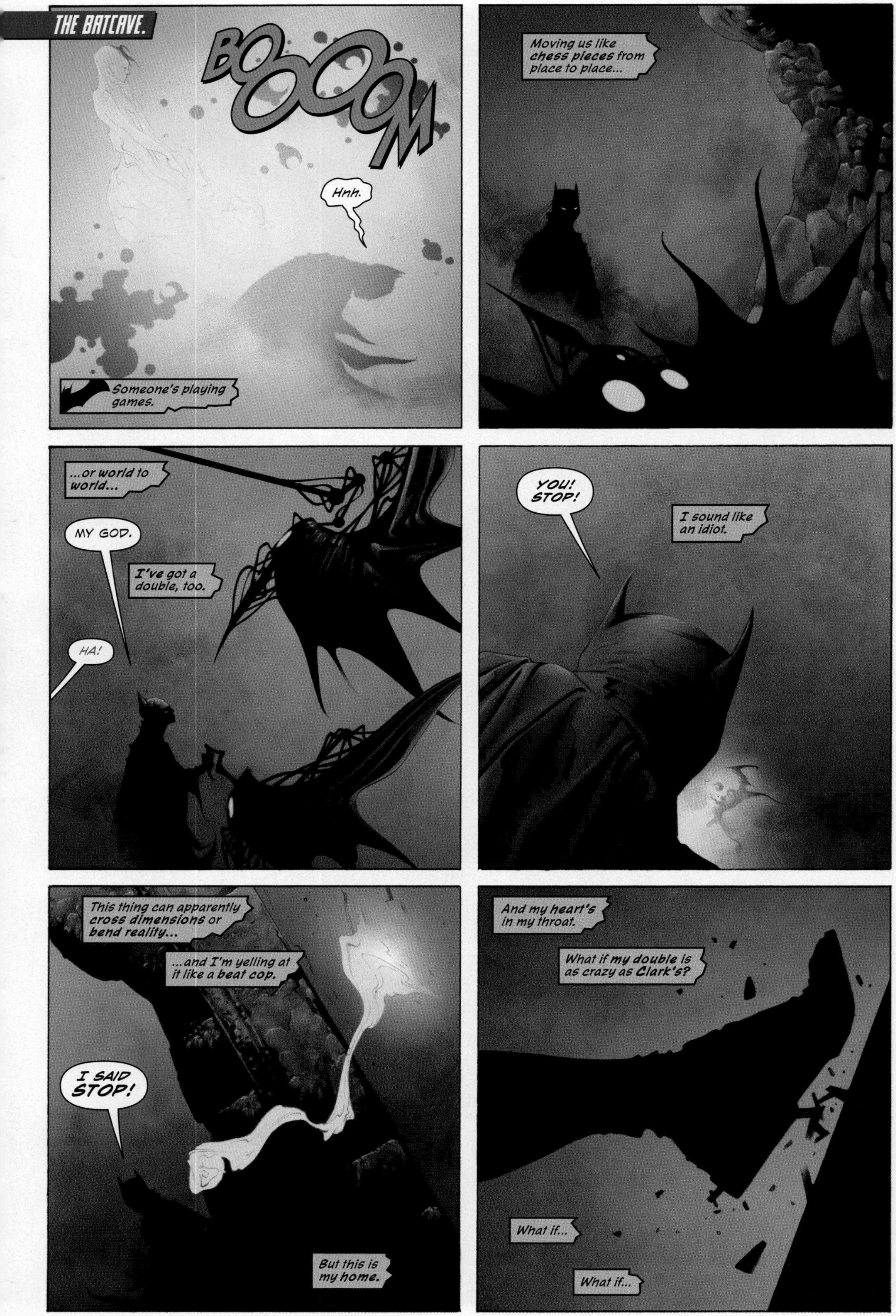
THE BATCAVE.
BOOOOOM
Hnh.
Someone's playing games.
Moving us like chess pieces from place to place...
...or world to world...
MY GOD.
I've got a double, too.
HA!
YOU! STOP!
I sound like an idiot.
This thing can apparently cross dimensions or bend reality...
...and I'm yelling at it like a beat cop.
I SAID STOP!
But this is my home.
And my heart's in my throat.
What if my double is as crazy as Clark's?
What if...
What if...

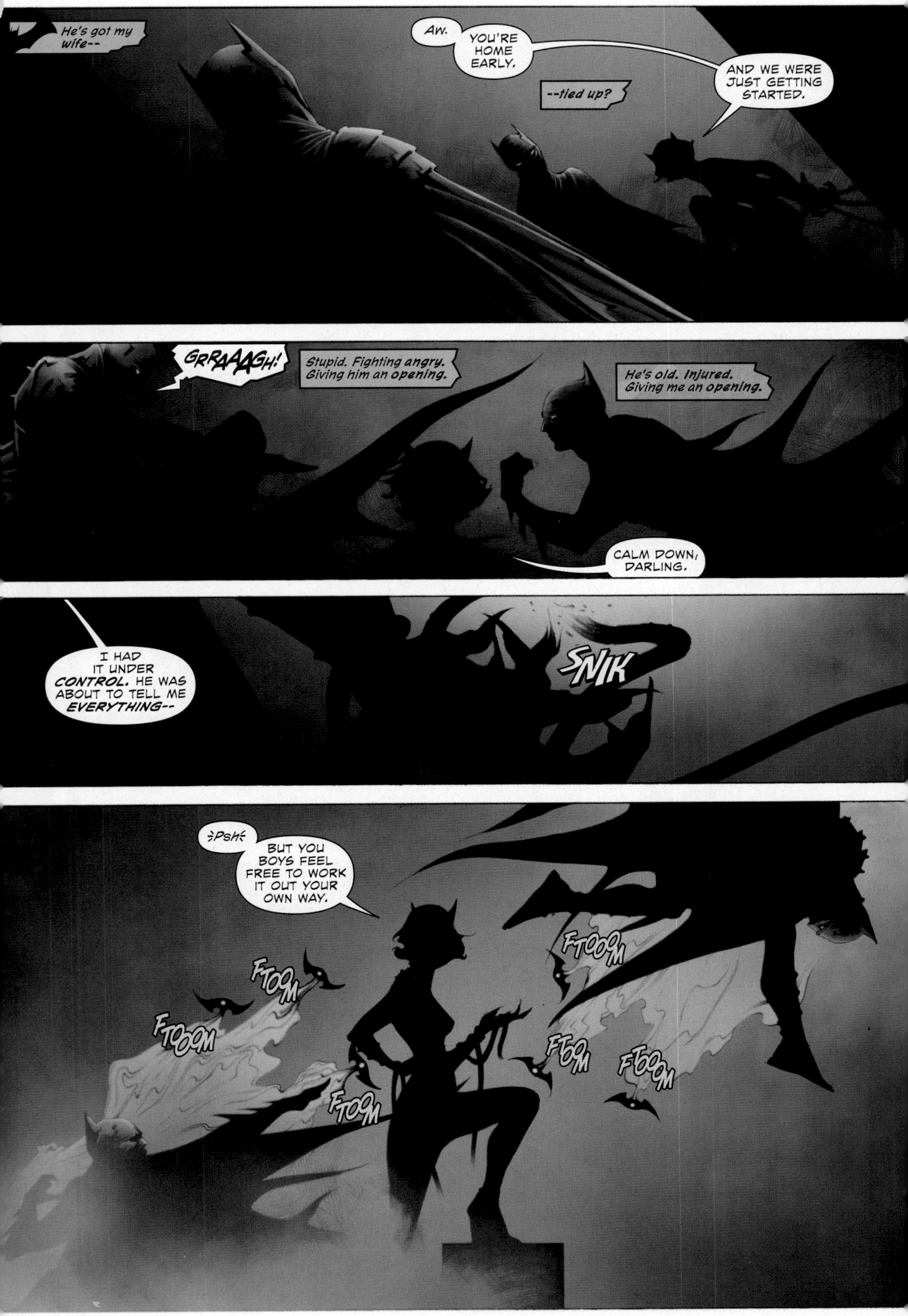
He's got my wife--
Aw.
YOU'RE HOME EARLY.
--tied up?
AND WE WERE JUST GETTING STARTED.
GRRAAAGH!
Stupid. Fighting angry. Giving him an opening.
He's old. Injured. Giving me an opening.
CALM DOWN, DARLING.
I HAD IT UNDER CONTROL. HE WAS ABOUT TO TELL ME EVERYTHING--
SNIK
Psh
BUT YOU BOYS FEEL FREE TO WORK IT OUT YOUR OWN WAY.
FTOOOM
FTOOM
FTOOOM
FTOOM
FTOOM
FTOOOM
FTOOOM

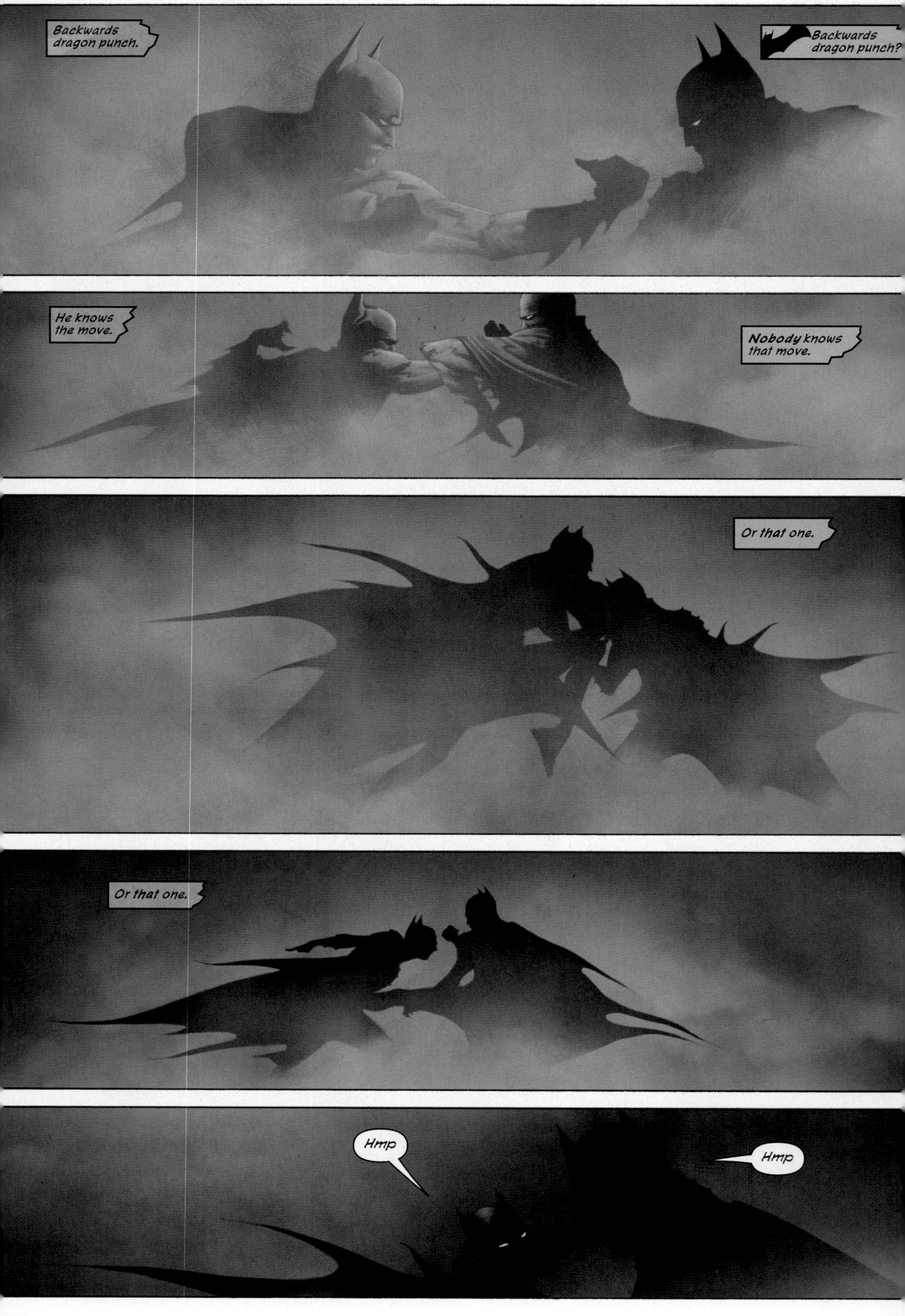
Backwards dragon punch.
Backwards dragon punch?
He knows the move.
Nobody knows that move.
Or that one.
Or that one.
Hmp
Hmp

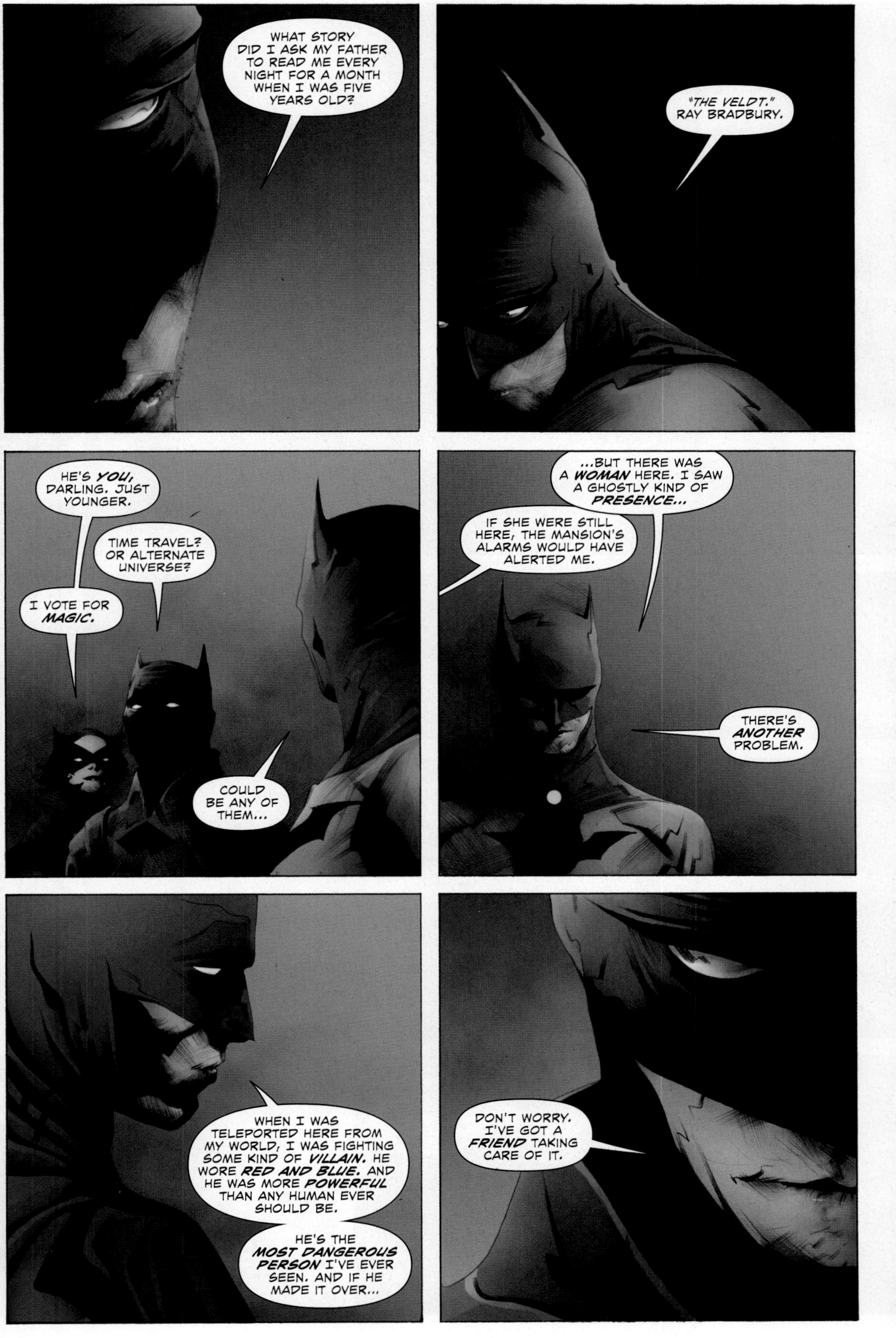
WHAT STORY DID I ASK MY FATHER TO READ ME EVERY NIGHT FOR A MONTH WHEN I WAS FIVE YEARS OLD?
"THE VELDT." RAY BRADBURY.
HE'S YOU, DARLING. JUST YOUNGER.
TIME TRAVEL? OR ALTERNATE UNIVERSE?
I VOTE FOR MAGIC.
COULD BE ANY OF THEM...
...BUT THERE WAS A WOMAN HERE. I SAW A GHOSTLY KIND OF PRESENCE...
IF SHE WERE STILL HERE, THE MANSION'S ALARMS WOULD HAVE ALERTED ME.
THERE'S ANOTHER PROBLEM.
WHEN I WAS TELEPORTED HERE FROM MY WORLD, I WAS FIGHTING SOME KIND OF VILLAIN. HE WORE RED AND BLUE. AND HE WAS MORE POWERFUL THAN ANY HUMAN EVER SHOULD BE.
HE'S THE MOST DANGEROUS PERSON I'VE EVER SEEN. AND IF HE MADE IT OVER...
DON'T WORRY. I'VE GOT A FRIEND TAKING CARE OF IT.

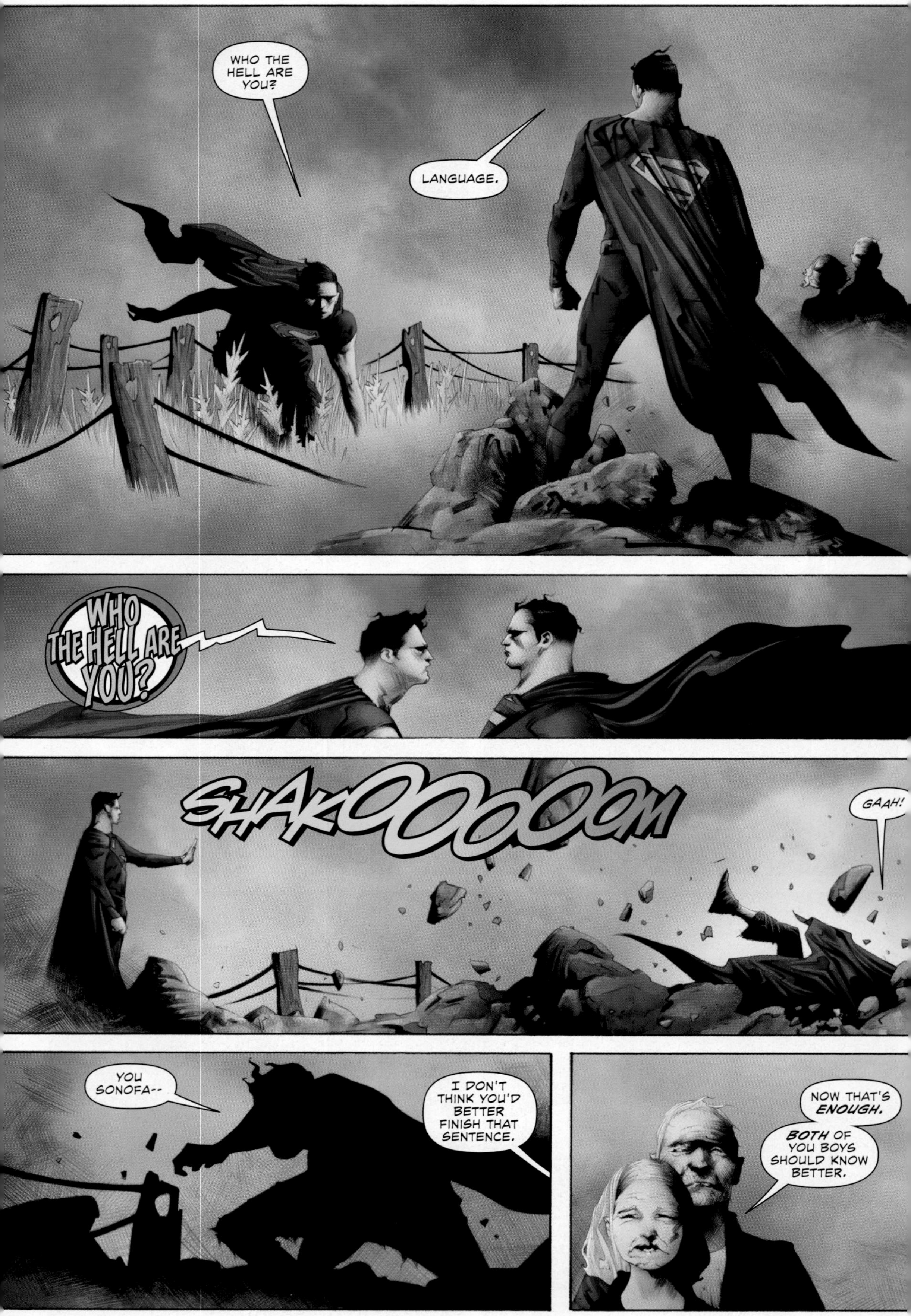
WHO THE HELL ARE YOU?
LANGUAGE.
WHO THE HELL ARE YOU?
SHAKOOOOOOOM
GAAH!
YOU SONOFA--
I DON'T THINK YOU'D BETTER FINISH THAT SENTENCE.
NOW THAT'S ENOUGH.
BOTH OF YOU BOYS SHOULD KNOW BETTER.

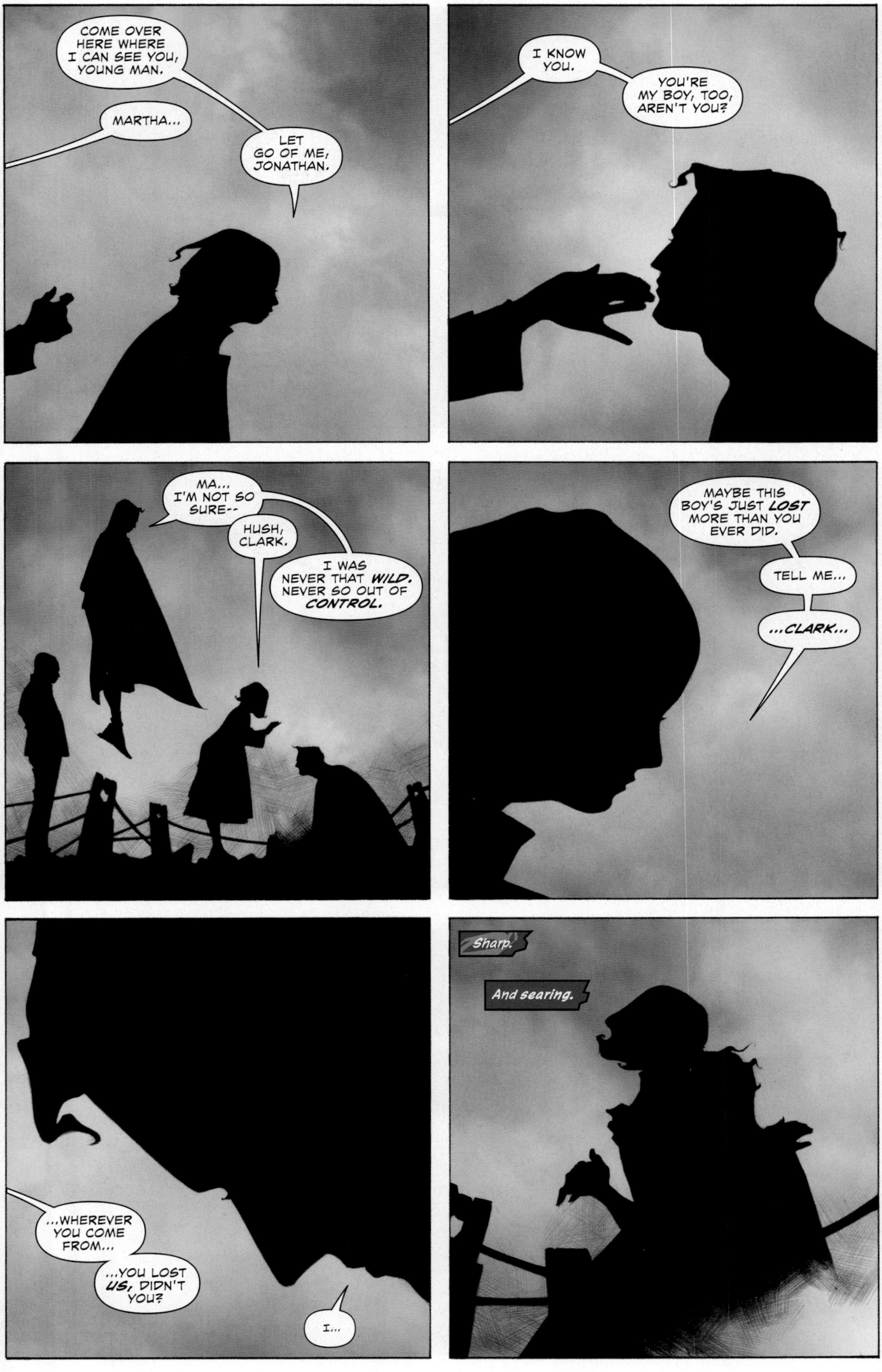
COME OVER HERE WHERE I CAN SEE YOU, YOUNG MAN.
MARTHA...
LET GO OF ME, JONATHAN.
I KNOW YOU.
YOU'RE MY BOY, TOO, AREN'T YOU?
MA... I'M NOT SO SURE--
HUSH, CLARK.
I WAS NEVER THAT WILD. NEVER SO OUT OF CONTROL.
MAYBE THIS BOY'S JUST LOST MORE THAN YOU EVER DID.
TELL ME...
...CLARK...
...WHEREVER YOU COME FROM...
...YOU LOST US, DIDN'T YOU?
I...
Sharp.
And searing.

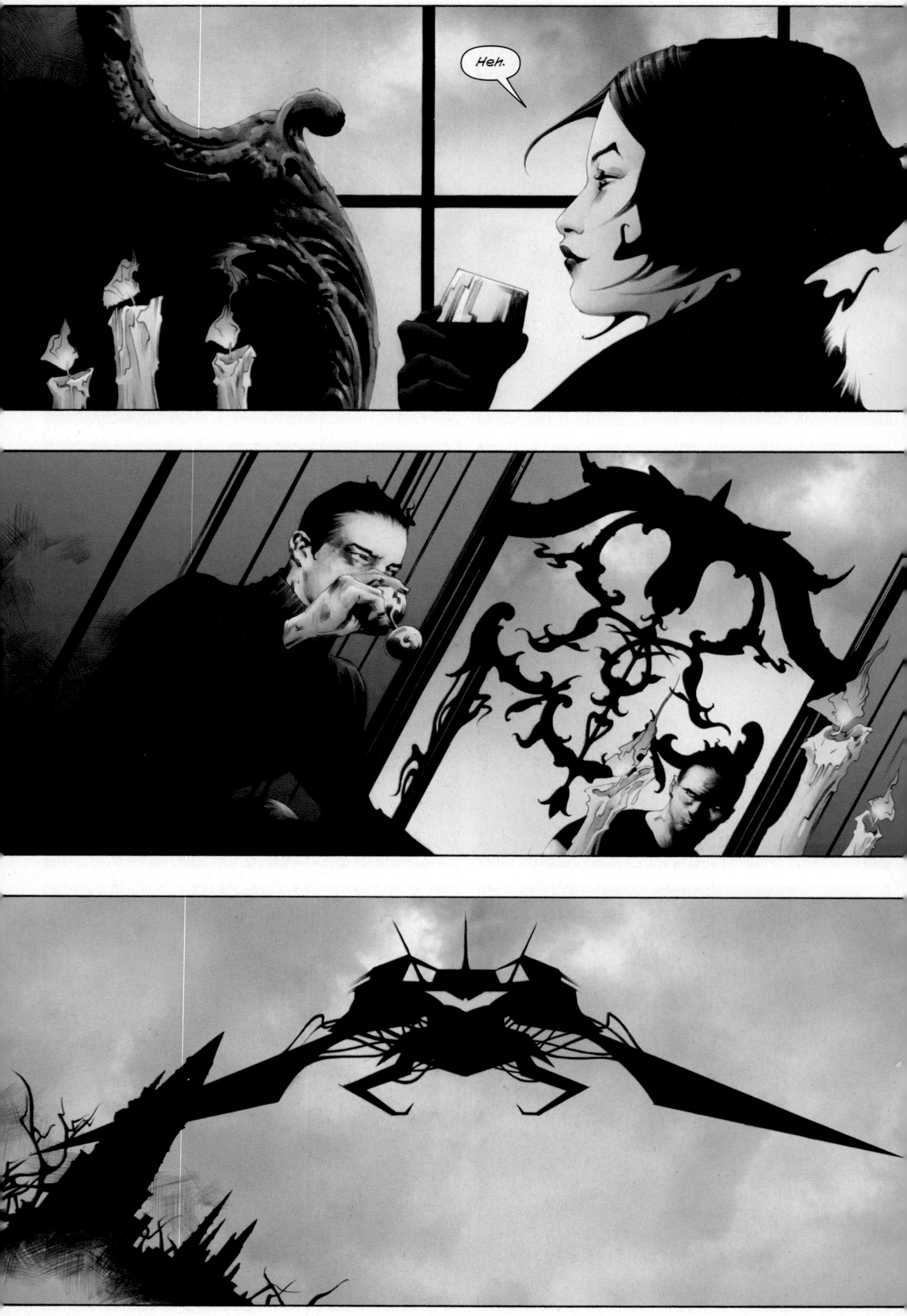
Heh.

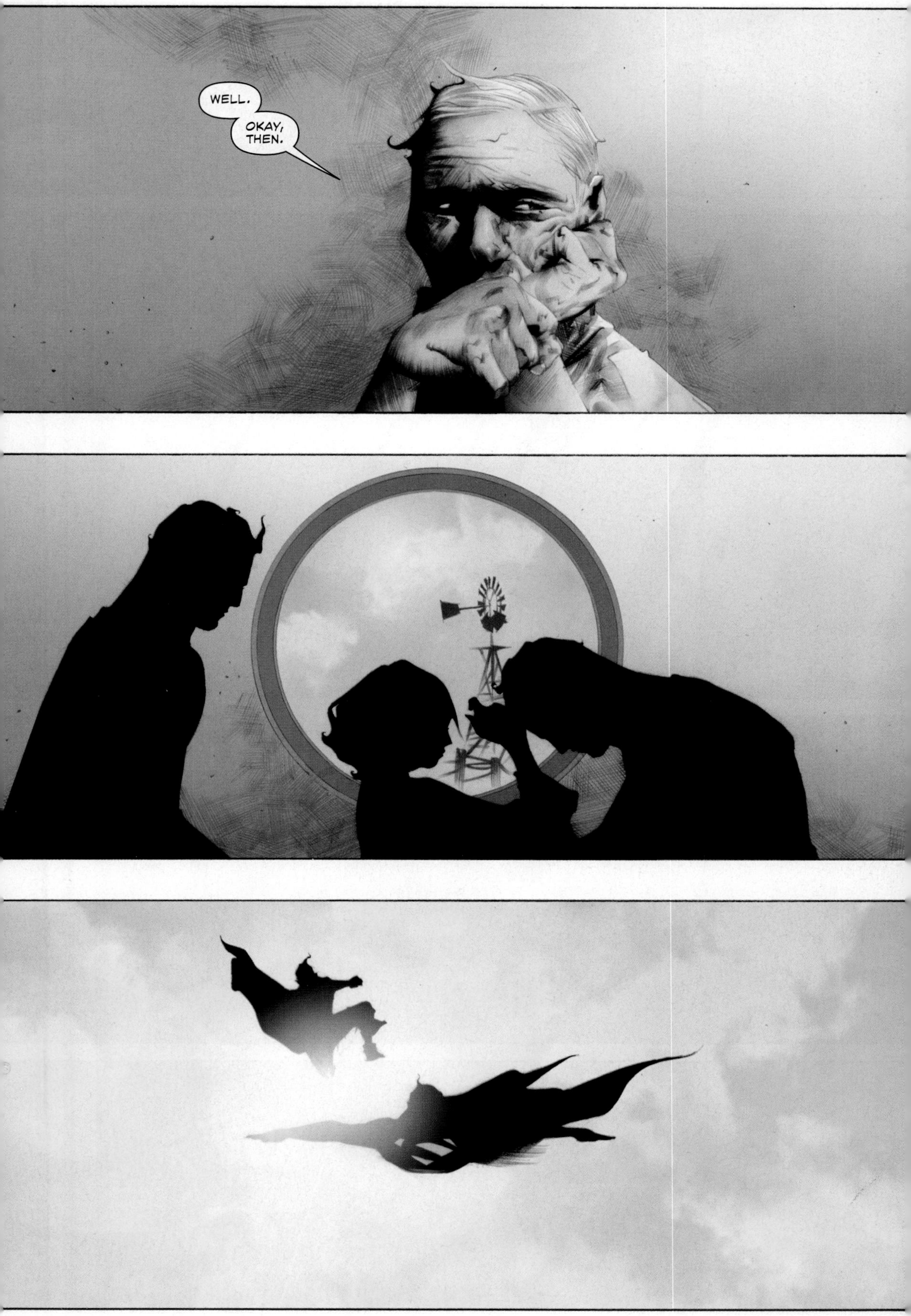
WELL.
OKAY, THEN.

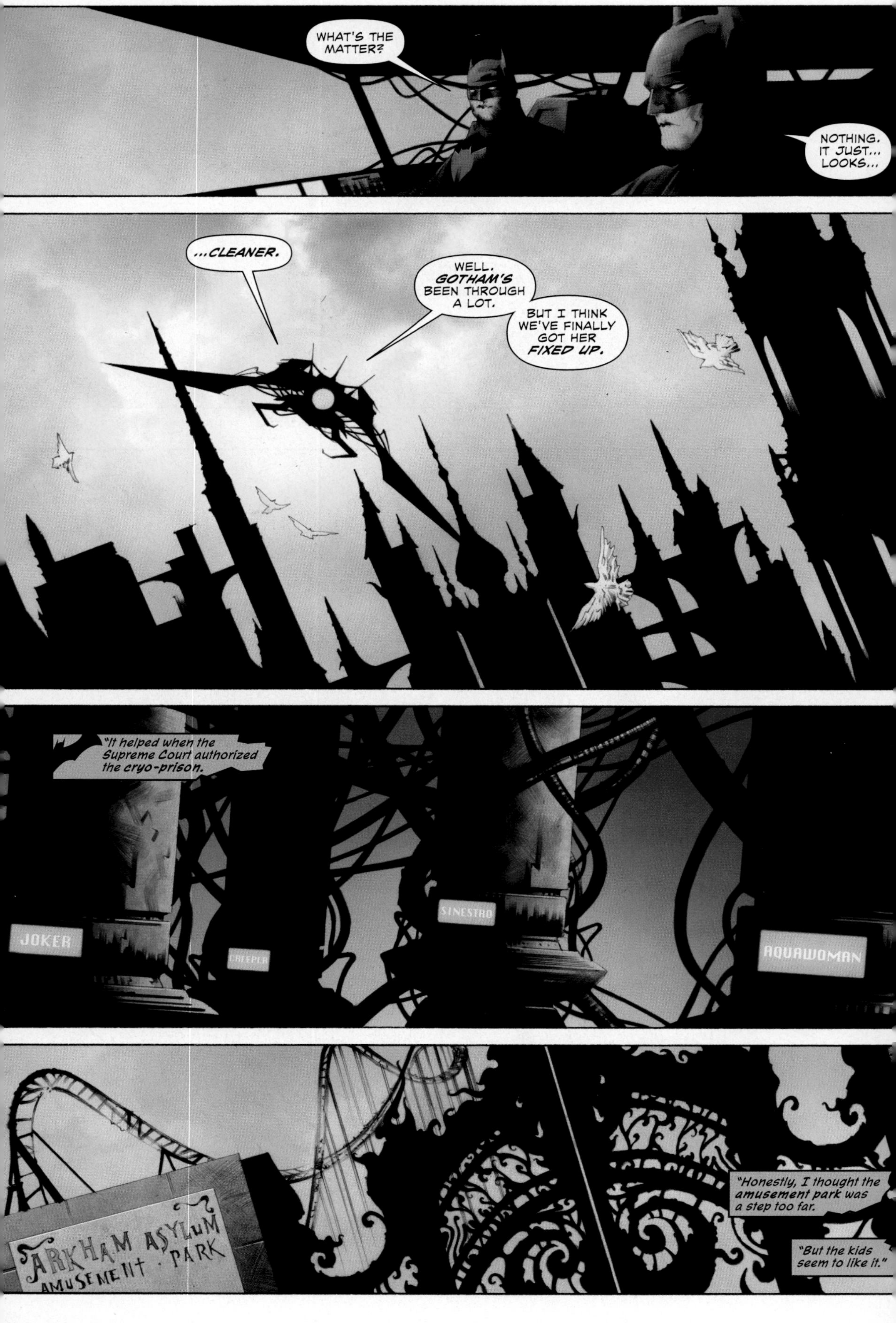

WHAT'S THE MATTER?
NOTHING. IT JUST... LOOKS...
...CLEANER.
WELL. GOTHAM'S BEEN THROUGH A LOT.
BUT I THINK WE'VE FINALLY GOT HER FIXED UP.
"It helped when the Supreme Court authorized the cryo-prison.
JOKER
CREEPER
SINESTRO
AQUAWOMAN
ARKHAM ASYLUM AMUSEMENT PARK
"Honestly, I thought the amusement park was a step too far.
"But the kids seem to like it."

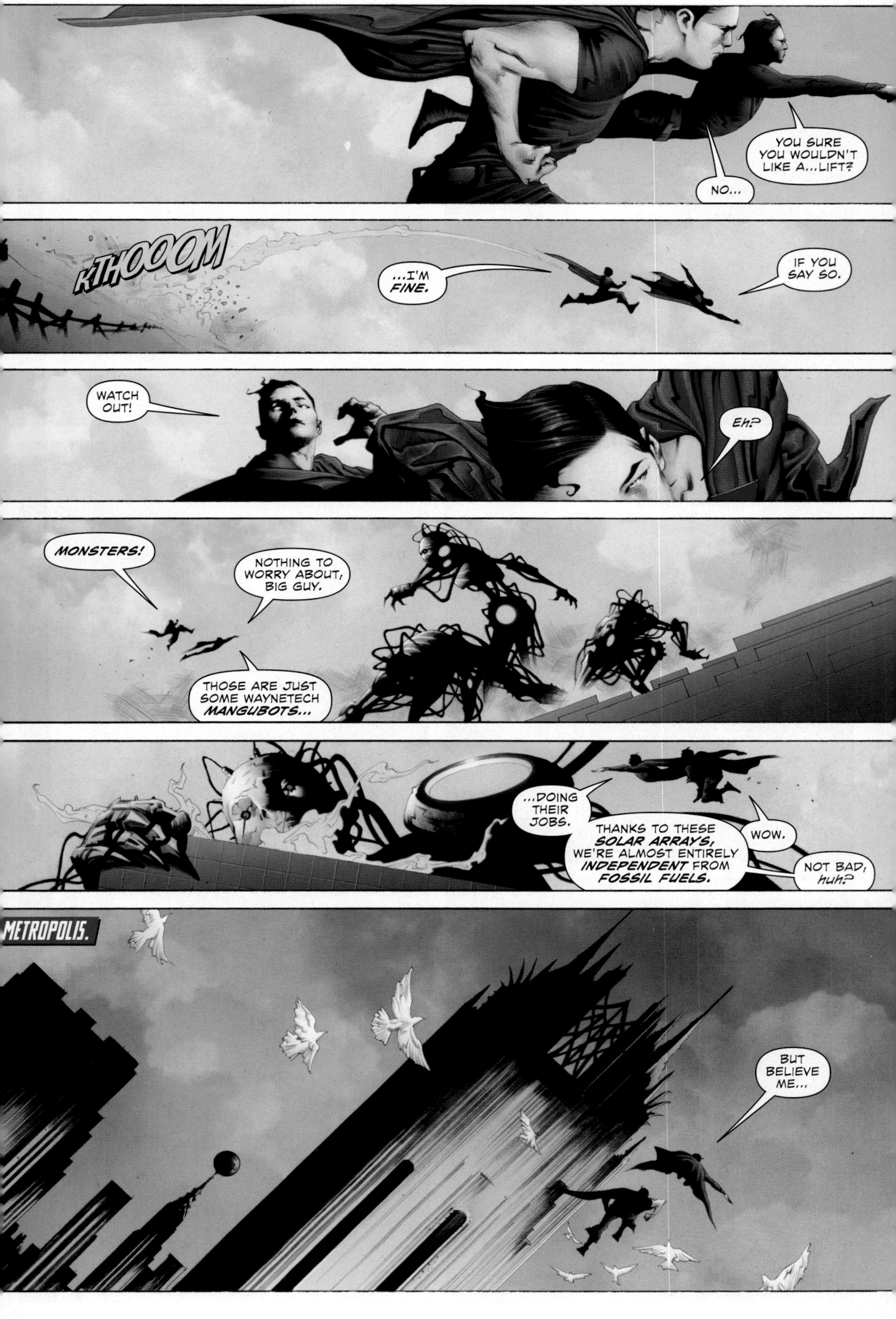
YOU SURE YOU WOULDN'T LIKE A...LIFT?
NO...
KTHOOOM
...I'M FINE.
IF YOU SAY SO.
WATCH OUT!
Eh?
MONSTERS!
NOTHING TO WORRY ABOUT, BIG GUY.
THOSE ARE JUST SOME WAYNETECH MANGUBOTS...
...DOING THEIR JOBS.
THANKS TO THESE SOLAR ARRAYS, WE'RE ALMOST ENTIRELY INDEPENDENT FROM FOSSIL FUELS.
WOW.
NOT BAD, huh?
METROPOLIS.
BUT BELIEVE ME...

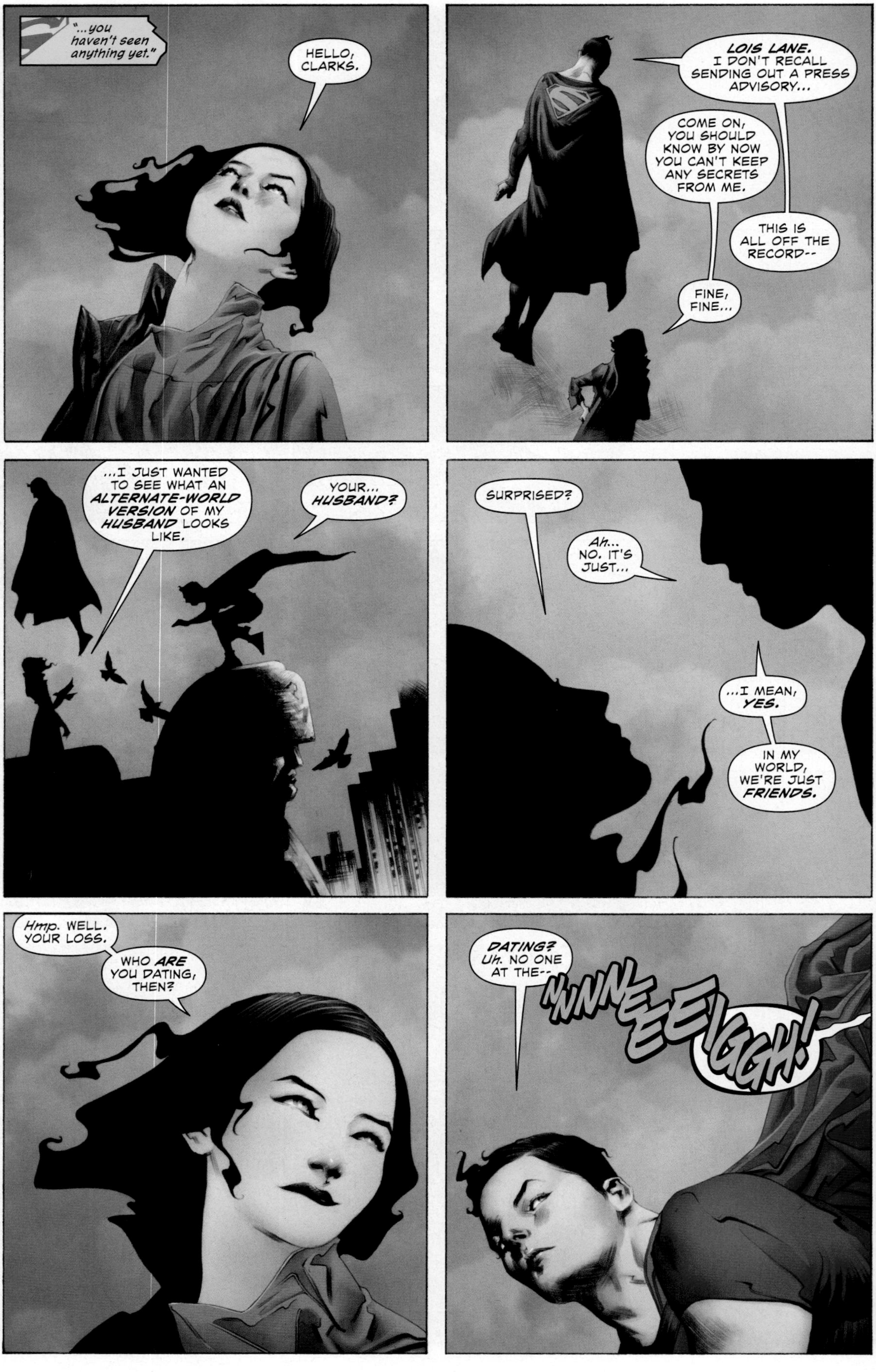
"...you haven't seen anything yet."
HELLO, CLARKS.
LOIS LANE. I DON'T RECALL SENDING OUT A PRESS ADVISORY...
COME ON, YOU SHOULD KNOW BY NOW YOU CAN'T KEEP ANY SECRETS FROM ME.
THIS IS ALL OFF THE RECORD--
FINE, FINE...
...I JUST WANTED TO SEE WHAT AN ALTERNATE-WORLD VERSION OF MY HUSBAND LOOKS LIKE.
YOUR... HUSBAND?
SURPRISED?
Ah... NO. IT'S JUST...
...I MEAN, YES.
IN MY WORLD, WE'RE JUST FRIENDS.
Hmp. WELL. YOUR LOSS.
WHO ARE YOU DATING, THEN?
DATING? Uh. NO ONE AT THE--
NNNNEEEIGGH!

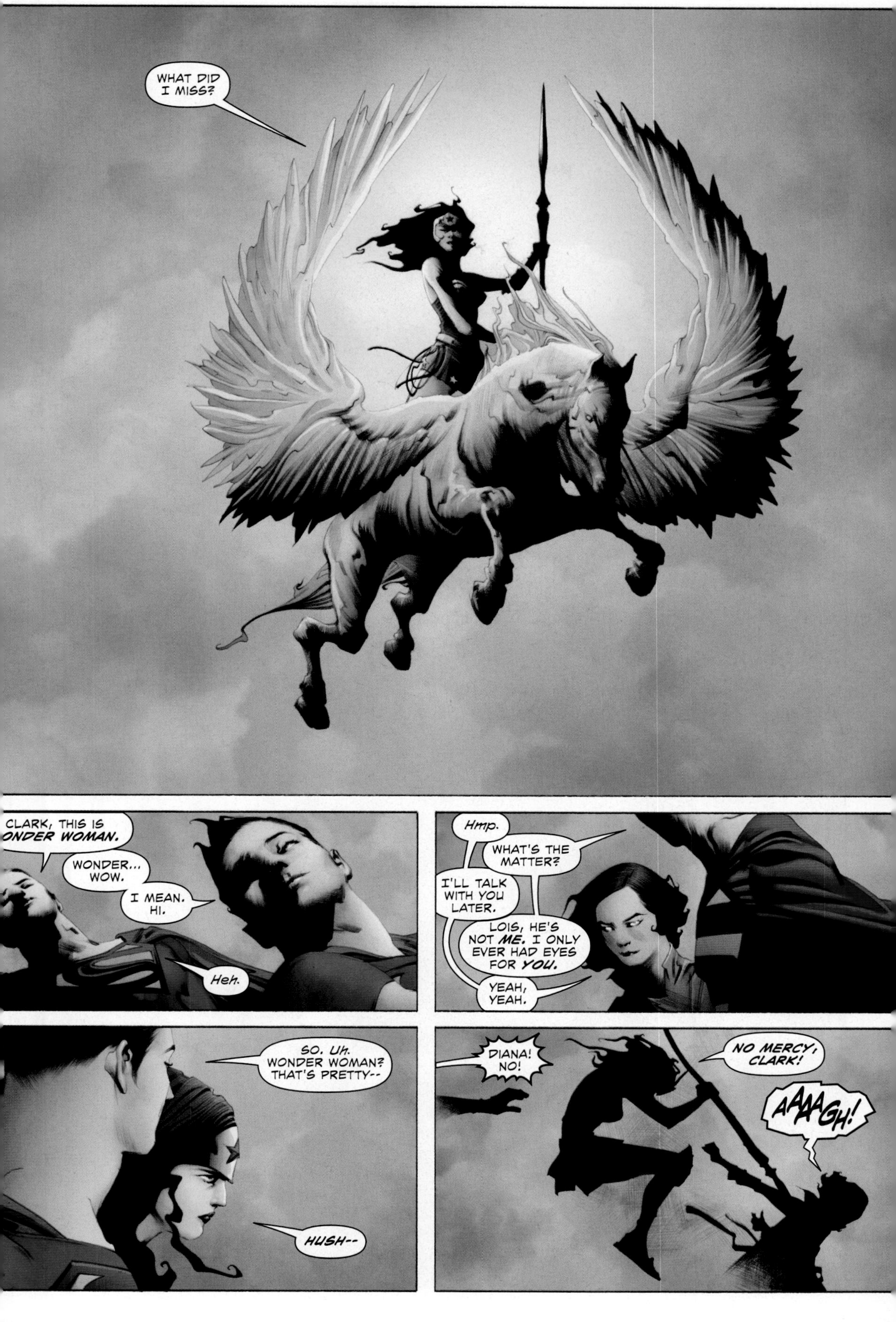
WHAT DID I MISS?
CLARK, THIS IS WONDER WOMAN.
WONDER... WOW.
I MEAN. HI.
Heh.
Hmp.
WHAT'S THE MATTER?
I'LL TALK WITH YOU LATER.
LOIS, HE'S NOT ME. I ONLY EVER HAD EYES FOR YOU.
YEAH, YEAH.
SO. Uh. WONDER WOMAN? THAT'S PRETTY--
HUSH--
DIANA! NO!
NO MERCY, CLARK!
AAAAGH!

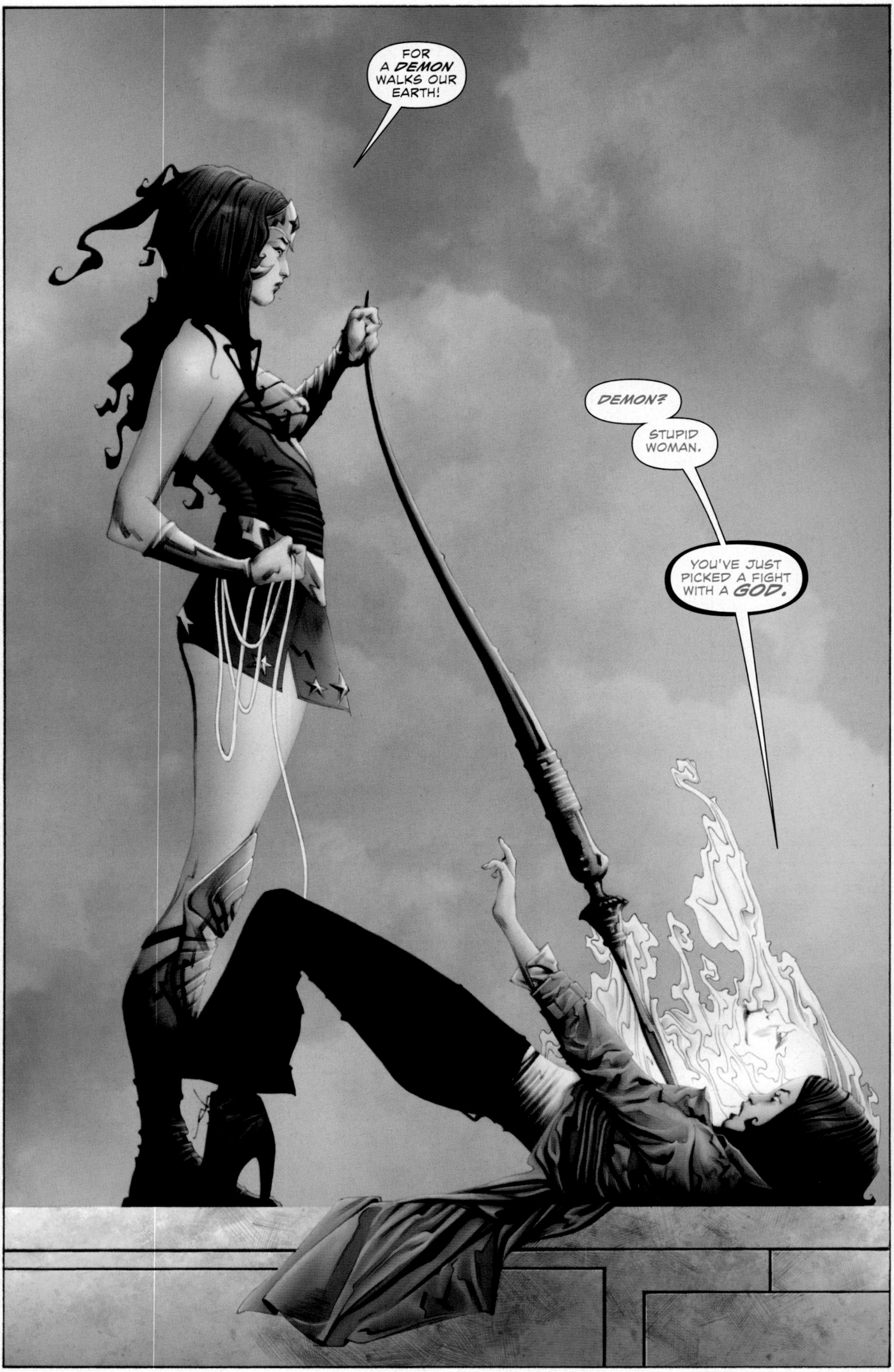
FOR A *DEMON* WALKS OUR EARTH!
DEMON?
STUPID WOMAN.
YOU'VE JUST PICKED A FIGHT WITH A ***GOD.***

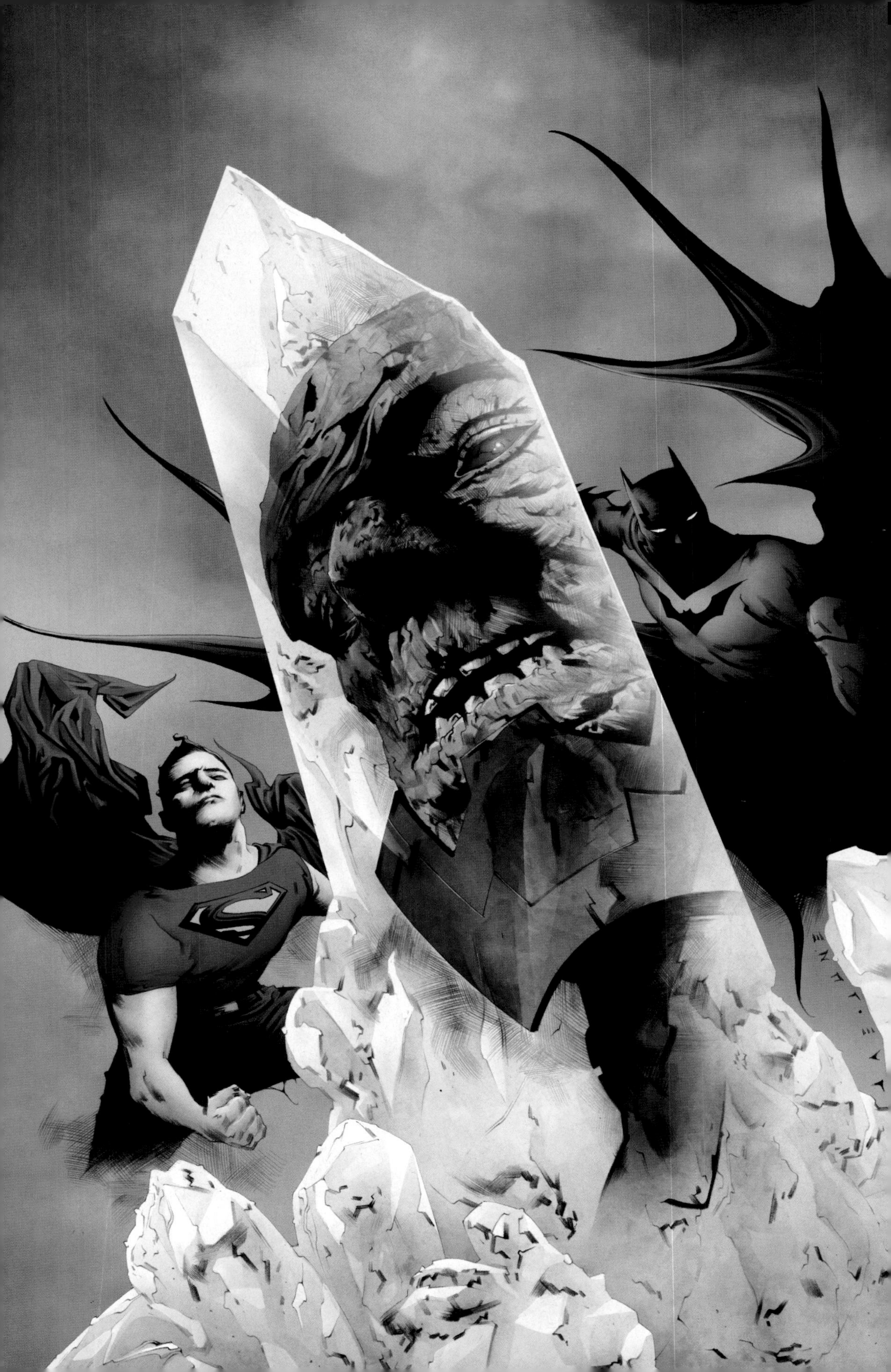

GREG PAK writer JAE LEE & YILDIRAY CINAR artists JUNE CHUNG, MATT YACKEY & JOHN KALISZ colorists cover by JAE LEE with JUNE CHUNG

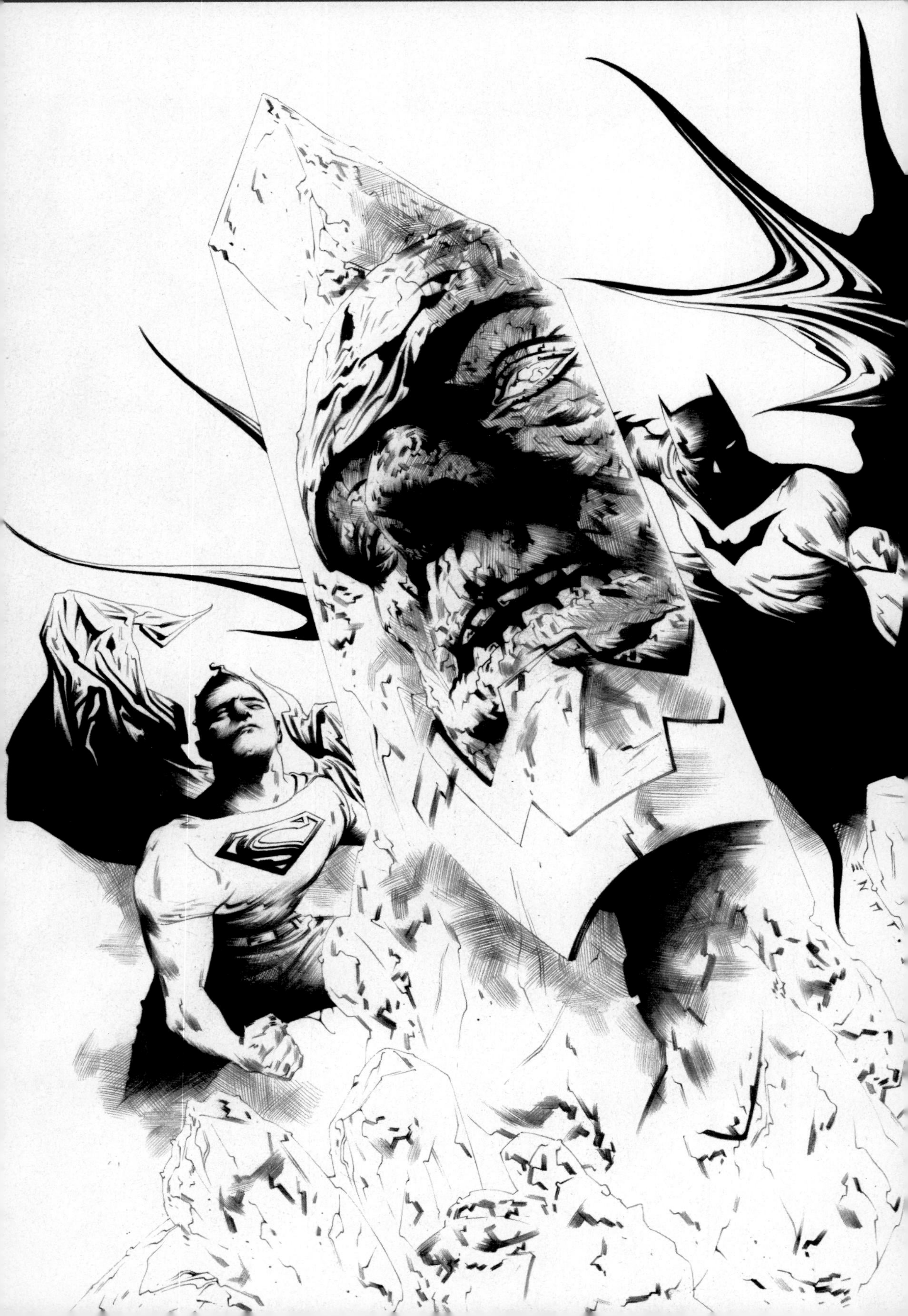

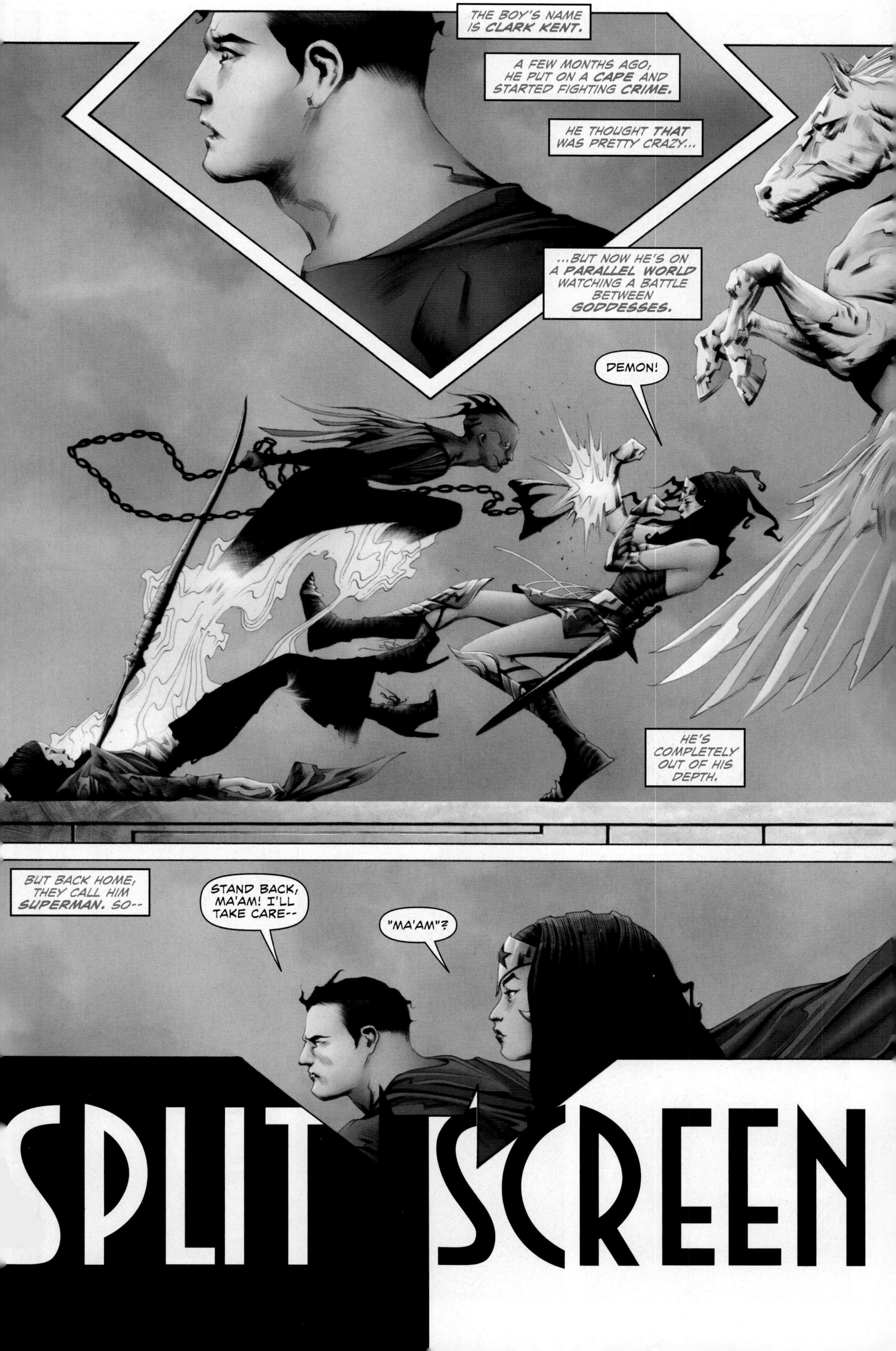
THE BOY'S NAME IS CLARK KENT.
A FEW MONTHS AGO, HE PUT ON A CAPE AND STARTED FIGHTING CRIME.
HE THOUGHT THAT WAS PRETTY CRAZY...
...BUT NOW HE'S ON A PARALLEL WORLD WATCHING A BATTLE BETWEEN GODDESSES.
DEMON!
HE'S COMPLETELY OUT OF HIS DEPTH.
BUT BACK HOME, THEY CALL HIM SUPERMAN. SO--
STAND BACK, MA'AM! I'LL TAKE CARE--
"MA'AM"?
SPLIT SCREEN

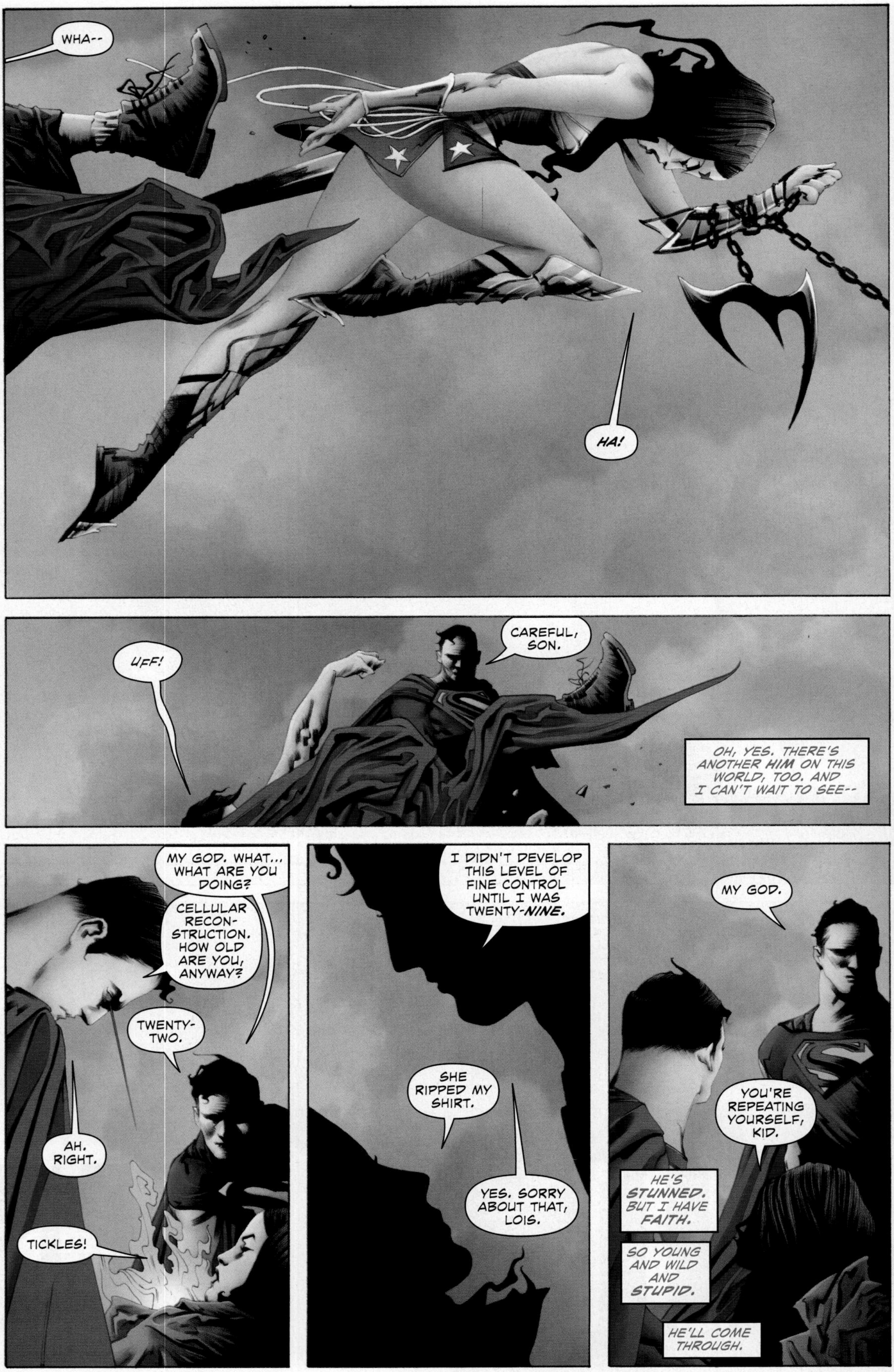
WHA--
HA!
CAREFUL, SON.
UFF!
OH, YES. THERE'S ANOTHER HIM ON THIS WORLD, TOO. AND I CAN'T WAIT TO SEE--
MY GOD. WHAT... WHAT ARE YOU DOING?
CELLULAR RECON-STRUCTION. HOW OLD ARE YOU, ANYWAY?
TWENTY-TWO.
AH. RIGHT.
TICKLES!
I DIDN'T DEVELOP THIS LEVEL OF FINE CONTROL UNTIL I WAS TWENTY-NINE.
SHE RIPPED MY SHIRT.
YES. SORRY ABOUT THAT, LOIS.
MY GOD.
YOU'RE REPEATING YOURSELF, KID.
HE'S STUNNED. BUT I HAVE FAITH.
SO YOUNG AND WILD AND STUPID.
HE'LL COME THROUGH.

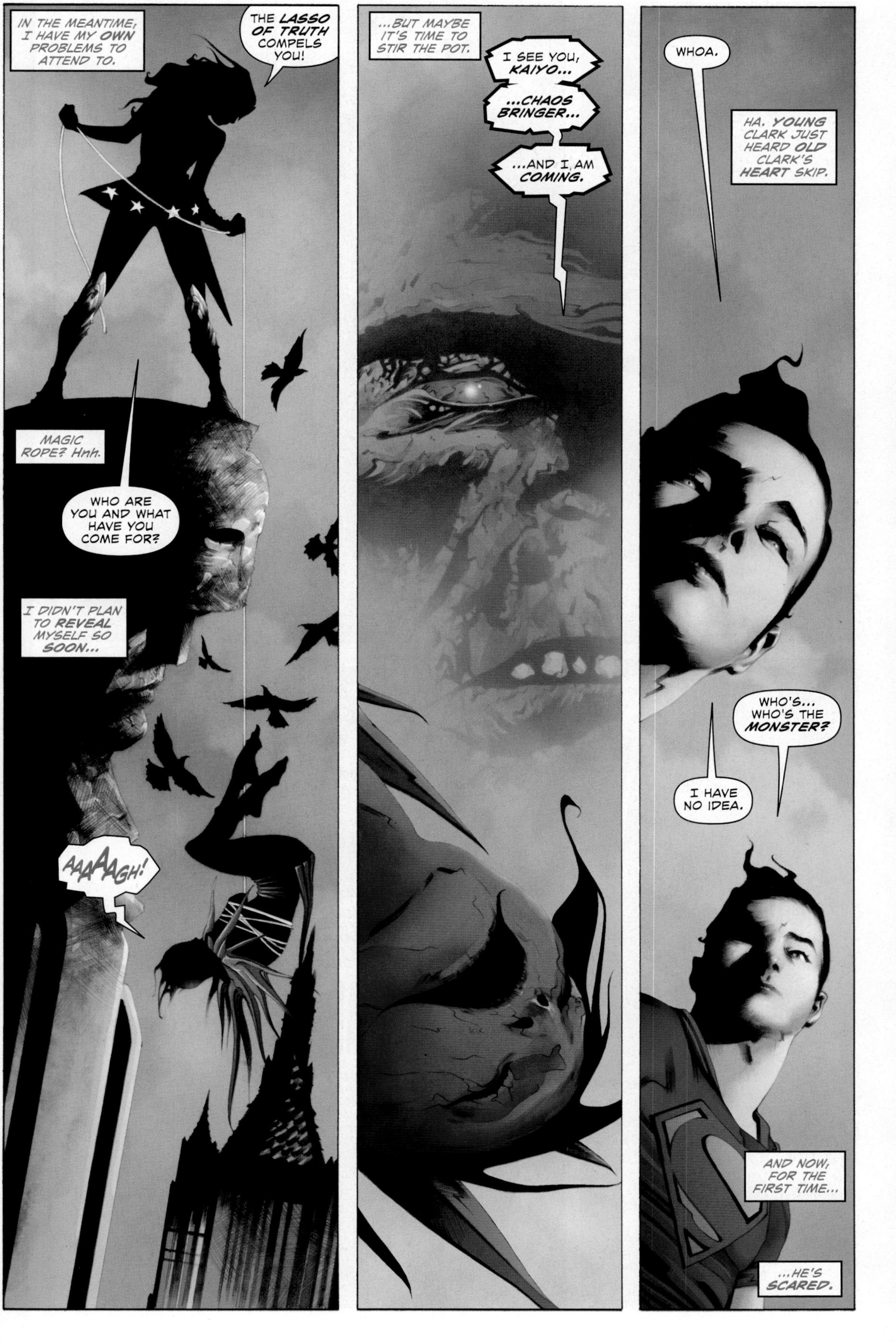
IN THE MEANTIME, I HAVE MY OWN PROBLEMS TO ATTEND TO.
THE LASSO OF TRUTH COMPELS YOU!
MAGIC ROPE? Hnh.
WHO ARE YOU AND WHAT HAVE YOU COME FOR?
I DIDN'T PLAN TO REVEAL MYSELF SO SOON...
AAAAAGH!
...BUT MAYBE IT'S TIME TO STIR THE POT.
I SEE YOU, KAIYO...
...CHAOS BRINGER...
...AND I AM COMING.
WHOA.
HA. YOUNG CLARK JUST HEARD OLD CLARK'S HEART SKIP.
WHO'S... WHO'S THE MONSTER?
I HAVE NO IDEA.
AND NOW, FOR THE FIRST TIME...
...HE'S SCARED.

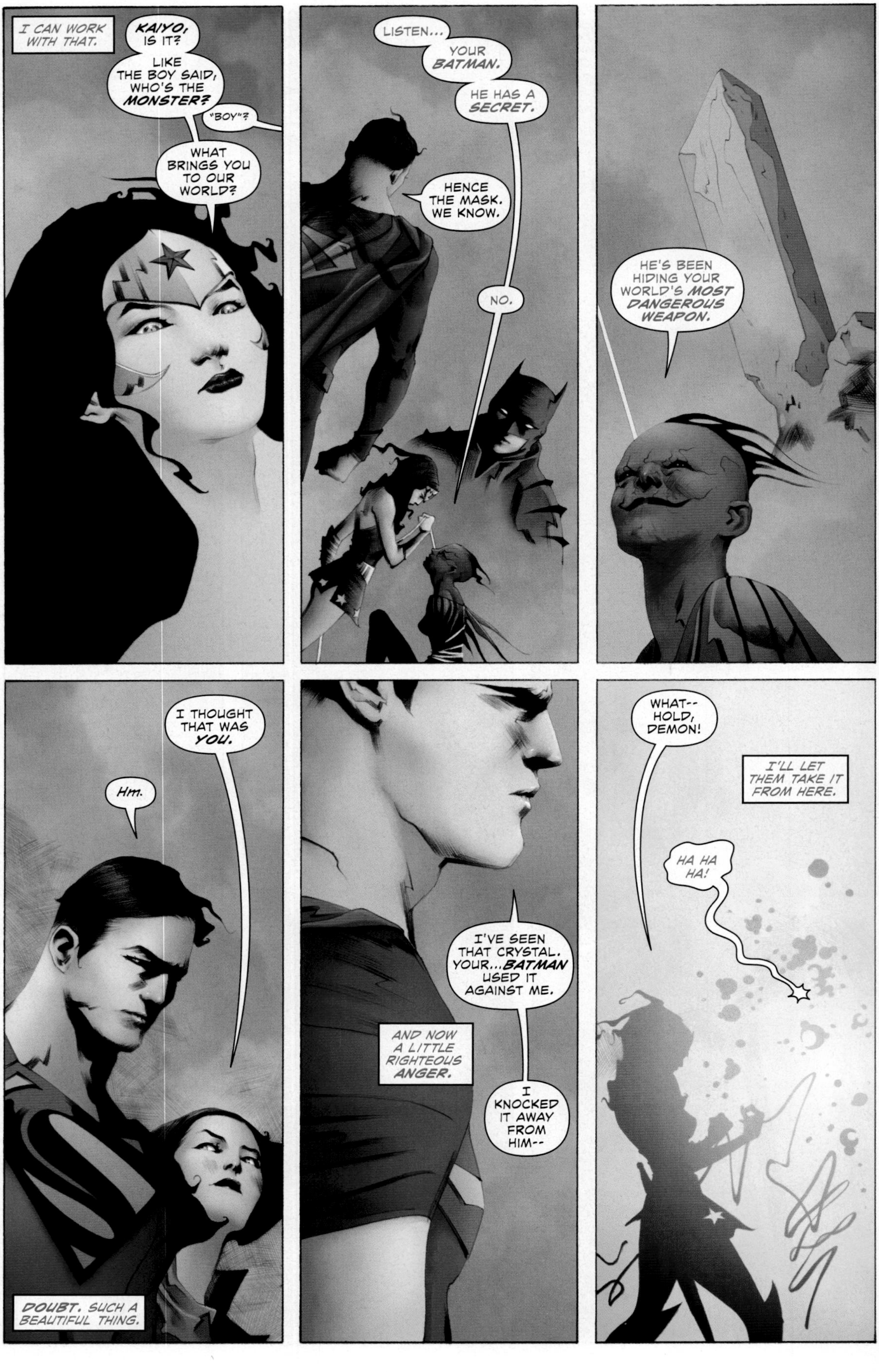

I CAN WORK WITH THAT.
KAIYO, IS IT?
LIKE THE BOY SAID, WHO'S THE MONSTER?
"BOY"?
WHAT BRINGS YOU TO OUR WORLD?
LISTEN...
YOUR BATMAN.
HE HAS A SECRET.
HENCE THE MASK. WE KNOW.
NO.
HE'S BEEN HIDING YOUR WORLD'S MOST DANGEROUS WEAPON.
I THOUGHT THAT WAS YOU.
Hm.
DOUBT. SUCH A BEAUTIFUL THING.
I'VE SEEN THAT CRYSTAL. YOUR...BATMAN USED IT AGAINST ME.
AND NOW A LITTLE RIGHTEOUS ANGER.
I KNOCKED IT AWAY FROM HIM--
WHAT-- HOLD, DEMON!
I'LL LET THEM TAKE IT FROM HERE.
HA HA HA!

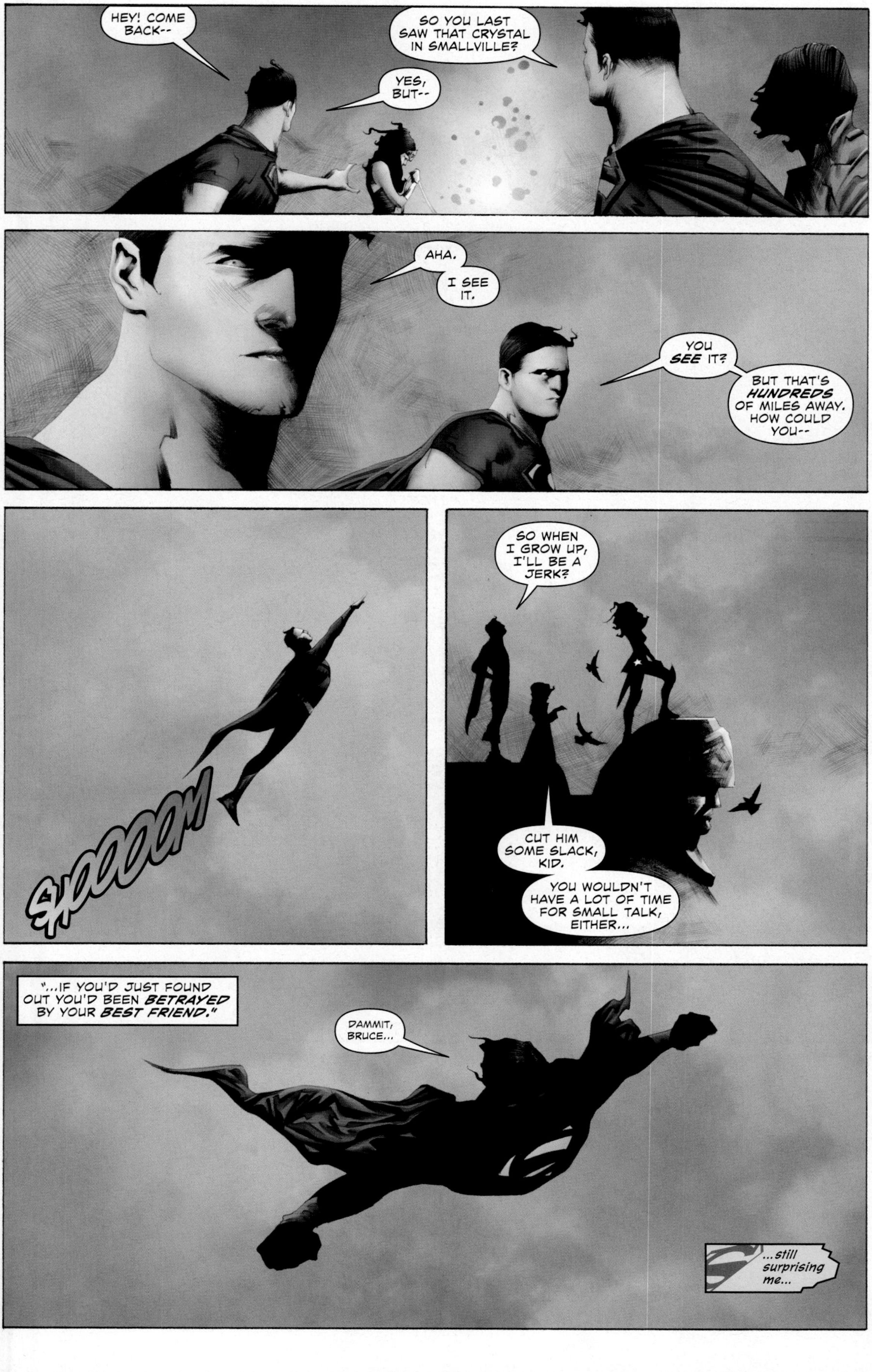
HEY! COME BACK--
SO YOU LAST SAW THAT CRYSTAL IN SMALLVILLE?
YES, BUT--
AHA.
I SEE IT.
YOU SEE IT?
BUT THAT'S HUNDREDS OF MILES AWAY. HOW COULD YOU--
SHOOOOM
SO WHEN I GROW UP, I'LL BE A JERK?
CUT HIM SOME SLACK, KID.
YOU WOULDN'T HAVE A LOT OF TIME FOR SMALL TALK, EITHER...
"...IF YOU'D JUST FOUND OUT YOU'D BEEN BETRAYED BY YOUR BEST FRIEND."
DAMMIT, BRUCE...
...still surprising me...

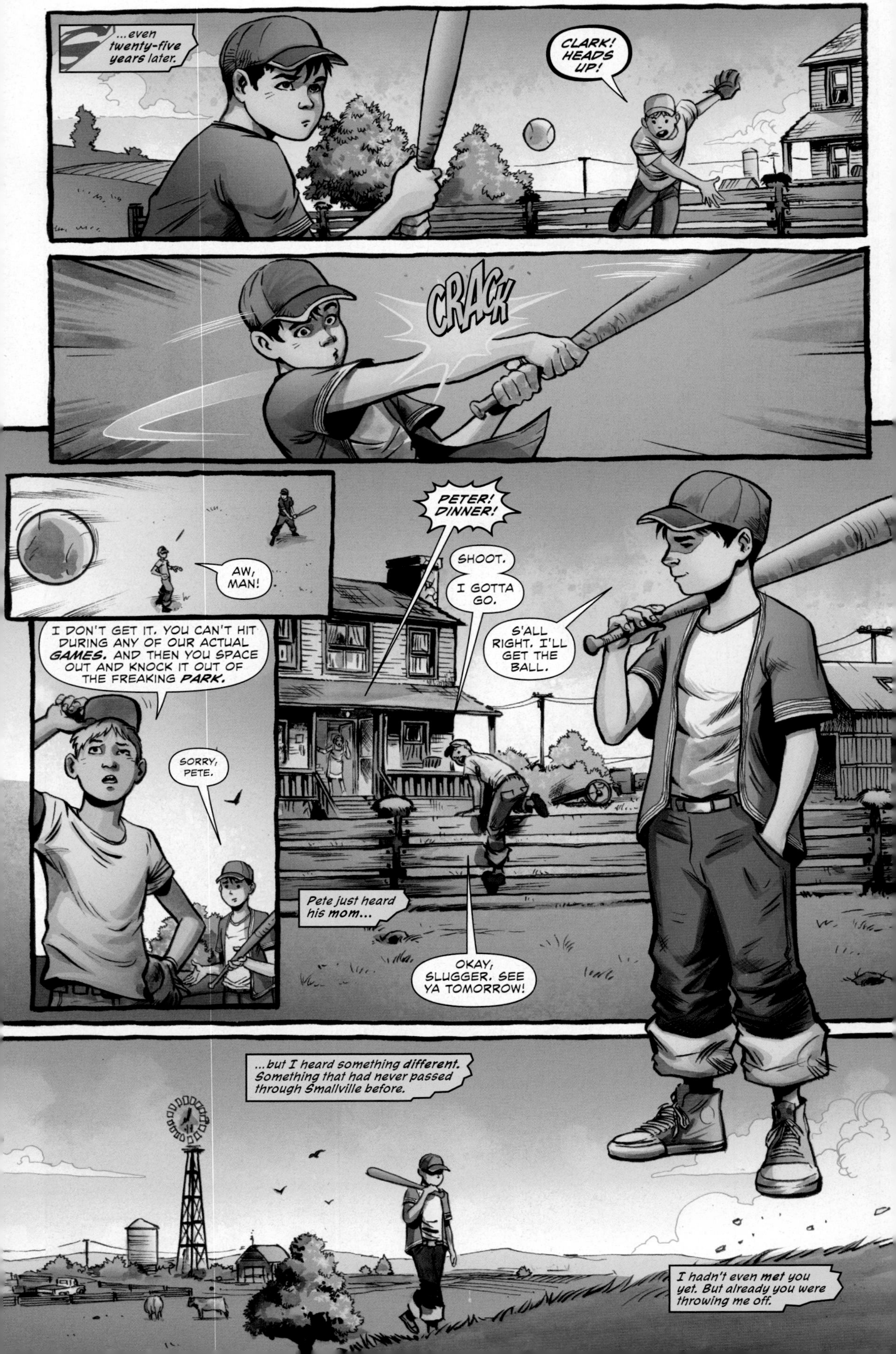
...even twenty-five years later.
CLARK! HEADS UP!
CRACK
AW, MAN!
I DON'T GET IT. YOU CAN'T HIT DURING ANY OF OUR ACTUAL GAMES. AND THEN YOU SPACE OUT AND KNOCK IT OUT OF THE FREAKING PARK.
SORRY, PETE.
PETER! DINNER!
SHOOT.
I GOTTA GO.
S'ALL RIGHT. I'LL GET THE BALL.
Pete just heard his mom...
OKAY, SLUGGER. SEE YA TOMORROW!
...but I heard something different. Something that had never passed through Smallville before.
I hadn't even met you yet. But already you were throwing me off.

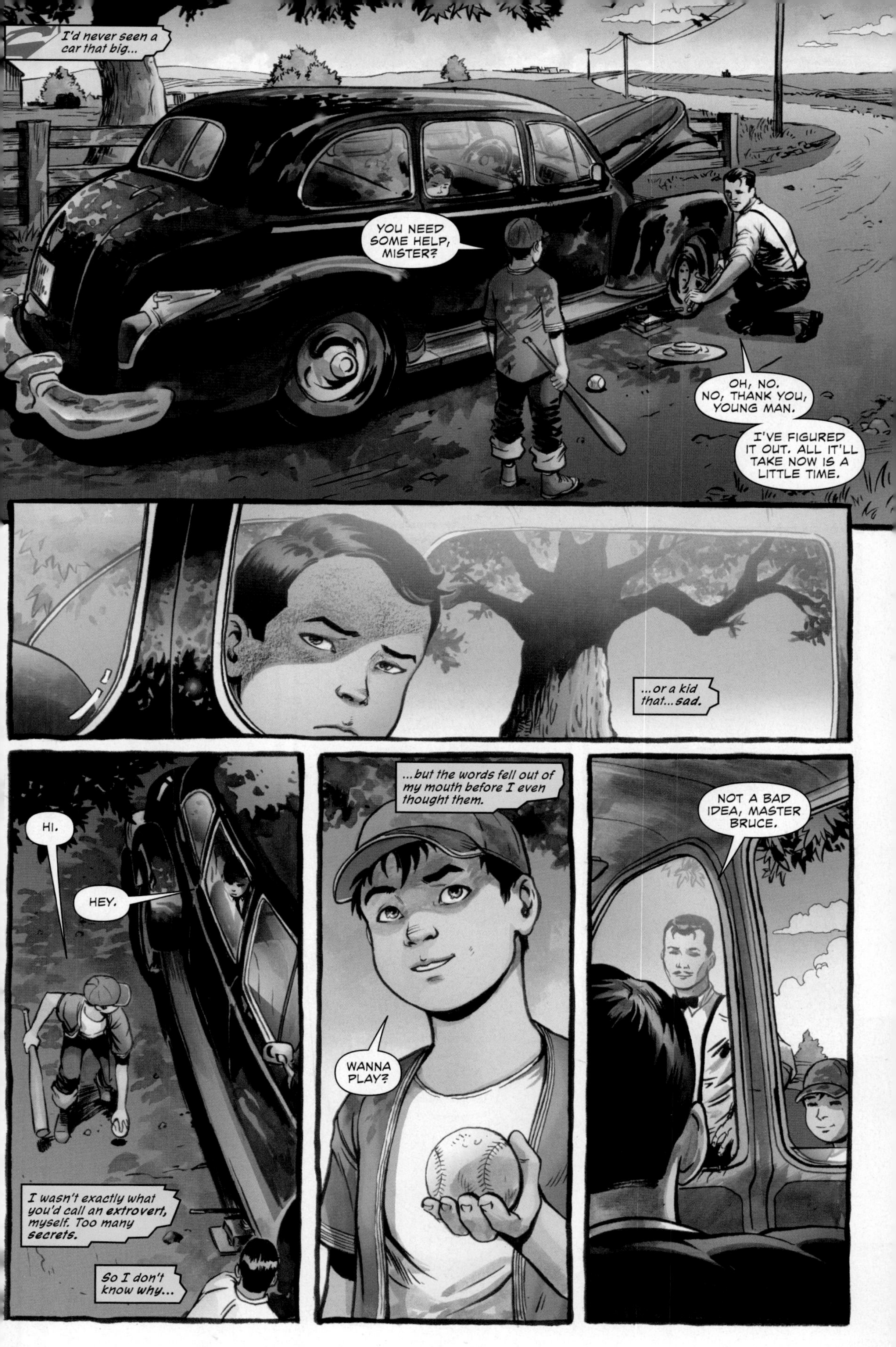

I'd never seen a car that big...
YOU NEED SOME HELP, MISTER?
OH, NO. NO, THANK YOU, YOUNG MAN.
I'VE FIGURED IT OUT. ALL IT'LL TAKE NOW IS A LITTLE TIME.
...or a kid that...sad.
HI.
HEY.
I wasn't exactly what you'd call an extrovert, myself. Too many secrets.
So I don't know why...
...but the words fell out of my mouth before I even thought them.
WANNA PLAY?
NOT A BAD IDEA, MASTER BRUCE.

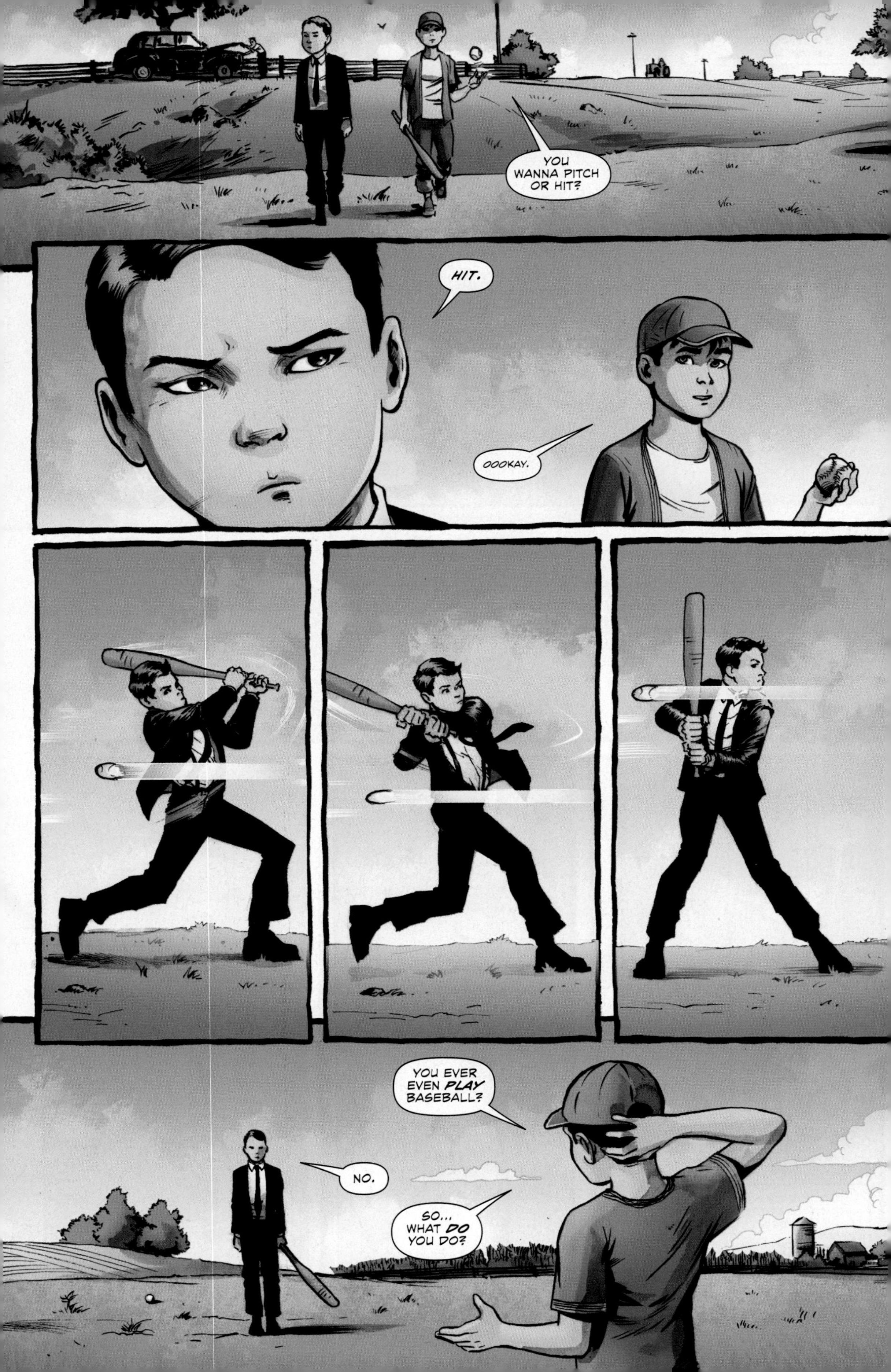
YOU WANNA PITCH OR HIT?
HIT.
OOOKAY.
YOU EVER EVEN PLAY BASEBALL?
NO.
SO... WHAT DO YOU DO?

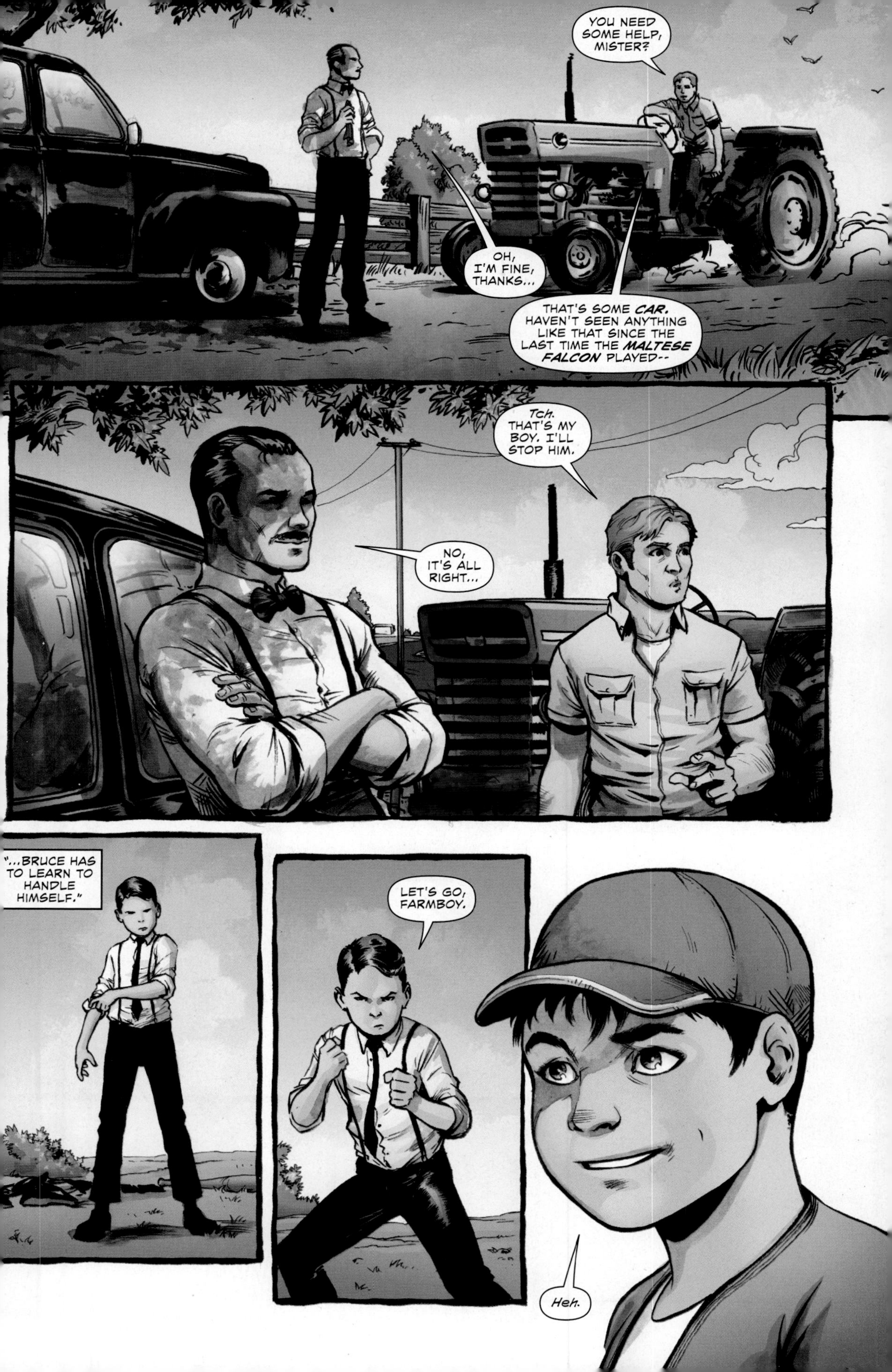
YOU NEED SOME HELP, MISTER?
OH, I'M FINE, THANKS...
THAT'S SOME *CAR.* HAVEN'T SEEN ANYTHING LIKE THAT SINCE THE LAST TIME THE *MALTESE FALCON* PLAYED--
Tch. THAT'S MY BOY. I'LL STOP HIM.
NO, IT'S ALL RIGHT...
"...BRUCE HAS TO LEARN TO HANDLE HIMSELF."
LET'S GO, FARMBOY.
Heh.

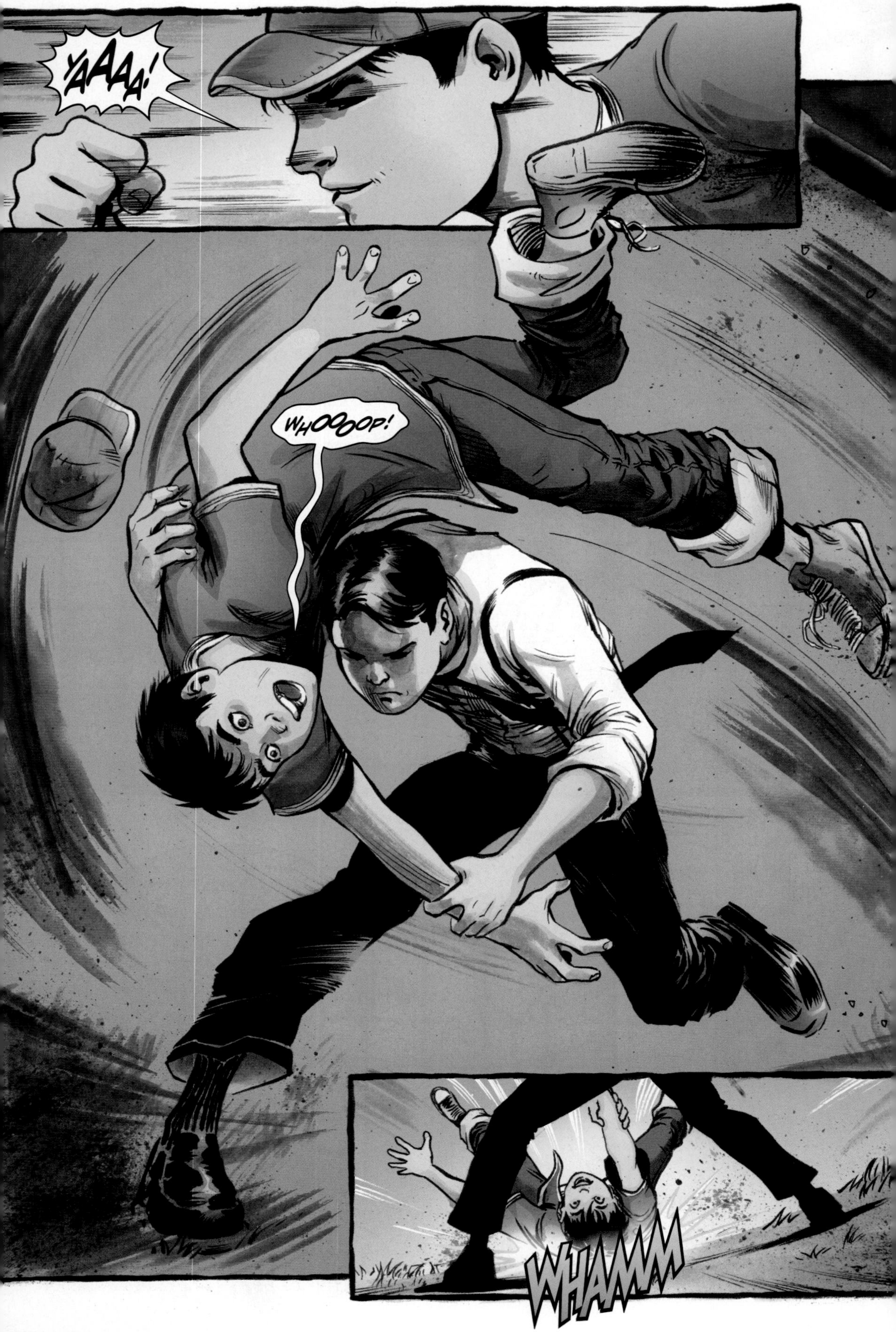
YAAAA!
WHOOOOP!
WHAMM

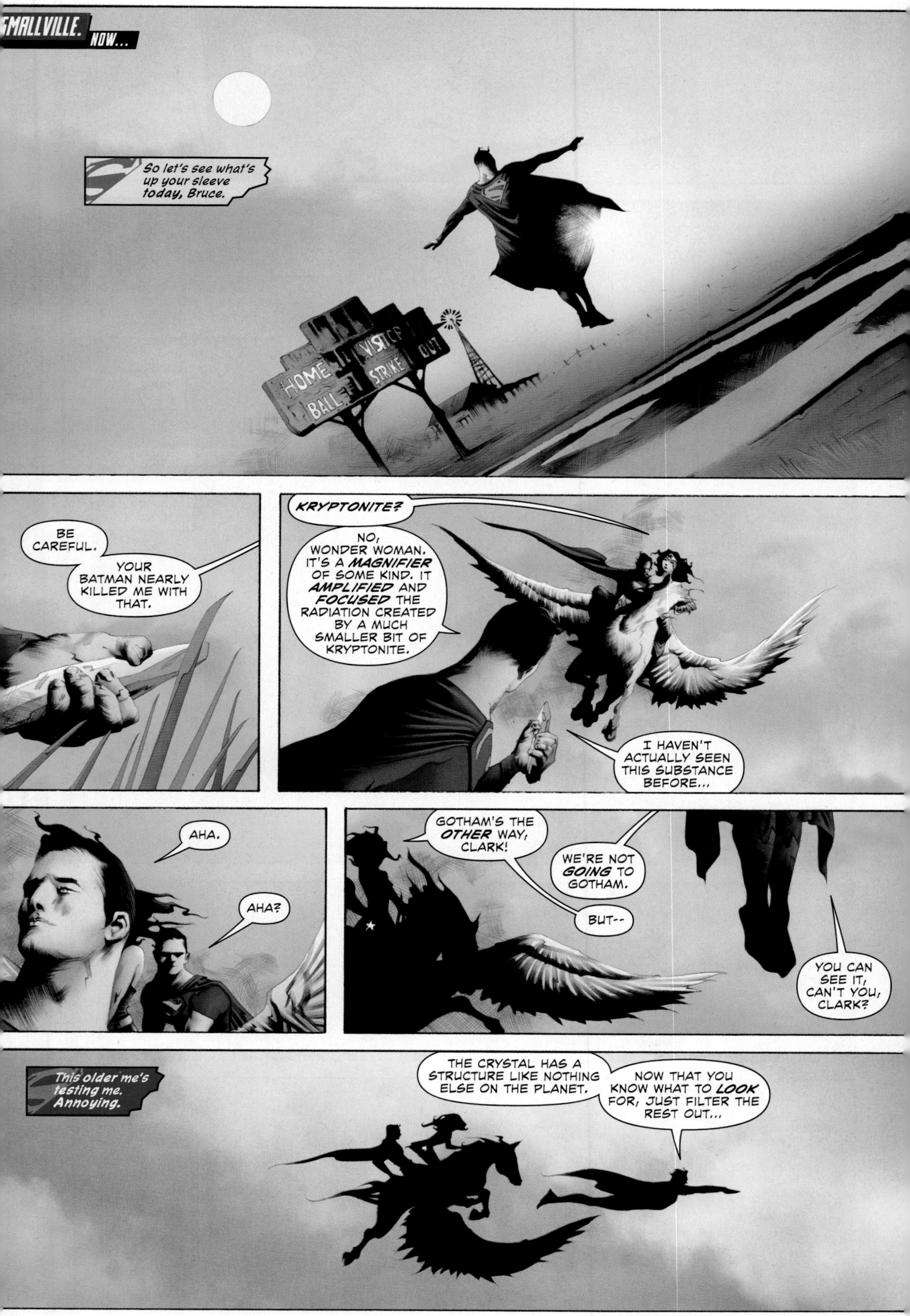
SMALLVILLE. NOW...
So let's see what's up your sleeve today, Bruce.
HOME
BALL
VISITOR
STRIKE
OUT
BE CAREFUL.
YOUR BATMAN NEARLY KILLED ME WITH THAT.
KRYPTONITE?
NO, WONDER WOMAN. IT'S A MAGNIFIER OF SOME KIND. IT AMPLIFIED AND FOCUSED THE RADIATION CREATED BY A MUCH SMALLER BIT OF KRYPTONITE.
I HAVEN'T ACTUALLY SEEN THIS SUBSTANCE BEFORE...
AHA.
AHA?
GOTHAM'S THE OTHER WAY, CLARK!
WE'RE NOT GOING TO GOTHAM.
BUT--
YOU CAN SEE IT, CAN'T YOU, CLARK?
This older me's testing me. Annoying.
THE CRYSTAL HAS A STRUCTURE LIKE NOTHING ELSE ON THE PLANET.
NOW THAT YOU KNOW WHAT TO LOOK FOR, JUST FILTER THE REST OUT...

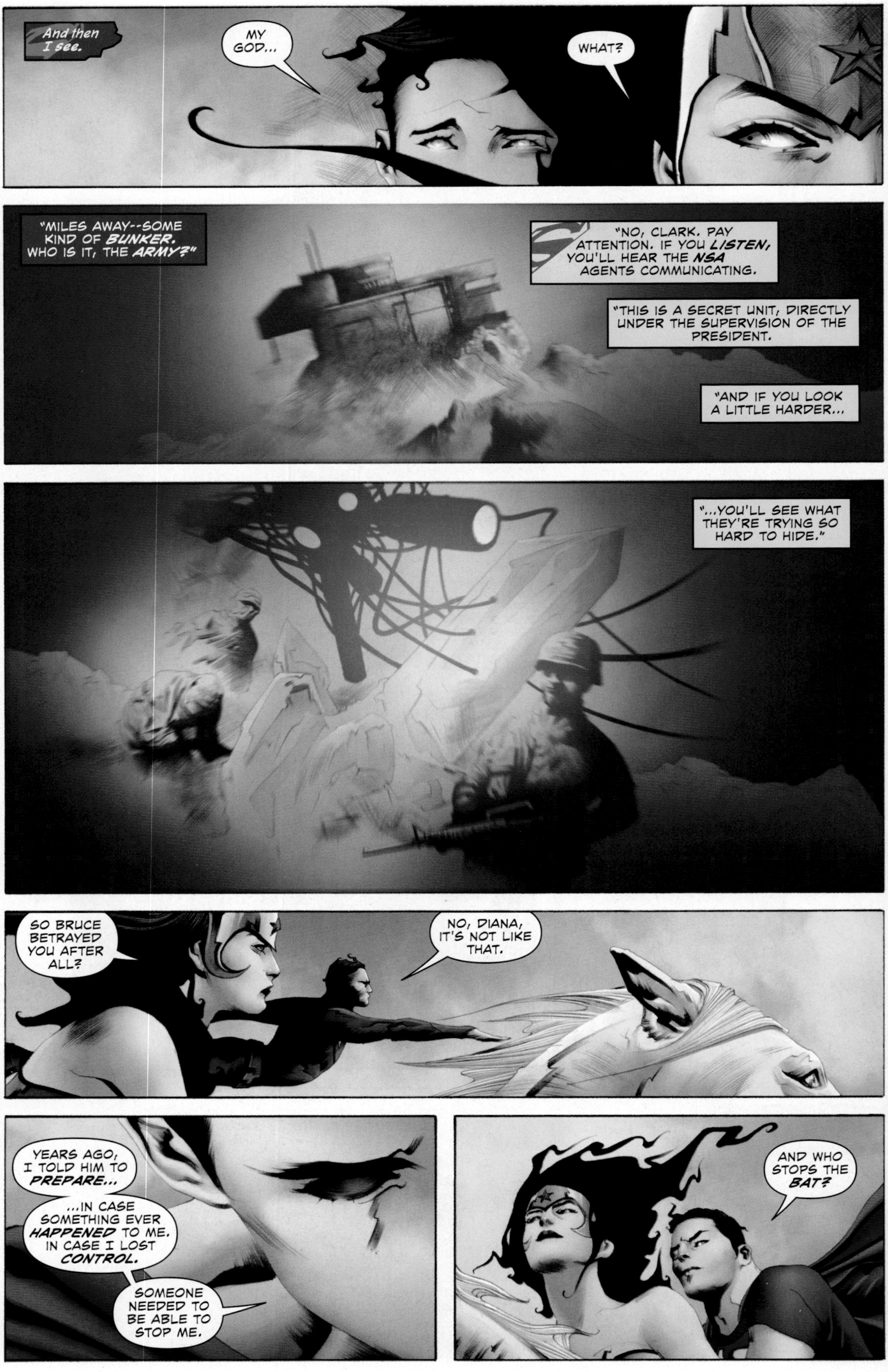

And then I see.
MY GOD...
WHAT?
"MILES AWAY--SOME KIND OF BUNKER. WHO IS IT, THE ARMY?"
"NO, CLARK. PAY ATTENTION. IF YOU LISTEN, YOU'LL HEAR THE NSA AGENTS COMMUNICATING.
"THIS IS A SECRET UNIT, DIRECTLY UNDER THE SUPERVISION OF THE PRESIDENT.
"AND IF YOU LOOK A LITTLE HARDER...
"...YOU'LL SEE WHAT THEY'RE TRYING SO HARD TO HIDE."
SO BRUCE BETRAYED YOU AFTER ALL?
NO, DIANA, IT'S NOT LIKE THAT.
YEARS AGO, I TOLD HIM TO PREPARE...
...IN CASE SOMETHING EVER HAPPENED TO ME. IN CASE I LOST CONTROL.
SOMEONE NEEDED TO BE ABLE TO STOP ME.
AND WHO STOPS THE BAT?

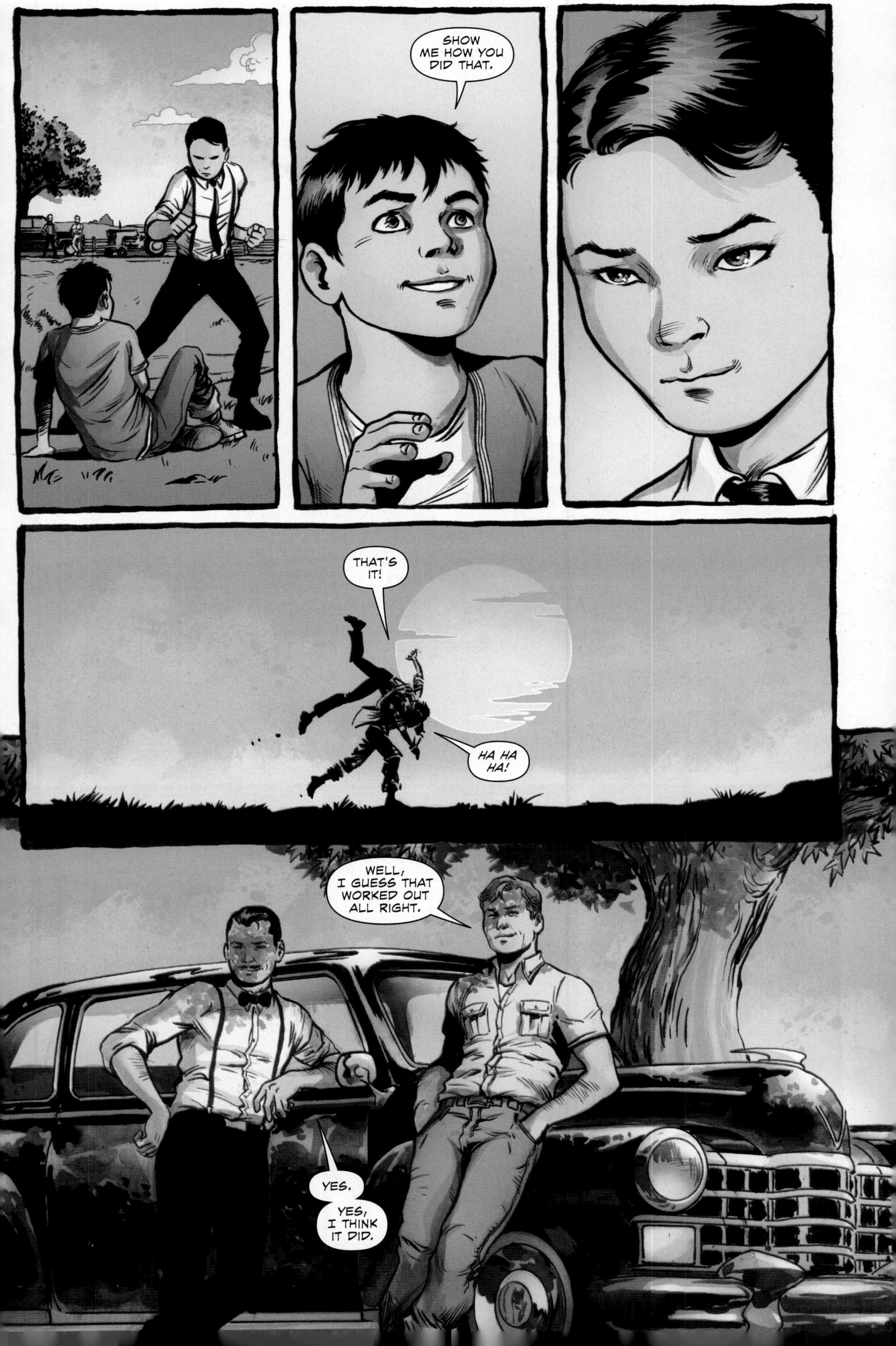
SHOW ME HOW YOU DID THAT.
THAT'S IT!
HA HA HA!
WELL, I GUESS THAT WORKED OUT ALL RIGHT.
YES.
YES, I THINK IT DID.

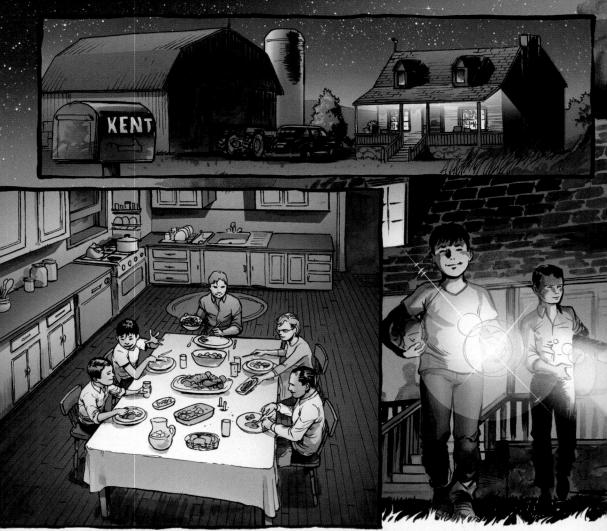

KENT

JONATHAN... I HAVE A CONFESSION TO MAKE.

Uh-oh. SOUNDS SERIOUS.

I COULD HAVE FIXED THE CAR BY NOW.

BUT IT'S BEEN SO LONG... I WANTED TO GIVE BRUCE A CHANCE...

...A CHANCE TO PLAY.

Hm.

YOU KNOW, IT MIGHT NOT BE SO OBVIOUS, ALFRED...

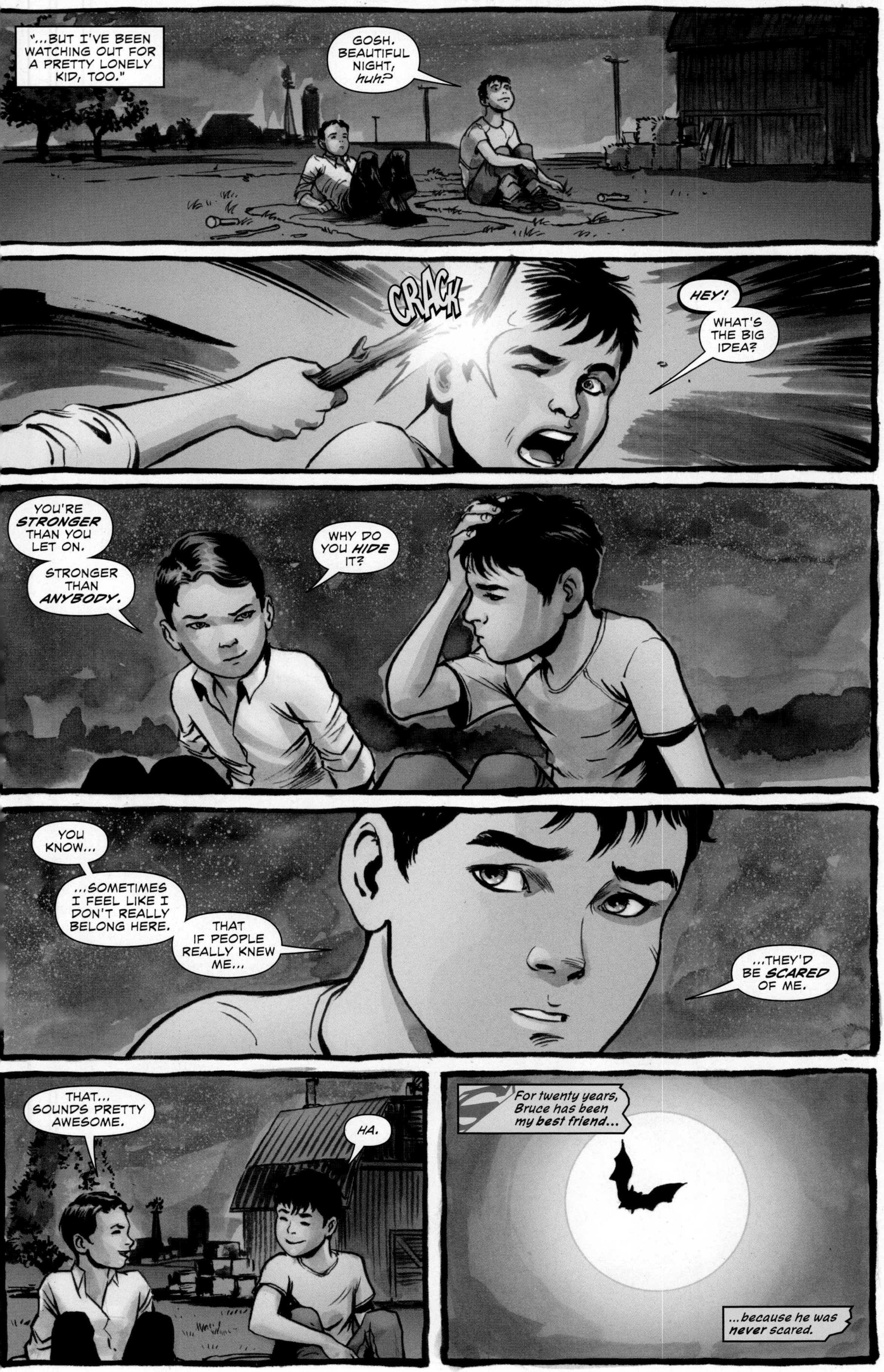
"...BUT I'VE BEEN WATCHING OUT FOR A PRETTY LONELY KID, TOO."
GOSH. BEAUTIFUL NIGHT, *huh?*
CRACK
HEY!
WHAT'S THE BIG IDEA?
YOU'RE **STRONGER** THAN YOU LET ON.
STRONGER THAN **ANYBODY.**
WHY DO YOU **HIDE** IT?
YOU KNOW...
...SOMETIMES I FEEL LIKE I DON'T REALLY BELONG HERE.
THAT IF PEOPLE REALLY KNEW ME...
...THEY'D BE **SCARED** OF ME.
THAT... SOUNDS PRETTY AWESOME.
HA.
For twenty years, Bruce has been my best friend...
*...because he was **never** scared.*

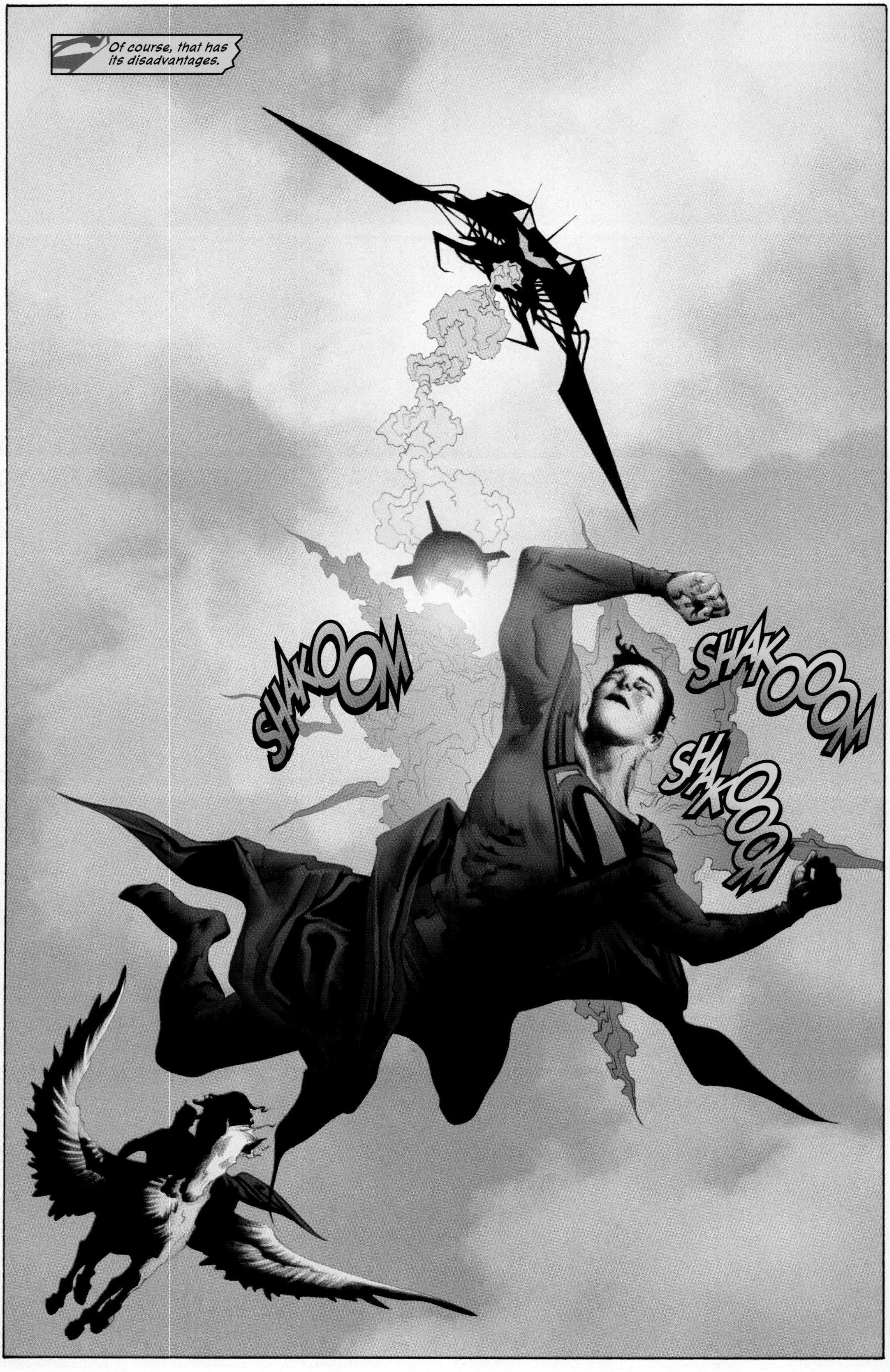
Of course, that has its disadvantages.
SHAKOOM
SHAKOOOM
SHAKOOOM

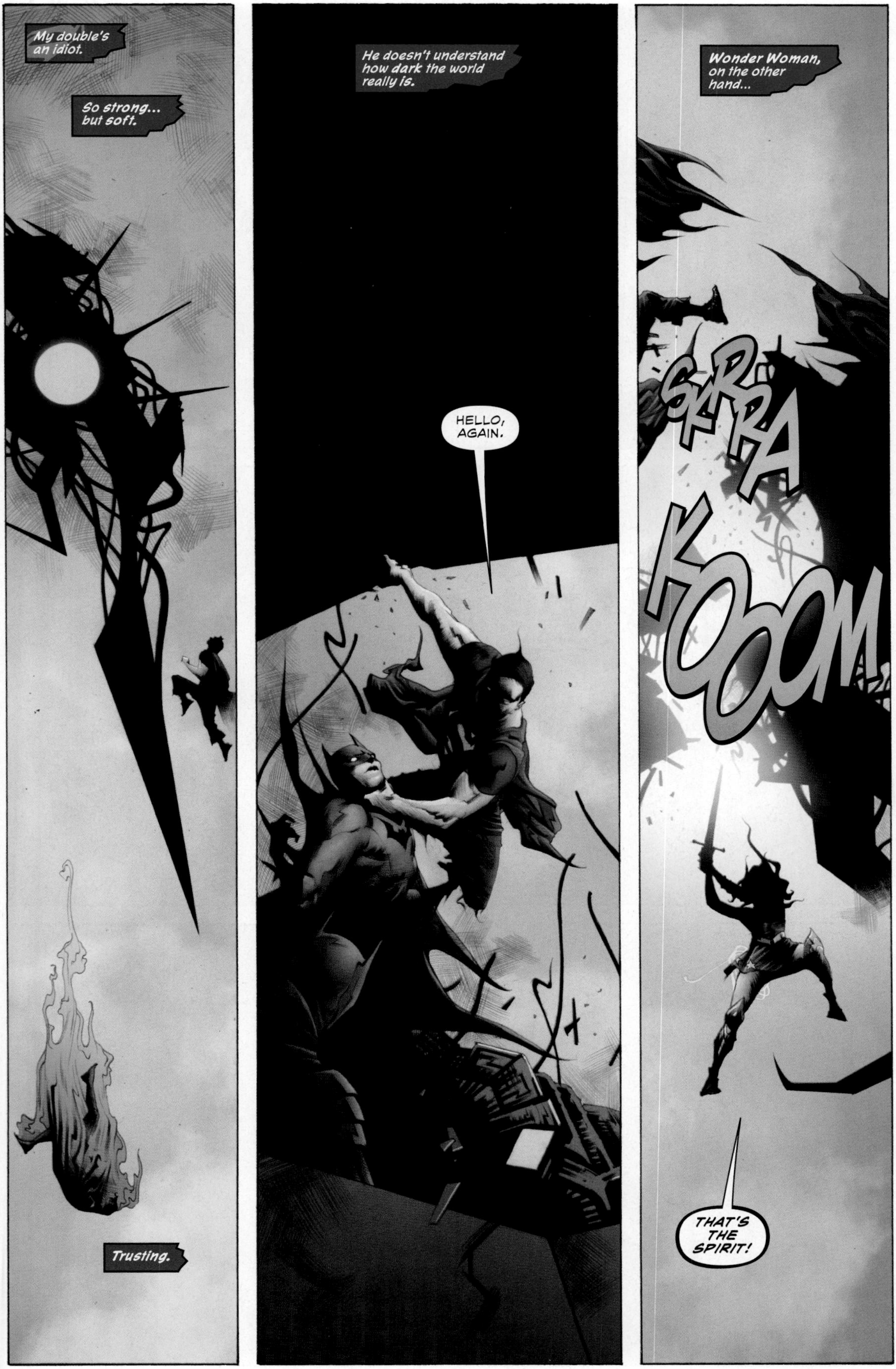

My double's an idiot.
So strong... but soft.
Trusting.
He doesn't understand how dark the world really is.
HELLO, AGAIN.
Wonder Woman, on the other hand...
SKRRA
KOOOM
THAT'S THE SPIRIT!

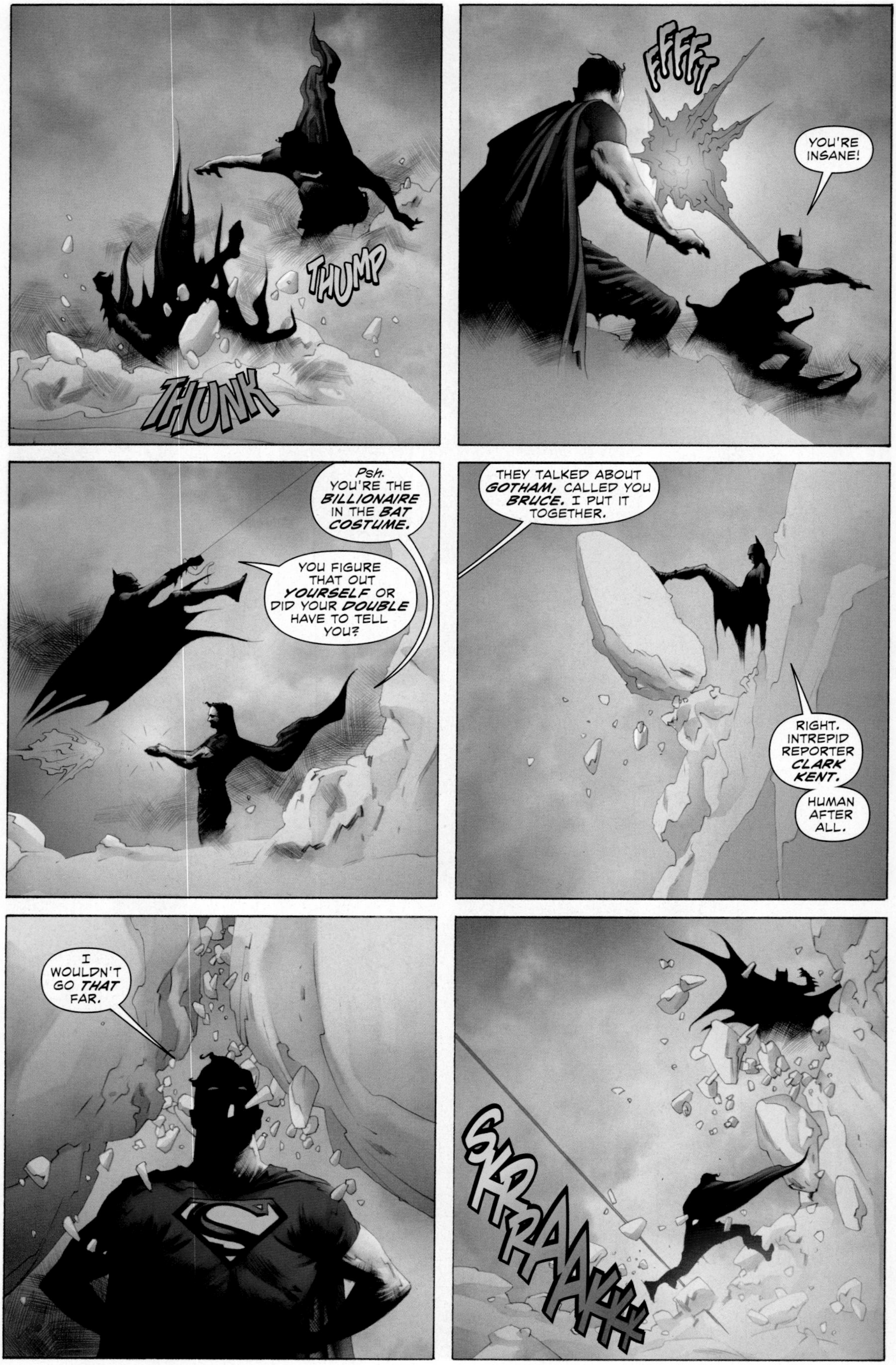
THUMP
THUNK
FFFFT
YOU'RE INSANE!
Psh. YOU'RE THE BILLIONAIRE IN THE BAT COSTUME.
YOU FIGURE THAT OUT YOURSELF OR DID YOUR DOUBLE HAVE TO TELL YOU?
THEY TALKED ABOUT GOTHAM, CALLED YOU BRUCE. I PUT IT TOGETHER.
RIGHT. INTREPID REPORTER CLARK KENT.
HUMAN AFTER ALL.
I WOULDN'T GO THAT FAR.
SKRAAKK

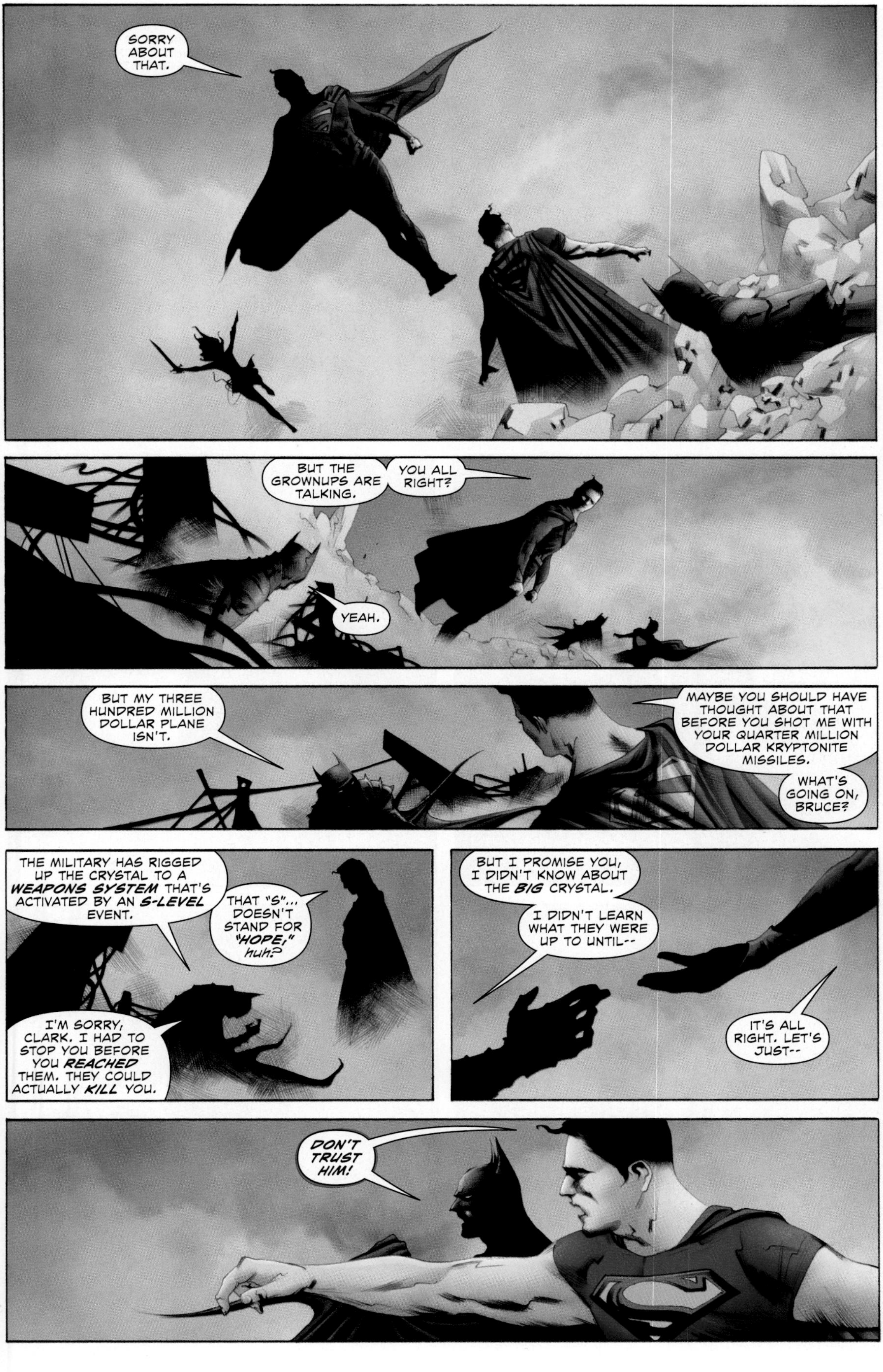
SORRY ABOUT THAT.
YOU ALL RIGHT?
BUT THE GROWNUPS ARE TALKING.
YEAH.
BUT MY THREE HUNDRED MILLION DOLLAR PLANE ISN'T.
MAYBE YOU SHOULD HAVE THOUGHT ABOUT THAT BEFORE YOU SHOT ME WITH YOUR QUARTER MILLION DOLLAR KRYPTONITE MISSILES.
WHAT'S GOING ON, BRUCE?
THE MILITARY HAS RIGGED UP THE CRYSTAL TO A WEAPONS SYSTEM THAT'S ACTIVATED BY AN S-LEVEL EVENT.
THAT "S"... DOESN'T STAND FOR "HOPE," huh?
I'M SORRY, CLARK. I HAD TO STOP YOU BEFORE YOU REACHED THEM. THEY COULD ACTUALLY KILL YOU.
BUT I PROMISE YOU, I DIDN'T KNOW ABOUT THE BIG CRYSTAL.
I DIDN'T LEARN WHAT THEY WERE UP TO UNTIL--
IT'S ALL RIGHT. LET'S JUST--
DON'T TRUST HIM!

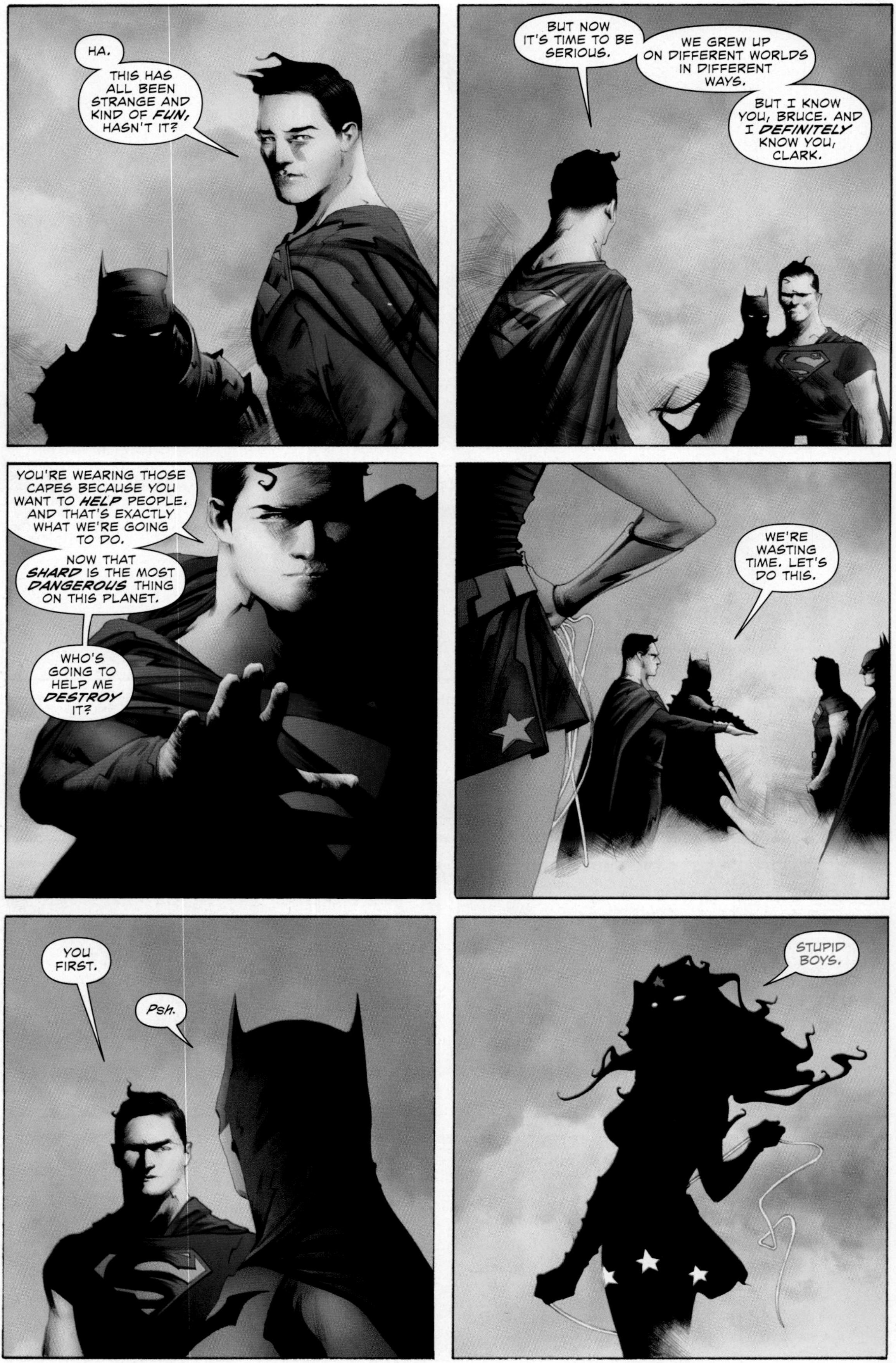
HA.
THIS HAS ALL BEEN STRANGE AND KIND OF *FUN,* HASN'T IT?
BUT NOW IT'S TIME TO BE SERIOUS.
WE GREW UP ON DIFFERENT WORLDS IN DIFFERENT WAYS.
BUT I KNOW YOU, BRUCE. AND I *DEFINITELY* KNOW YOU, CLARK.
YOU'RE WEARING THOSE CAPES BECAUSE YOU WANT TO *HELP* PEOPLE. AND THAT'S EXACTLY WHAT WE'RE GOING TO DO.
NOW THAT *SHARD* IS THE MOST *DANGEROUS* THING ON THIS PLANET.
WHO'S GOING TO HELP ME *DESTROY* IT?
WE'RE WASTING TIME. LET'S DO THIS.
YOU FIRST.
Psh.
STUPID BOYS.

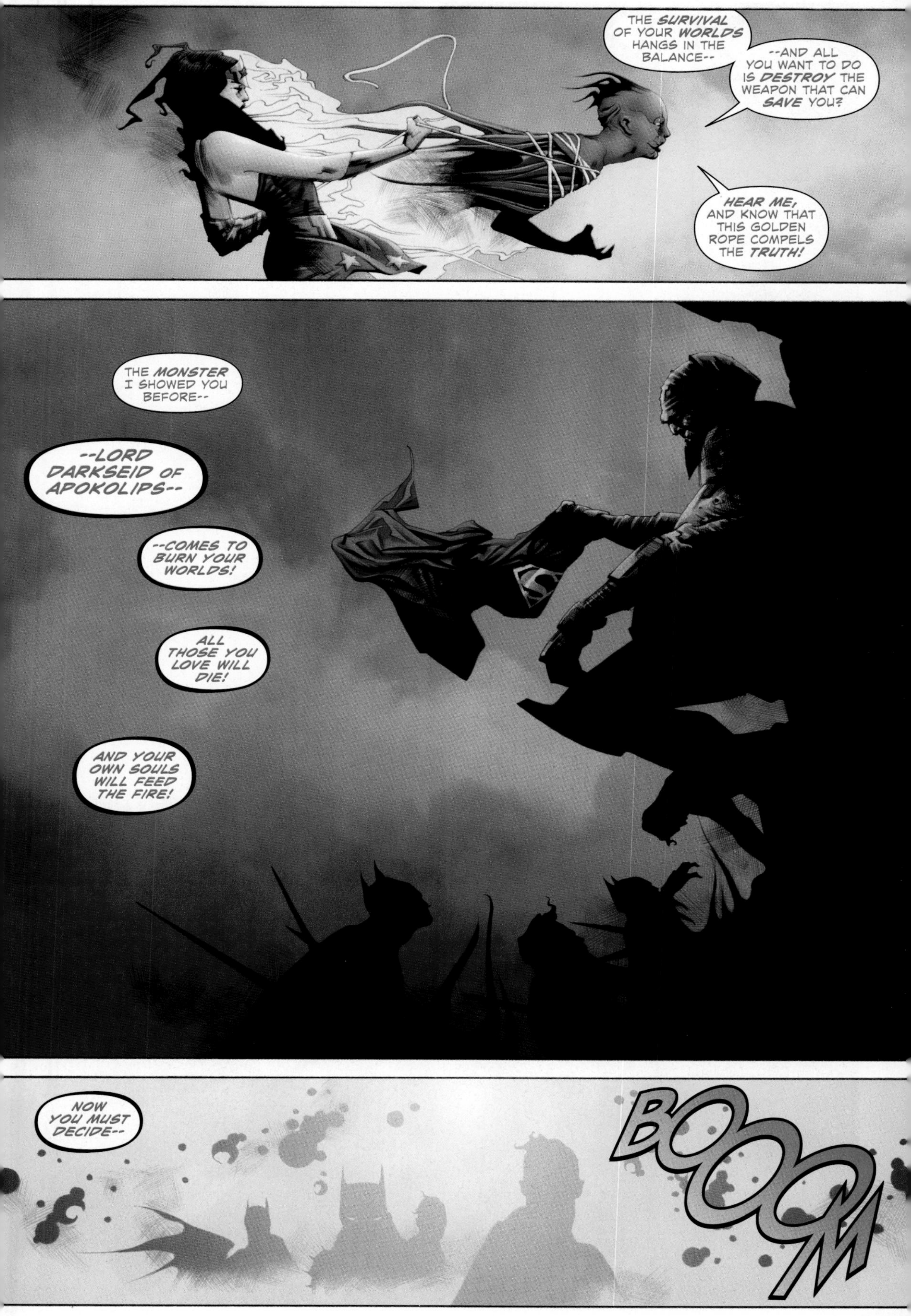
THE SURVIVAL OF YOUR WORLDS HANGS IN THE BALANCE--
--AND ALL YOU WANT TO DO IS DESTROY THE WEAPON THAT CAN SAVE YOU?
HEAR ME, AND KNOW THAT THIS GOLDEN ROPE COMPELS THE TRUTH!
THE MONSTER I SHOWED YOU BEFORE--
--LORD DARKSEID OF APOKOLIPS--
--COMES TO BURN YOUR WORLDS!
ALL THOSE YOU LOVE WILL DIE!
AND YOUR OWN SOULS WILL FEED THE FIRE!
NOW YOU MUST DECIDE--
BOOOM

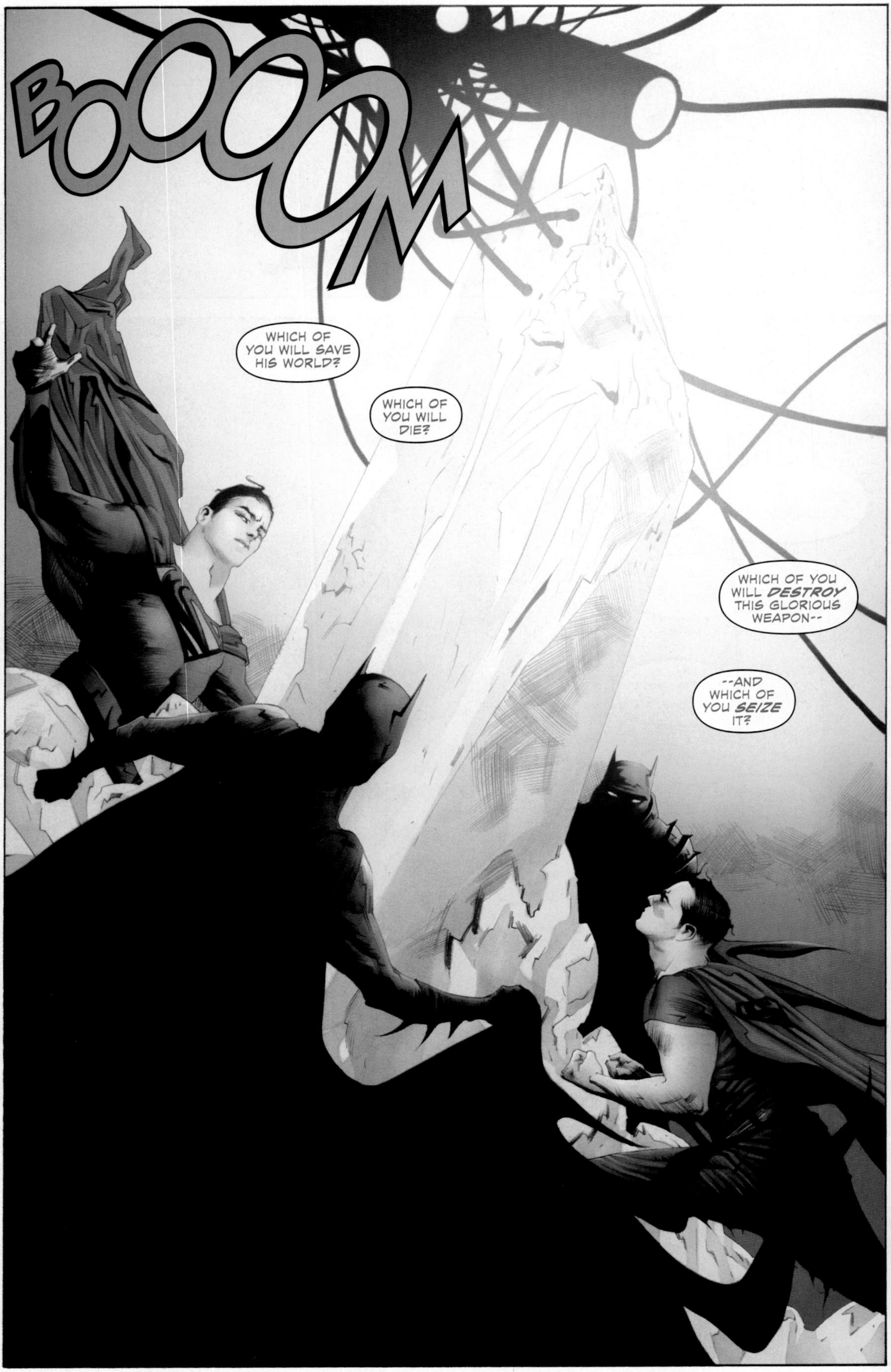
BOOOOOM
WHICH OF YOU WILL SAVE HIS WORLD?
WHICH OF YOU WILL DIE?
WHICH OF YOU WILL DESTROY THIS GLORIOUS WEAPON--
--AND WHICH OF YOU SEIZE IT?

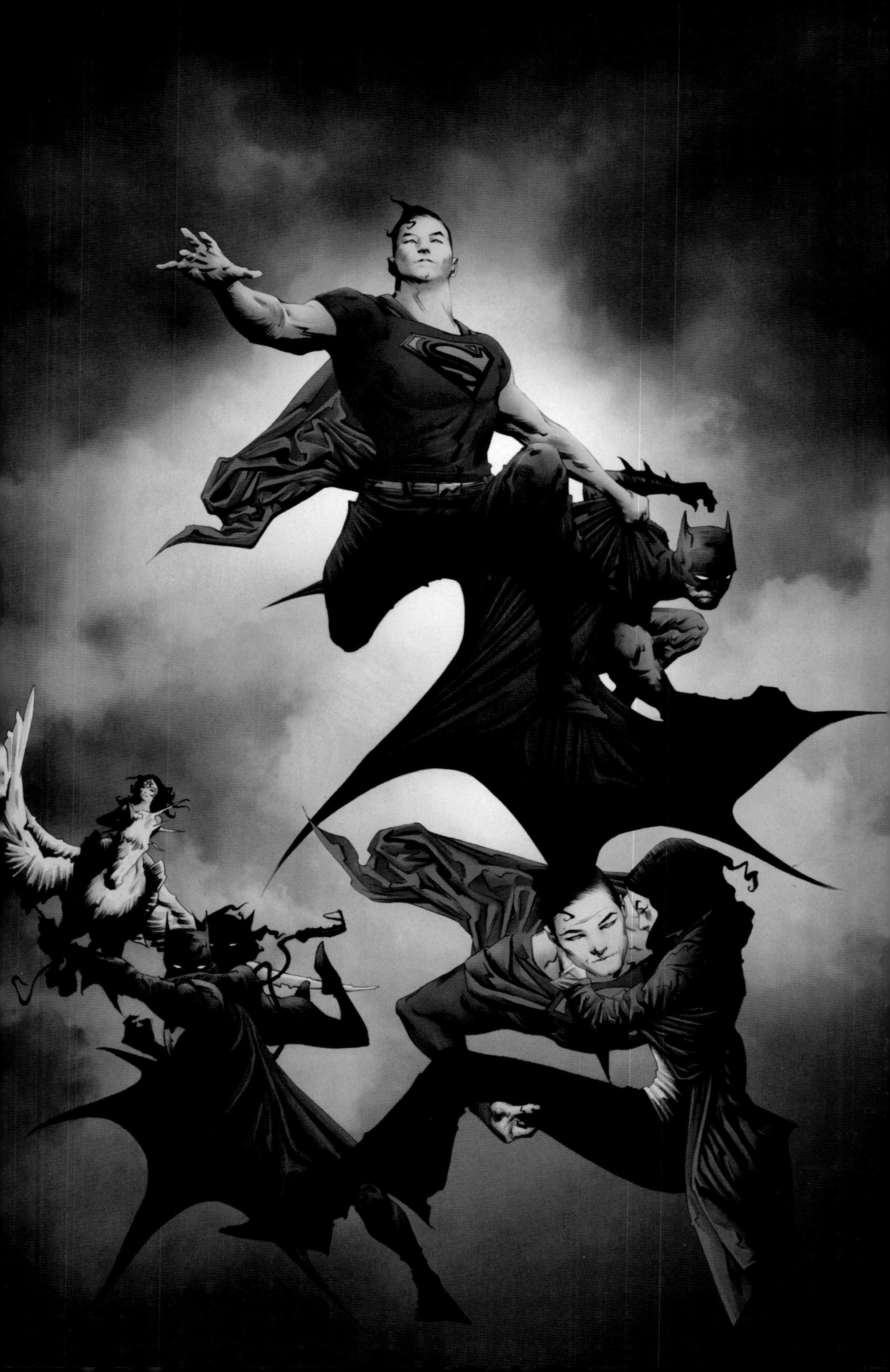

GREG PAK writer **JAE LEE BEN OLIVER** artists **JUNE CHUNG DANIEL BROWN** colorists cover by **JAE LEE** with **JUNE CHUNG**

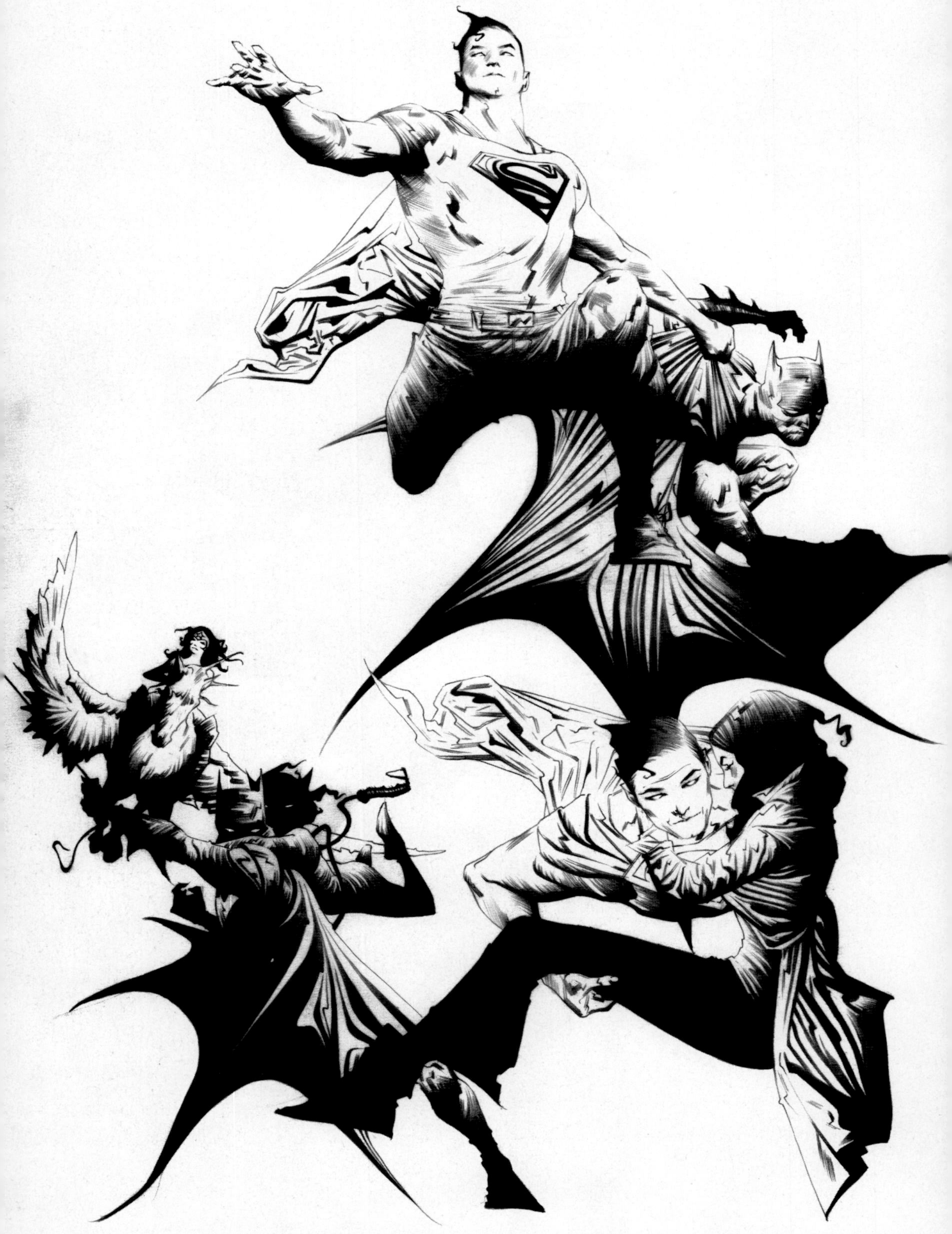

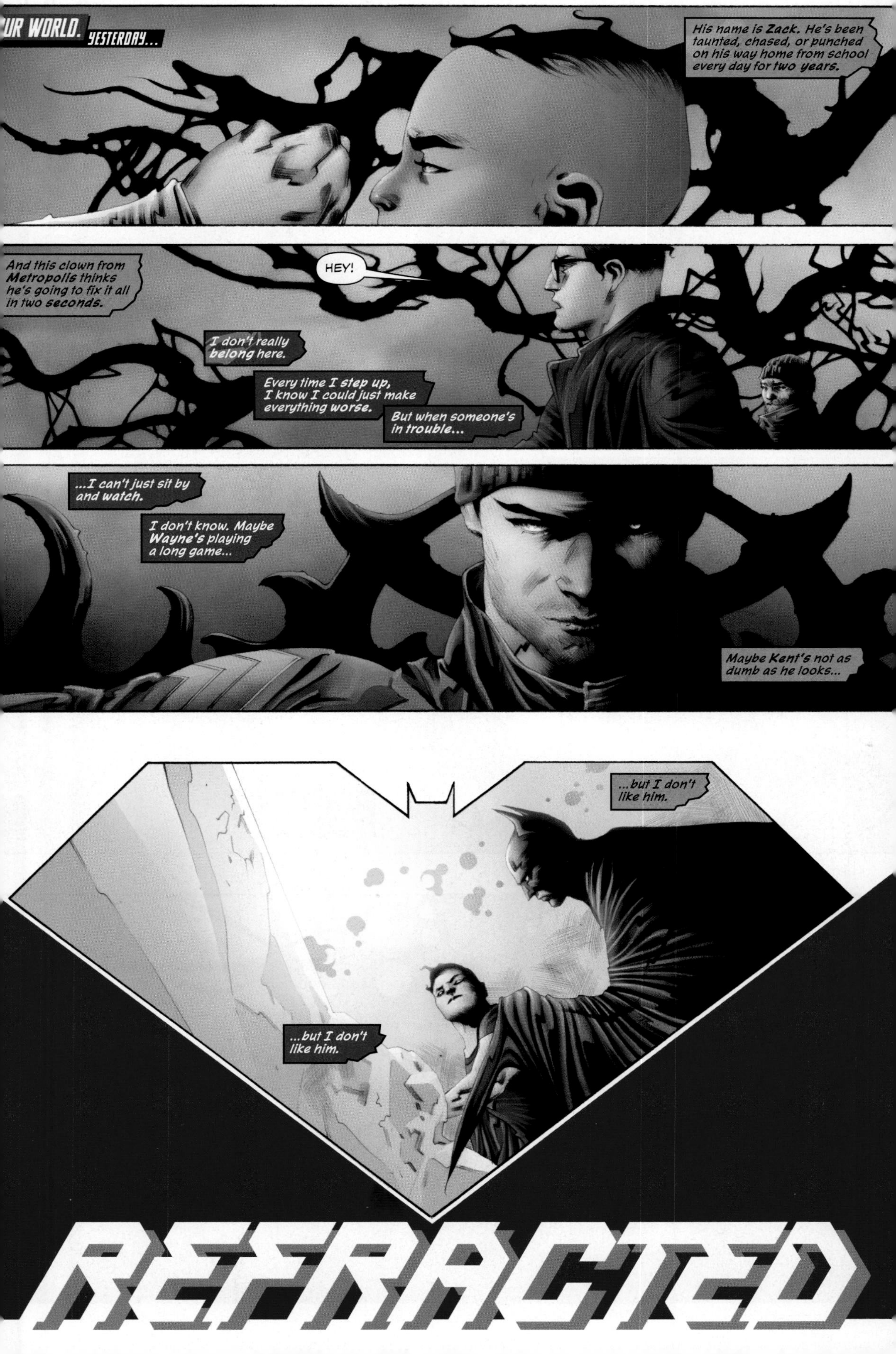

OUR WORLD. YESTERDAY...
His name is Zack. He's been taunted, chased, or punched on his way home from school every day for two years.
And this clown from Metropolis thinks he's going to fix it all in two seconds.
HEY!
I don't really belong here.
Every time I step up, I know I could just make everything worse.
But when someone's in trouble...
...I can't just sit by and watch.
I don't know. Maybe Wayne's playing a long game...
Maybe Kent's not as dumb as he looks...
...but I don't like him.
...but I don't like him.
REFRACTED

Which makes the current situation even more... annoying.

We're on another world-- with another me and another him...

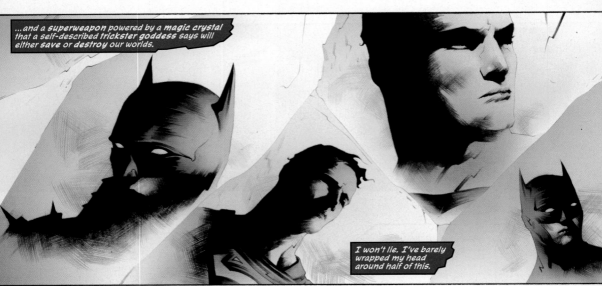

...and a *superweapon* powered by a *magic crystal* that a self-described *trickster goddess* says will either *save* or *destroy* our worlds.

I won't lie. I've barely wrapped my head around half of this.

SLADE! FIRE IT UP!

YES, SIR!

But now it's time for *action*.

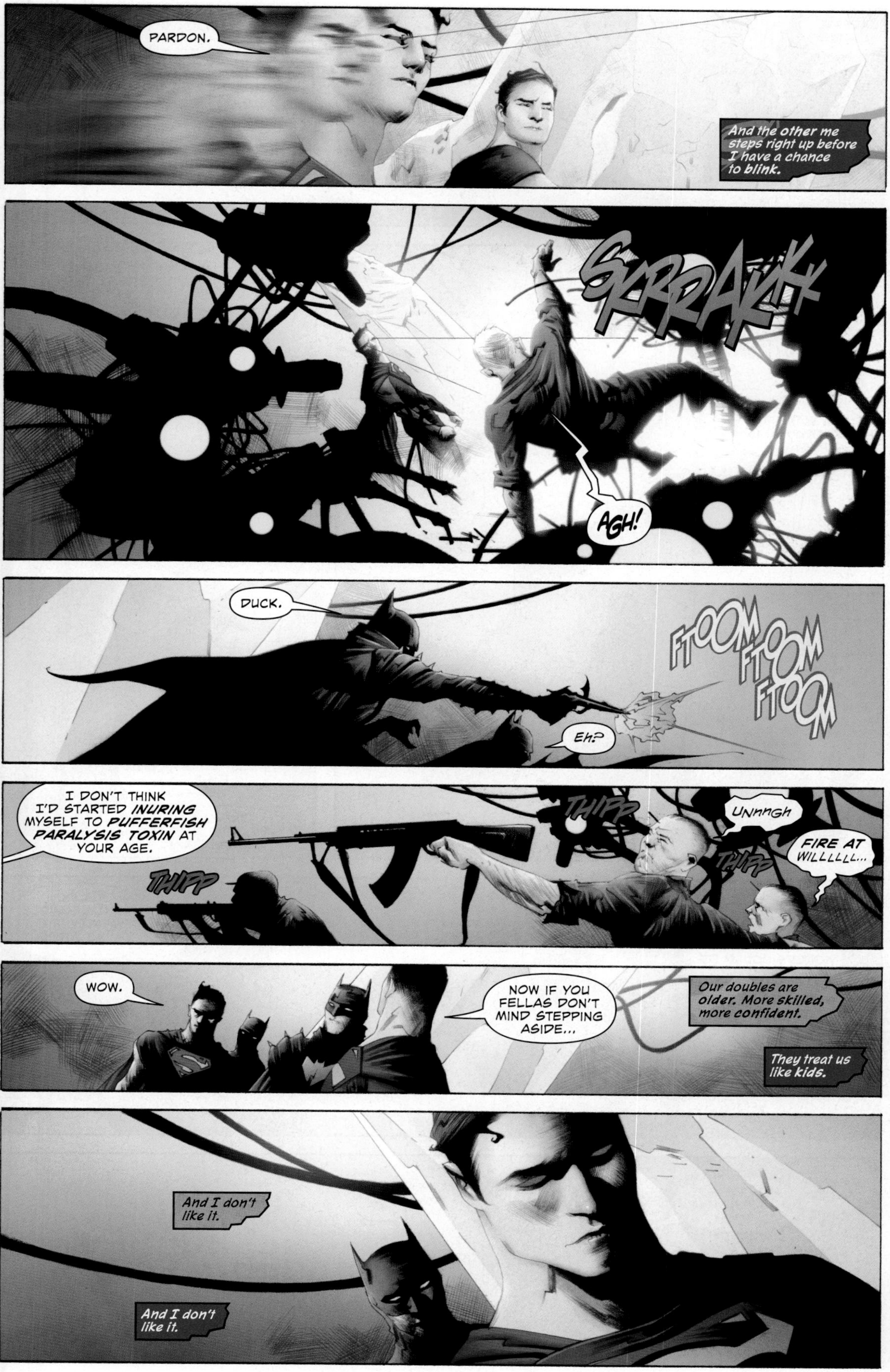
PARDON.
And the other me steps right up before I have a chance to blink.
SKRRAKKK
AGH!
DUCK.
FTOOM FTOOM FTOOM
Eh?
I DON'T THINK I'D STARTED INURING MYSELF TO PUFFERFISH PARALYSIS TOXIN AT YOUR AGE.
THIPP
THIPP
Unnngh
THIPP
FIRE AT WILLLLLL...
WOW.
NOW IF YOU FELLAS DON'T MIND STEPPING ASIDE...
Our doubles are older. More skilled, more confident.
They treat us like kids.
And I don't like it.
And I don't like it.

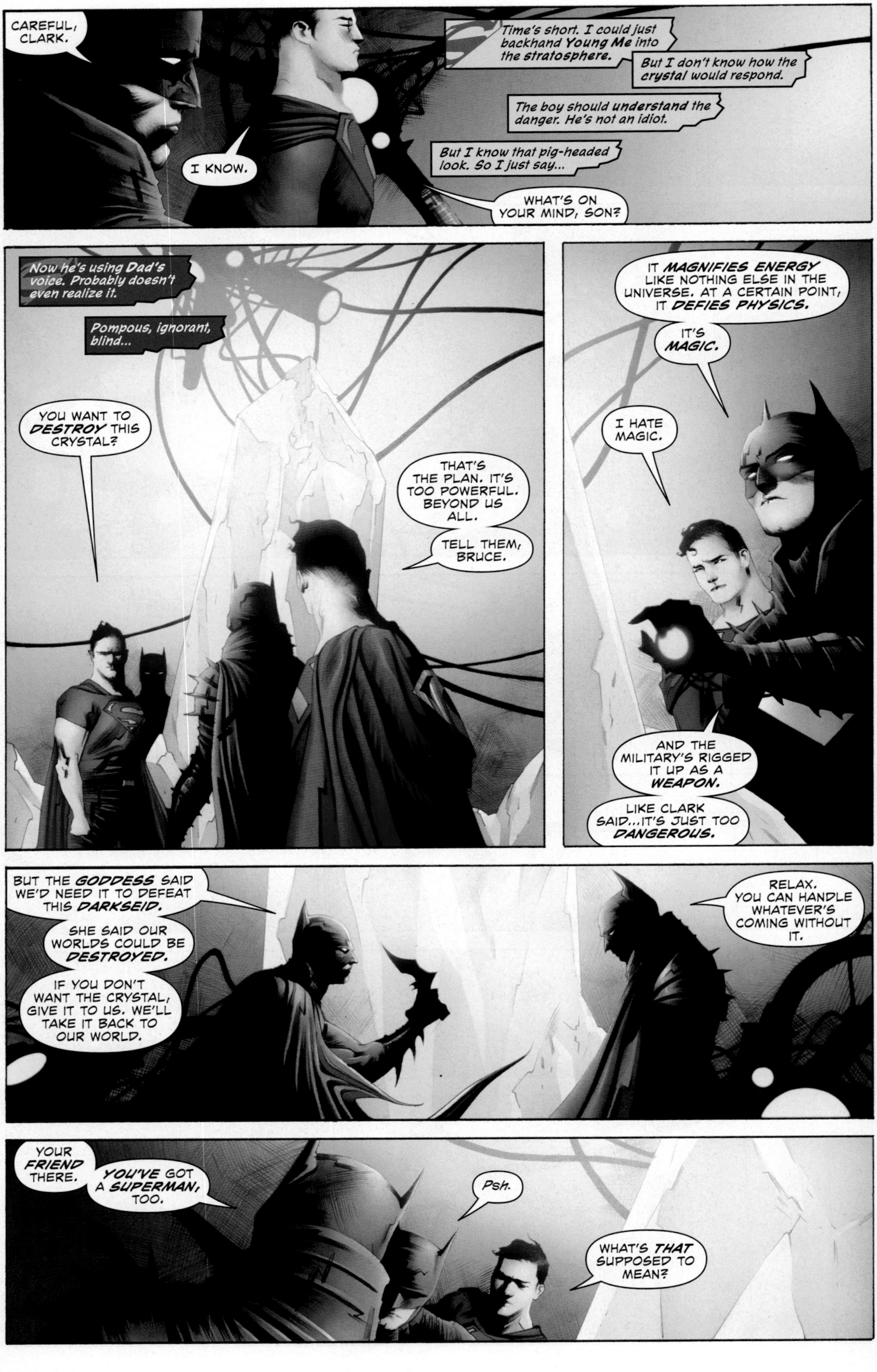
CAREFUL, CLARK.
I KNOW.
Time's short. I could just backhand Young Me into the stratosphere.
But I don't know how the crystal would respond.
The boy should understand the danger. He's not an idiot.
But I know that pig-headed look. So I just say...
WHAT'S ON YOUR MIND, SON?
Now he's using Dad's voice. Probably doesn't even realize it.
Pompous, ignorant, blind...
YOU WANT TO DESTROY THIS CRYSTAL?
THAT'S THE PLAN. IT'S TOO POWERFUL. BEYOND US ALL.
TELL THEM, BRUCE.
IT MAGNIFIES ENERGY LIKE NOTHING ELSE IN THE UNIVERSE. AT A CERTAIN POINT, IT DEFIES PHYSICS.
IT'S MAGIC.
I HATE MAGIC.
AND THE MILITARY'S RIGGED IT UP AS A WEAPON.
LIKE CLARK SAID...IT'S JUST TOO DANGEROUS.
BUT THE GODDESS SAID WE'D NEED IT TO DEFEAT THIS DARKSEID.
SHE SAID OUR WORLDS COULD BE DESTROYED.
IF YOU DON'T WANT THE CRYSTAL, GIVE IT TO US. WE'LL TAKE IT BACK TO OUR WORLD.
RELAX. YOU CAN HANDLE WHATEVER'S COMING WITHOUT IT.
YOUR FRIEND THERE.
YOU'VE GOT A SUPERMAN, TOO.
Psh.
WHAT'S THAT SUPPOSED TO MEAN?

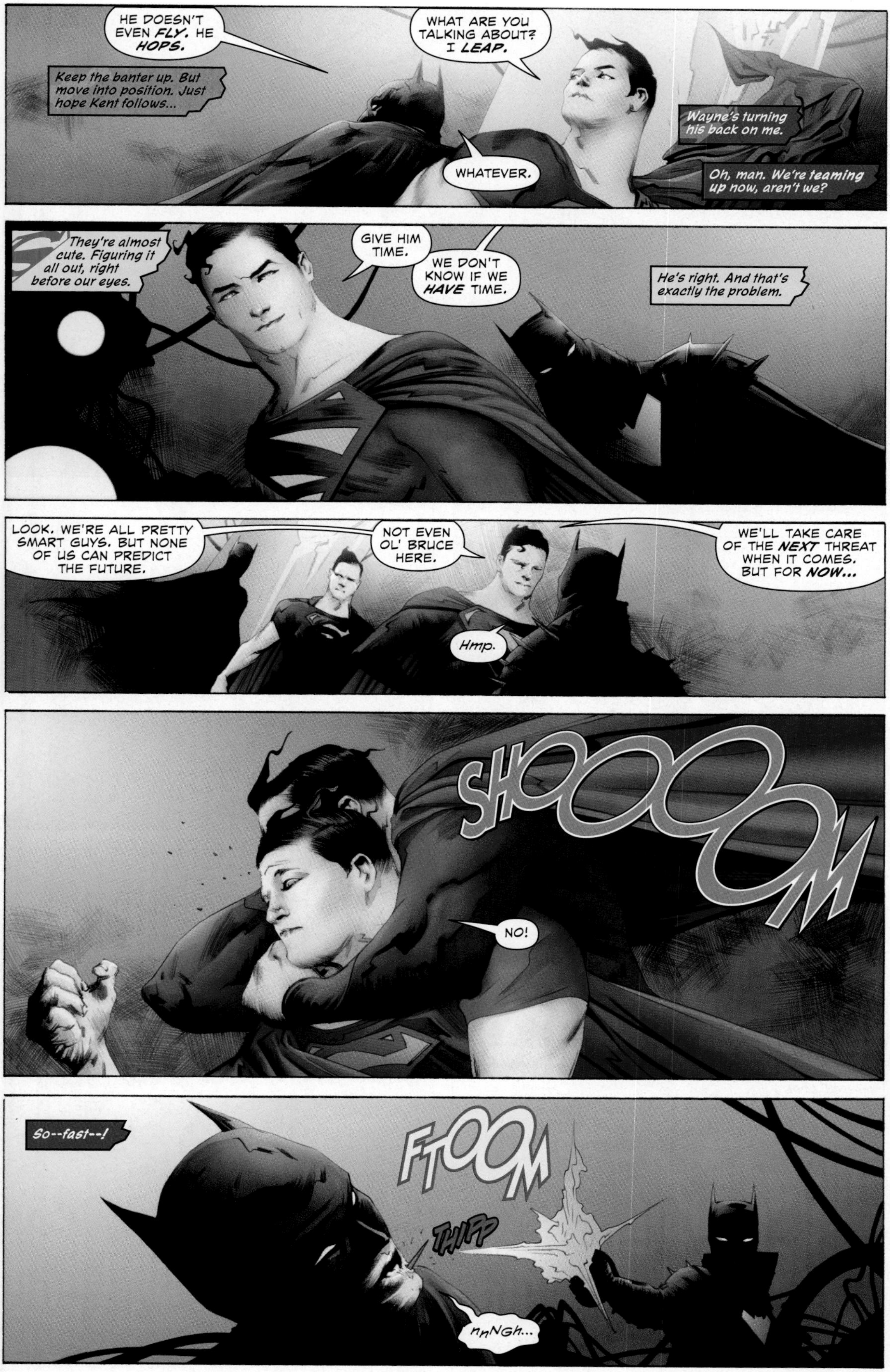
HE DOESN'T EVEN FLY. HE HOPS.
WHAT ARE YOU TALKING ABOUT? I LEAP.
Keep the banter up. But move into position. Just hope Kent follows...
WHATEVER.
Wayne's turning his back on me.
Oh, man. We're teaming up now, aren't we?
They're almost cute. Figuring it all out, right before our eyes.
GIVE HIM TIME.
WE DON'T KNOW IF WE HAVE TIME.
He's right. And that's exactly the problem.
LOOK. WE'RE ALL PRETTY SMART GUYS. BUT NONE OF US CAN PREDICT THE FUTURE.
NOT EVEN OL' BRUCE HERE.
WE'LL TAKE CARE OF THE NEXT THREAT WHEN IT COMES. BUT FOR NOW...
Hmp.
SHOOOOOM
NO!
So--fast--!
FTOOM
THIPP
nnNGh...

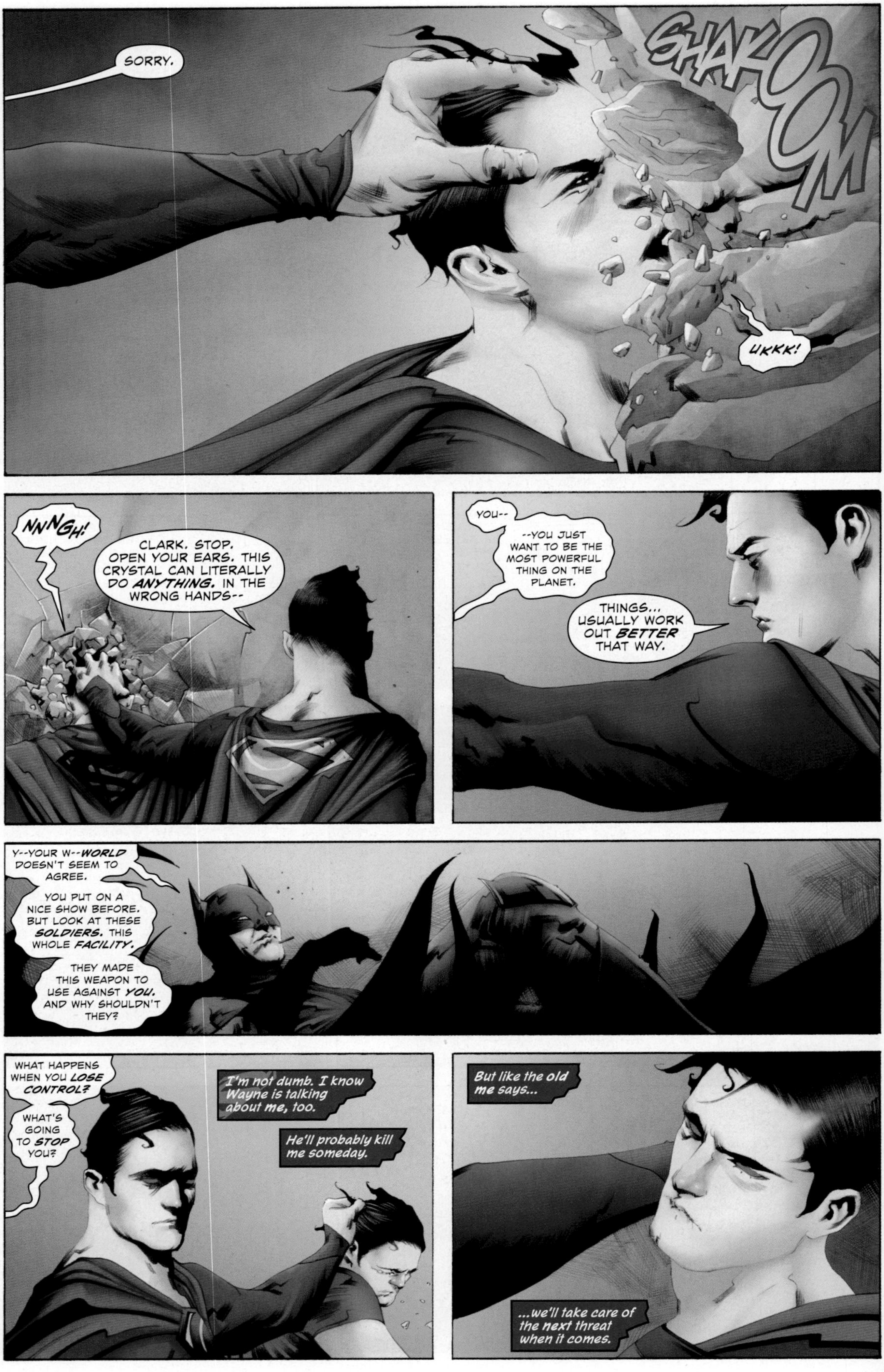
SORRY.
SHAKOOM
UKKK!
NNNGH!
CLARK. STOP. OPEN YOUR EARS. THIS CRYSTAL CAN LITERALLY DO ANYTHING. IN THE WRONG HANDS--
YOU--
--YOU JUST WANT TO BE THE MOST POWERFUL THING ON THE PLANET.
THINGS... USUALLY WORK OUT BETTER THAT WAY.
Y--YOUR W--WORLD DOESN'T SEEM TO AGREE.
YOU PUT ON A NICE SHOW BEFORE. BUT LOOK AT THESE SOLDIERS. THIS WHOLE FACILITY.
THEY MADE THIS WEAPON TO USE AGAINST YOU. AND WHY SHOULDN'T THEY?
WHAT HAPPENS WHEN YOU LOSE CONTROL?
WHAT'S GOING TO STOP YOU?
I'm not dumb. I know Wayne is talking about me, too.
He'll probably kill me someday.
But like the old me says...
...we'll take care of the next threat when it comes.

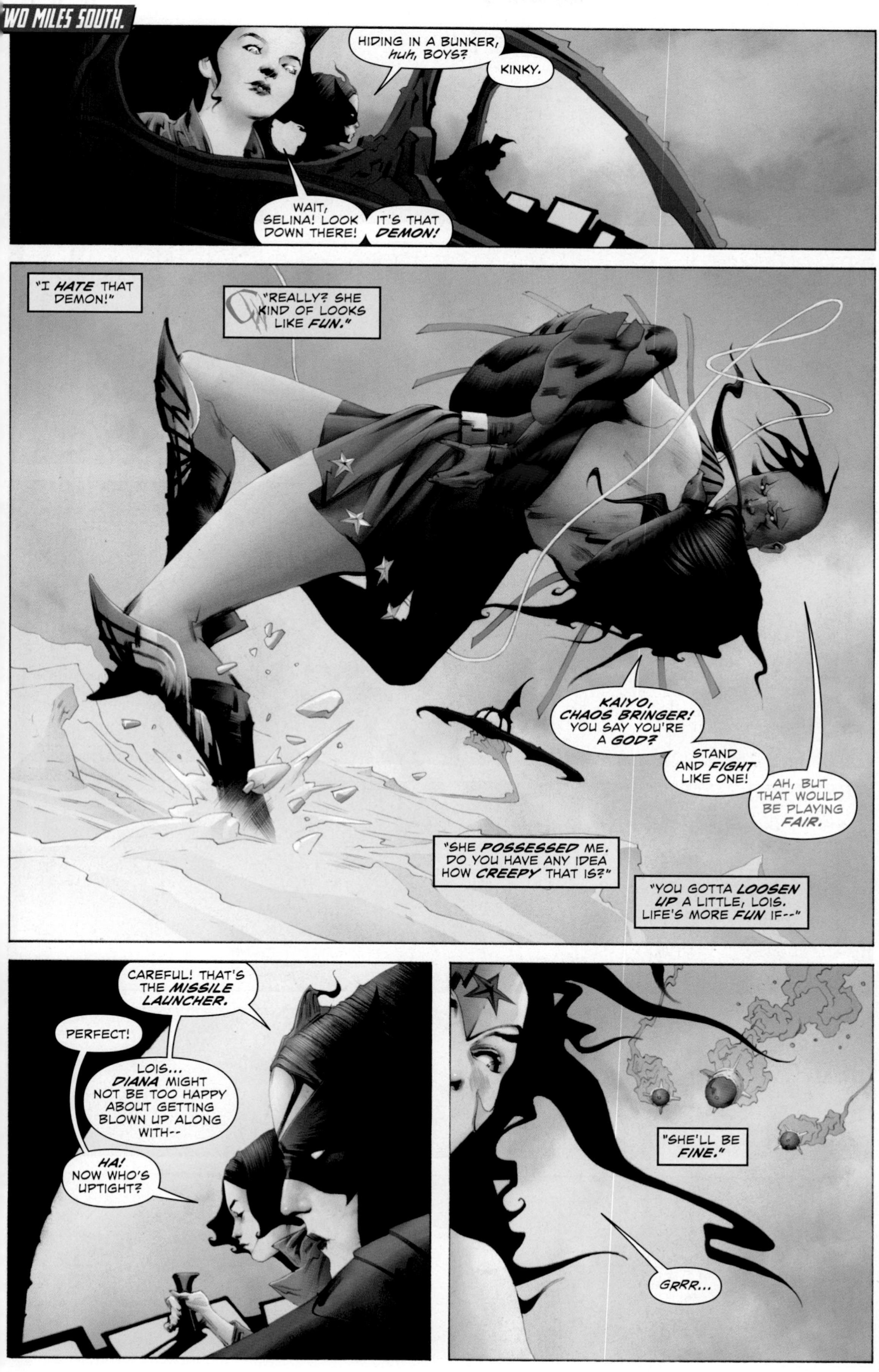
WO MILES SOUTH.
HIDING IN A BUNKER, *huh*, BOYS?
KINKY.
WAIT, SELINA! LOOK DOWN THERE!
IT'S THAT *DEMON!*
"I *HATE* THAT DEMON!"
"REALLY? SHE KIND OF LOOKS LIKE *FUN.*"
KAIYO, CHAOS BRINGER! YOU SAY YOU'RE A *GOD?*
STAND AND *FIGHT* LIKE ONE!
AH, BUT THAT WOULD BE PLAYING *FAIR.*
"SHE *POSSESSED* ME. DO YOU HAVE ANY IDEA HOW *CREEPY* THAT IS?"
"YOU GOTTA *LOOSEN UP* A LITTLE, LOIS. LIFE'S MORE *FUN* IF--"
CAREFUL! THAT'S THE *MISSILE LAUNCHER.*
PERFECT!
LOIS... *DIANA* MIGHT NOT BE TOO HAPPY ABOUT GETTING BLOWN UP ALONG WITH--
HA! NOW WHO'S UPTIGHT?
"SHE'LL BE *FINE.*"
GRRR...

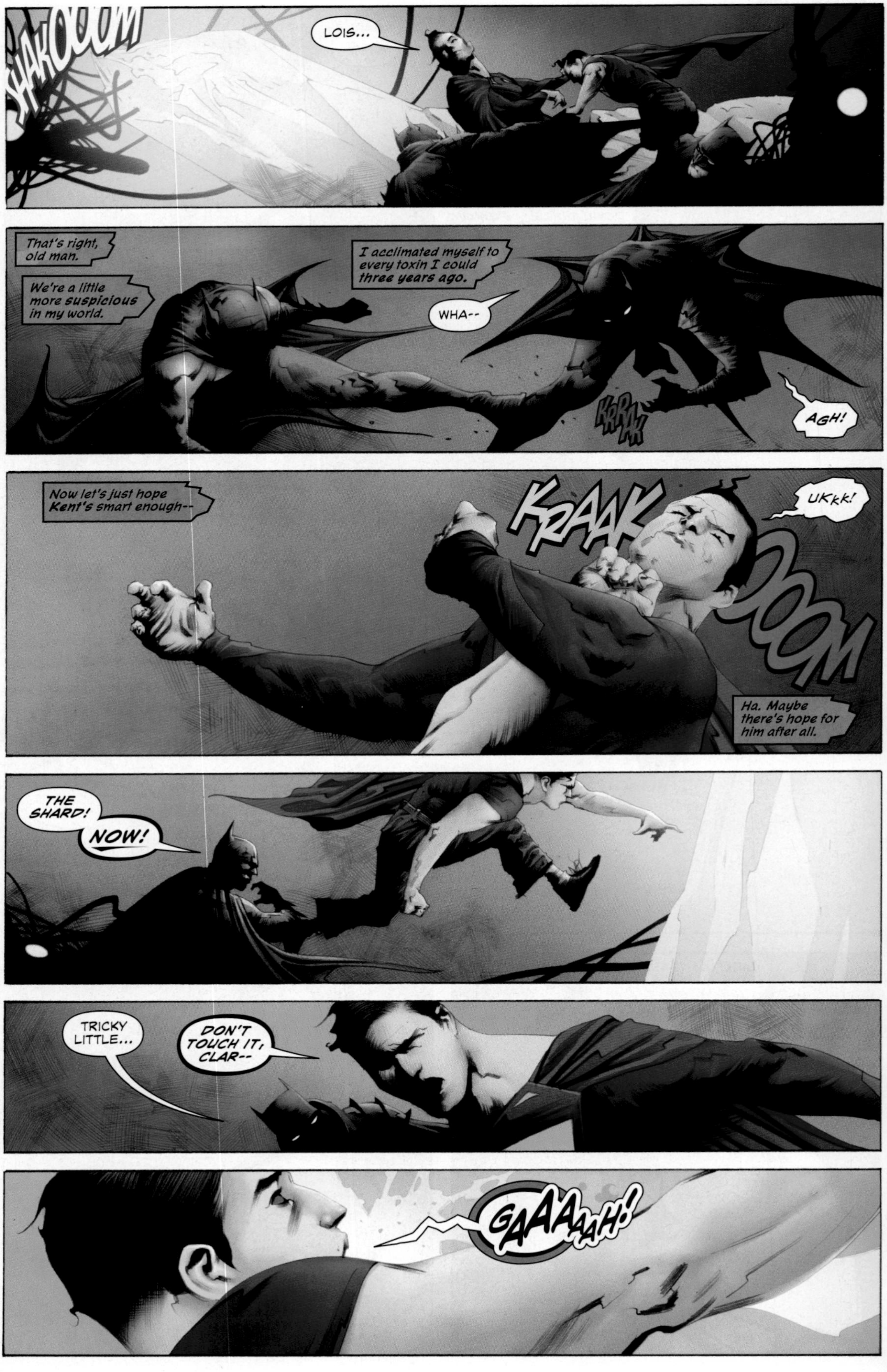
SHAROOOM
LOIS...
That's right, old man.
We're a little more suspicious in my world.
I acclimated myself to every toxin I could three years ago.
WHA--
KRRAK
AGH!
Now let's just hope Kent's smart enough--
KRAAK
UKkk!
OOOM
Ha. Maybe there's hope for him after all.
THE SHARD!
NOW!
TRICKY LITTLE...
DON'T TOUCH IT, CLAR--
GAAAAAH!

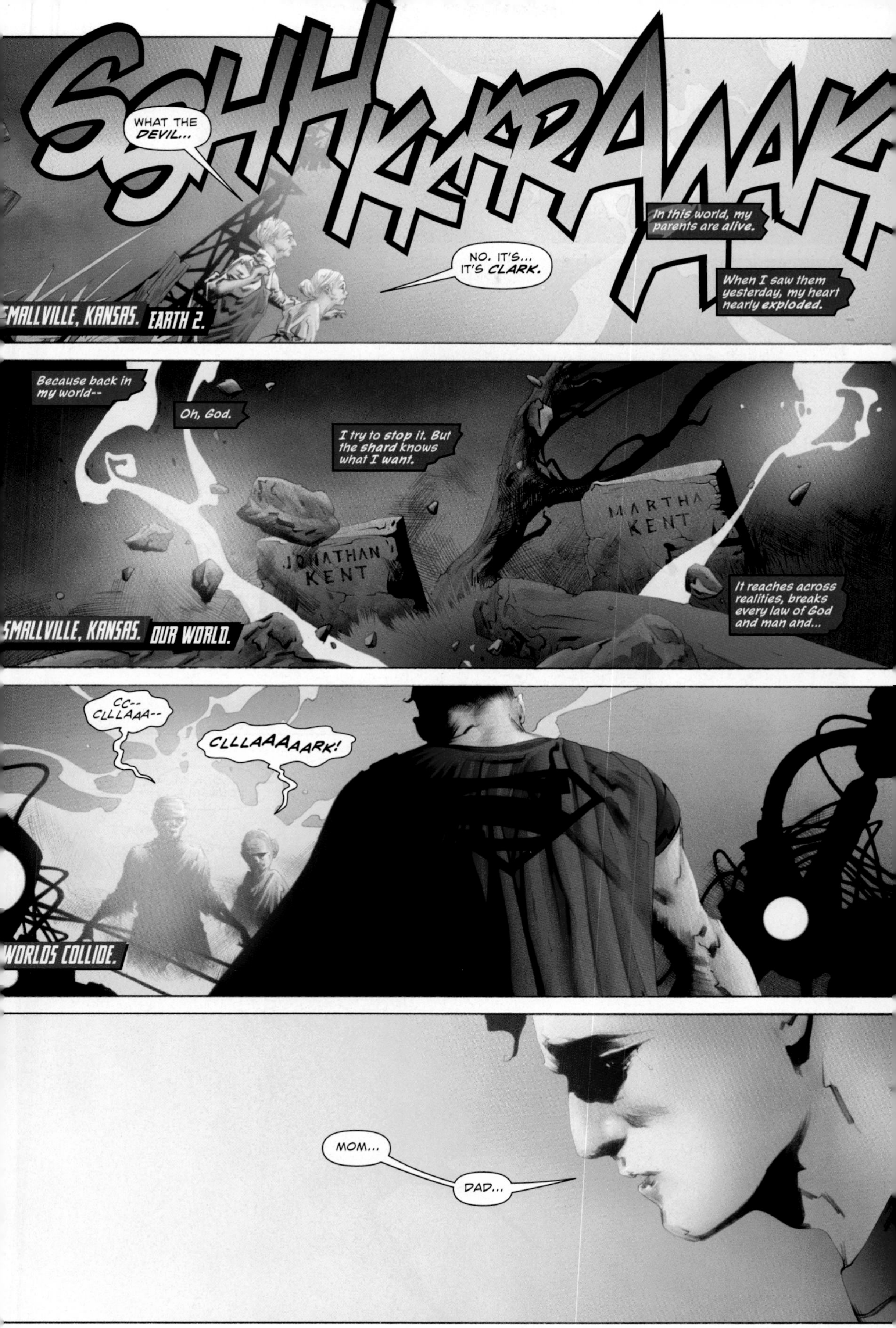
SSHKKRAAAK
WHAT THE DEVIL...
NO. IT'S... IT'S CLARK.
In this world, my parents are alive.
When I saw them yesterday, my heart nearly exploded.
SMALLVILLE, KANSAS. EARTH 2.
Because back in my world--
Oh, God.
I try to stop it. But the shard knows what I want.
MARTHA KENT
JONATHAN KENT
It reaches across realities, breaks every law of God and man and...
SMALLVILLE, KANSAS. OUR WORLD.
CC-- CLLLAAA--
CLLLAAAAARK!
WORLDS COLLIDE.
MOM...
DAD...

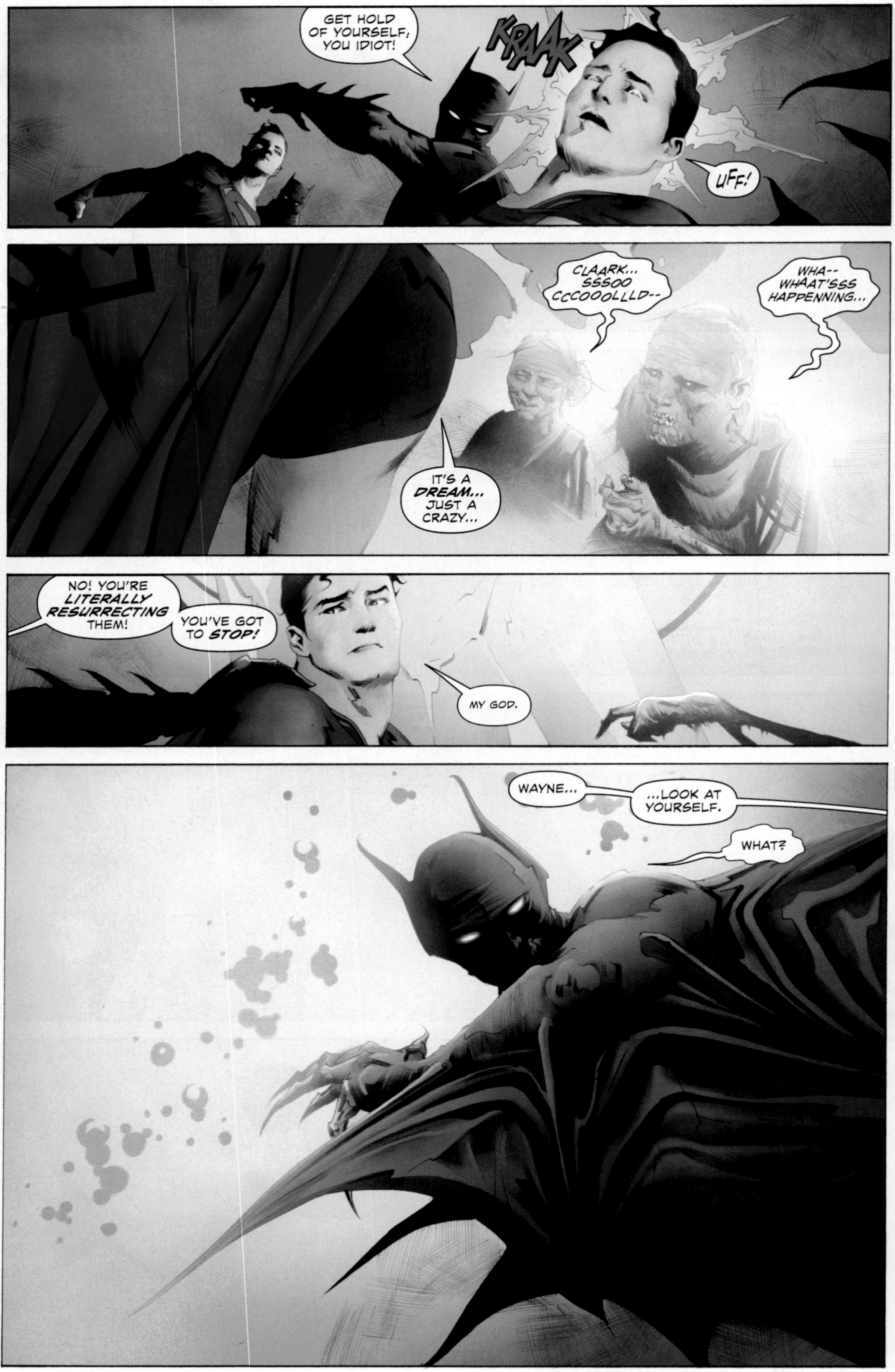
GET HOLD OF YOURSELF, YOU IDIOT!
KRAAK
UFF!
CLAARK... SSSOO CCCOOOLLLLD--
WHA-- WHAAT'SSS HAPPENNING...
IT'S A DREAM... JUST A CRAZY...
NO! YOU'RE LITERALLY RESURRECTING THEM!
YOU'VE GOT TO STOP!
MY GOD.
WAYNE...
...LOOK AT YOURSELF.
WHAT?

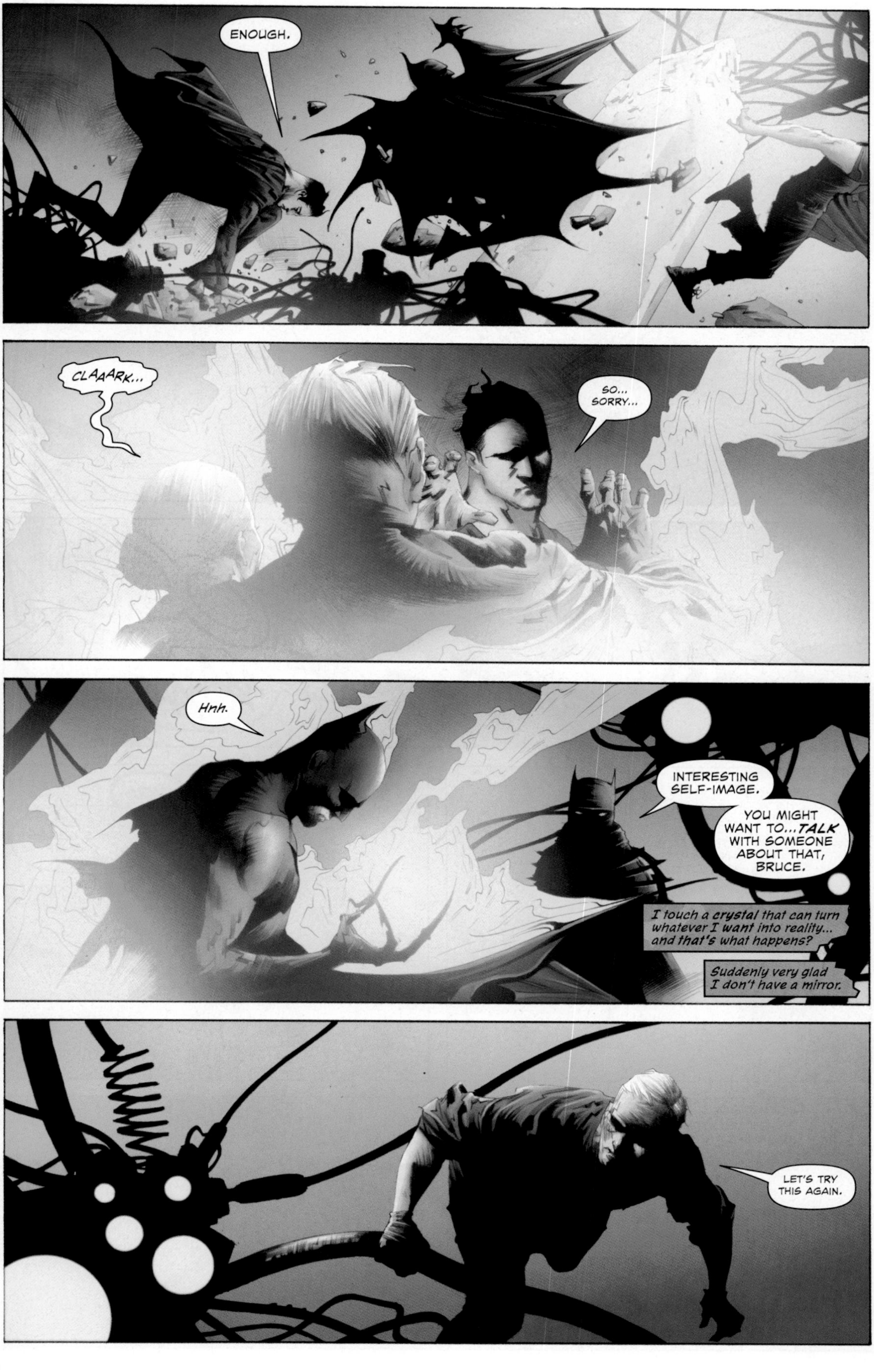
ENOUGH.
CLAAARK...
SO... SORRY...
Hnh.
INTERESTING SELF-IMAGE.
YOU MIGHT WANT TO...TALK WITH SOMEONE ABOUT THAT, BRUCE.
I touch a crystal that can turn whatever I want into reality... and that's what happens?
Suddenly very glad I don't have a mirror.
LET'S TRY THIS AGAIN.

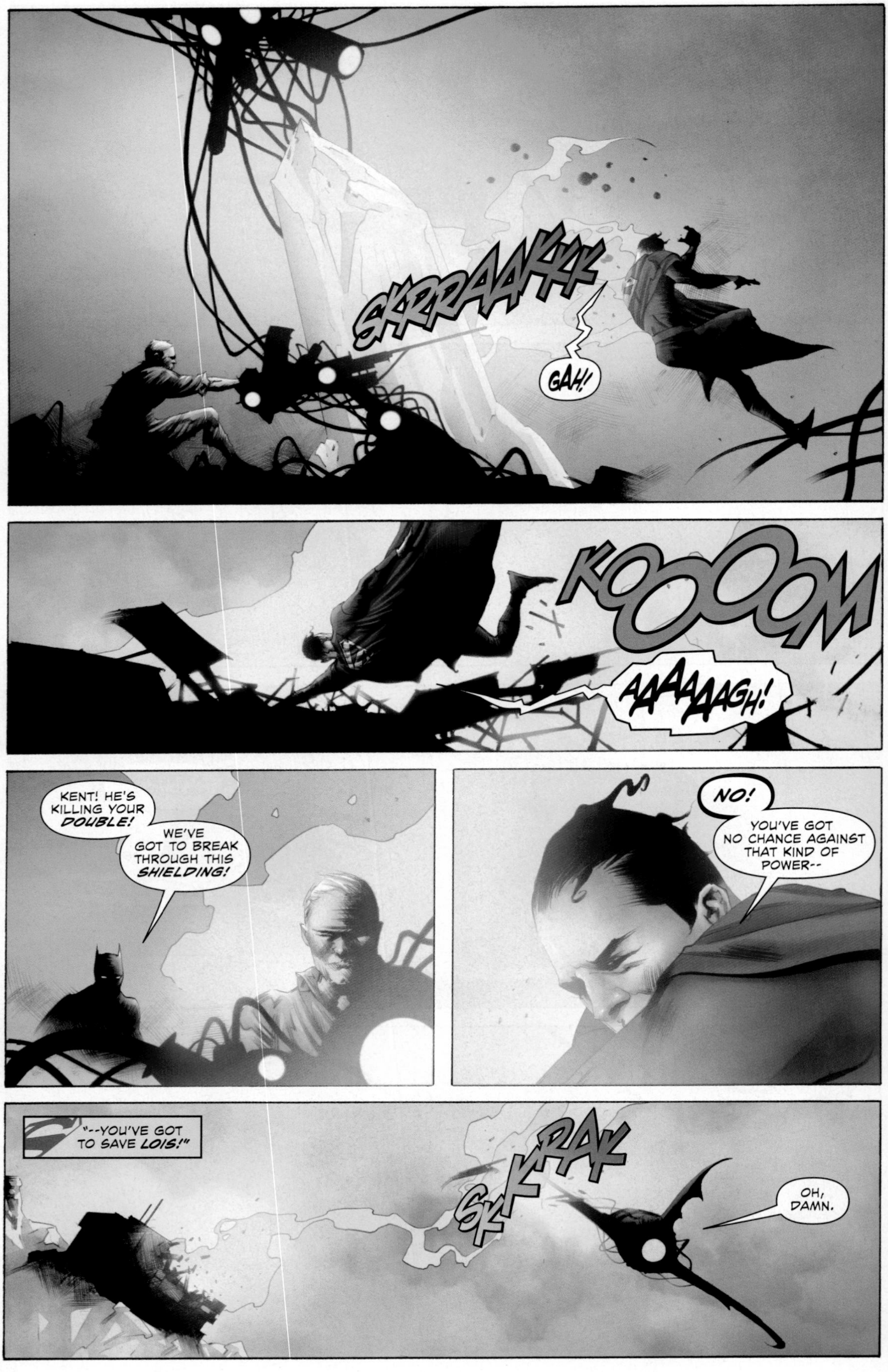
SKRRAAKKK
GAH!
KOOOOM
AAAAAAGH!
KENT! HE'S KILLING YOUR *DOUBLE!*
WE'VE GOT TO BREAK THROUGH THIS *SHIELDING!*
NO!
YOU'VE GOT NO CHANCE AGAINST THAT KIND OF POWER--
"--YOU'VE GOT TO SAVE *LOIS!*"
SKKRAK
OH, DAMN.

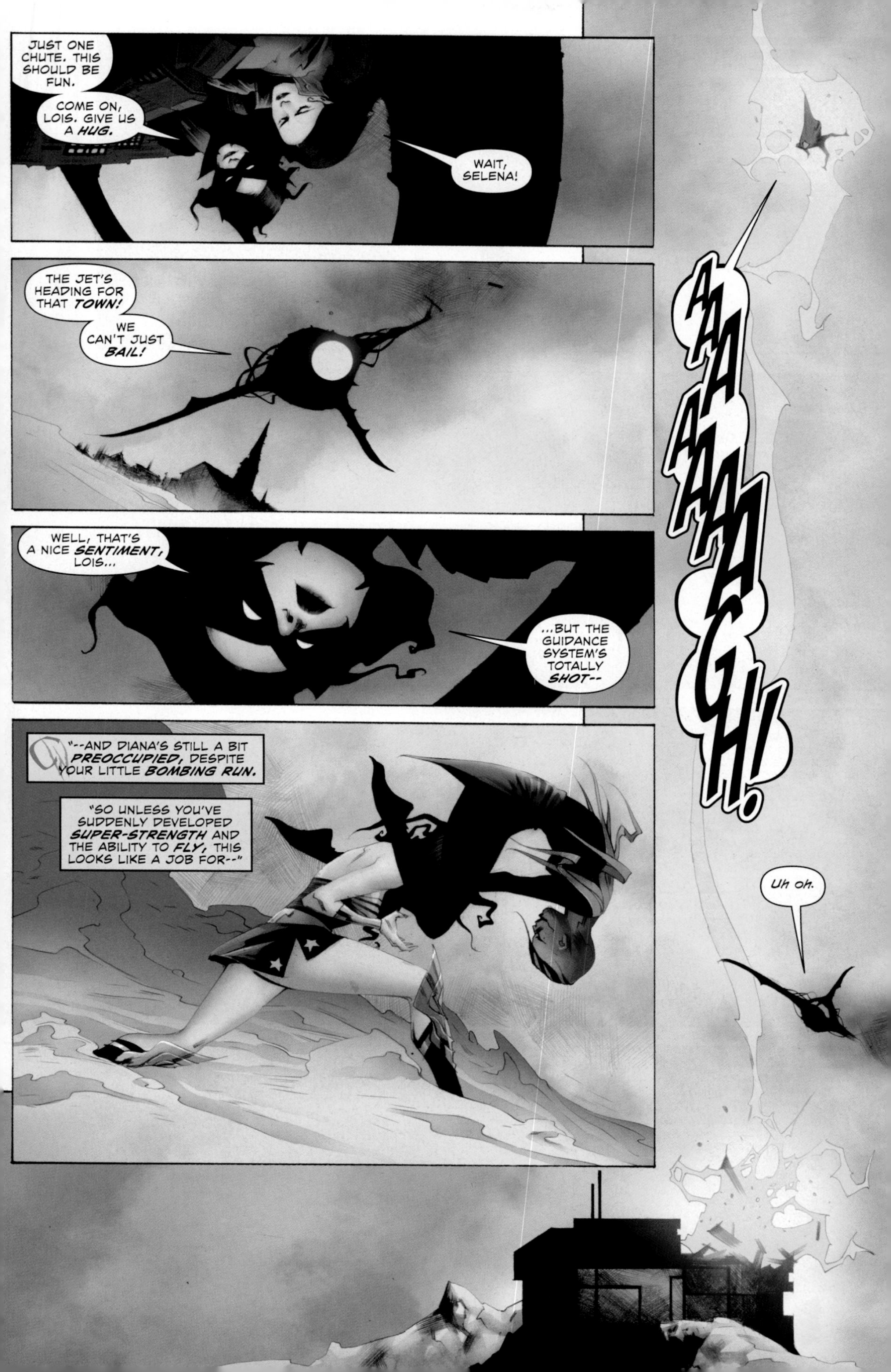
JUST ONE CHUTE. THIS SHOULD BE FUN.
COME ON, LOIS. GIVE US A HUG.
WAIT, SELENA!
THE JET'S HEADING FOR THAT TOWN!
WE CAN'T JUST BAIL!
WELL, THAT'S A NICE SENTIMENT, LOIS...
...BUT THE GUIDANCE SYSTEM'S TOTALLY SHOT--
"--AND DIANA'S STILL A BIT PREOCCUPIED, DESPITE YOUR LITTLE BOMBING RUN.
"SO UNLESS YOU'VE SUDDENLY DEVELOPED SUPER-STRENGTH AND THE ABILITY TO FLY, THIS LOOKS LIKE A JOB FOR--"
AAAAAAAGH!
Uh oh.

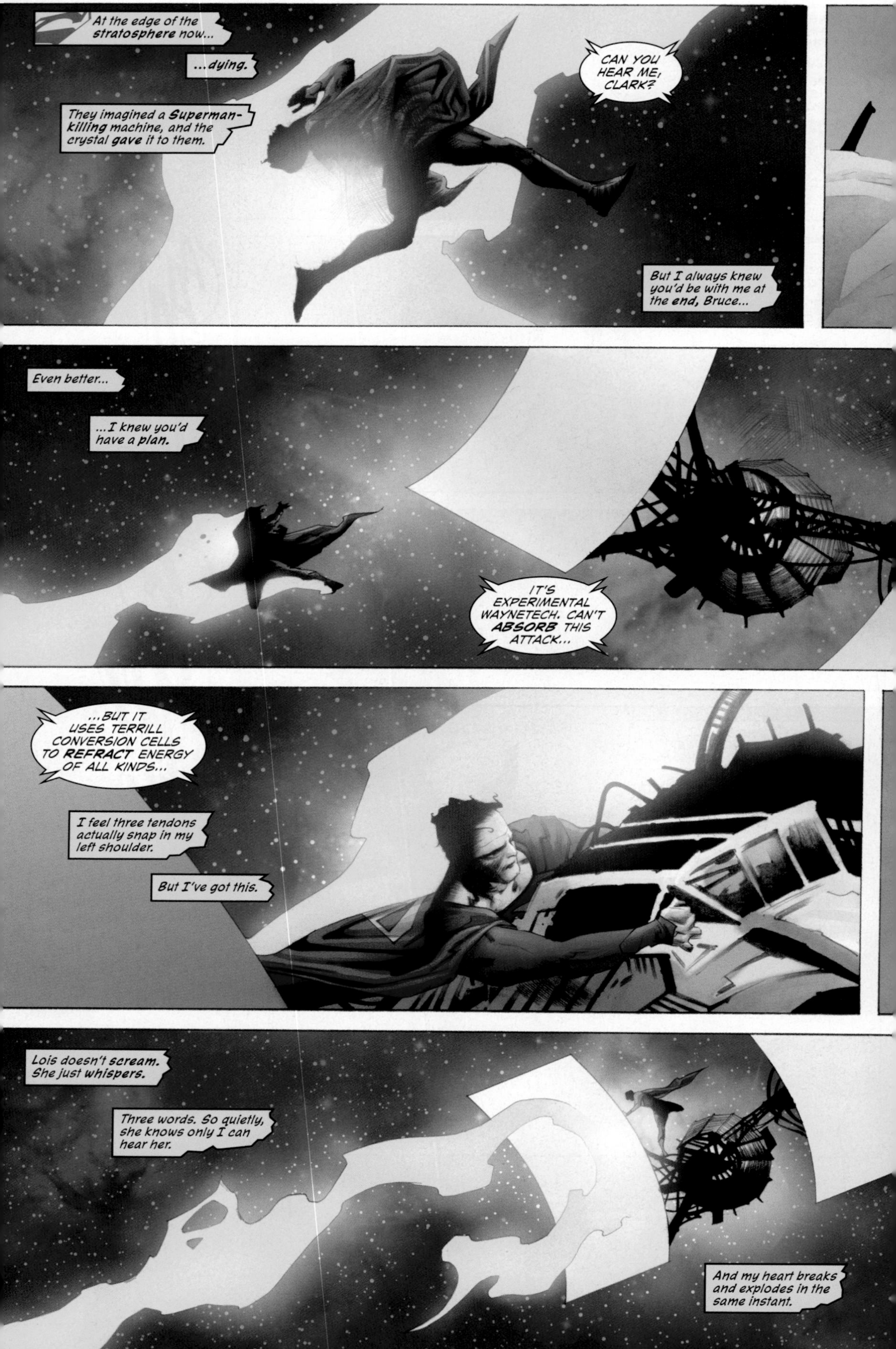

At the edge of the stratosphere now...
...dying.
They imagined a Superman-killing machine, and the crystal gave it to them.
CAN YOU HEAR ME, CLARK?
But I always knew you'd be with me at the end, Bruce...
Even better...
...I knew you'd have a plan.
IT'S EXPERIMENTAL WAYNETECH. CAN'T ABSORB THIS ATTACK...
...BUT IT USES TERRILL CONVERSION CELLS TO REFRACT ENERGY OF ALL KINDS...
I feel three tendons actually snap in my left shoulder.
But I've got this.
Lois doesn't scream. She just whispers.
Three words. So quietly, she knows only I can hear her.
And my heart breaks and explodes in the same instant.

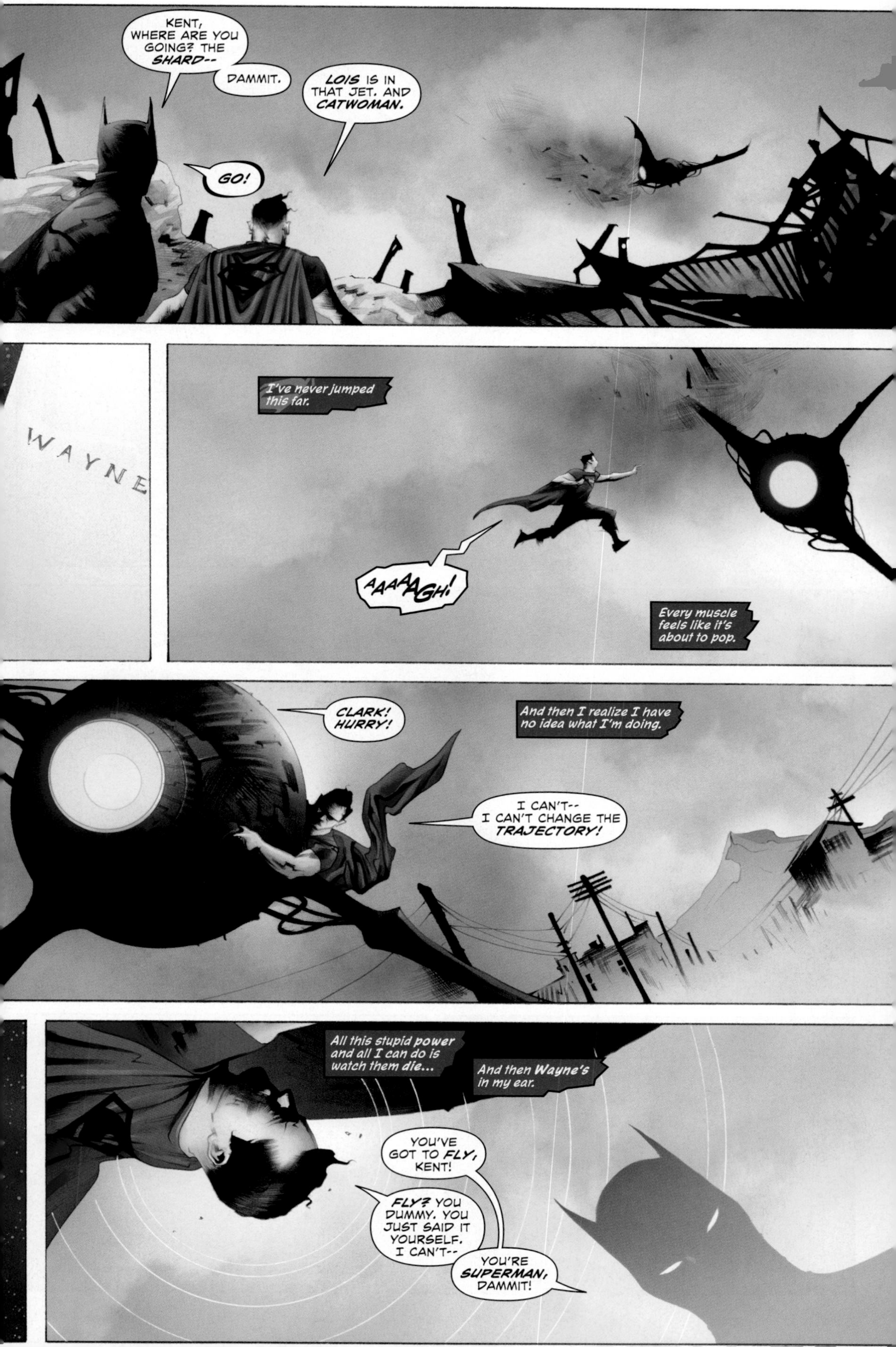
KENT, WHERE ARE YOU GOING? THE SHARD--
DAMMIT.
LOIS IS IN THAT JET. AND CATWOMAN.
GO!
WAYNE
I've never jumped this far.
AAAAAGH!
Every muscle feels like it's about to pop.
CLARK! HURRY!
And then I realize I have no idea what I'm doing.
I CAN'T-- I CAN'T CHANGE THE TRAJECTORY!
All this stupid power and all I can do is watch them die...
And then Wayne's in my ear.
YOU'VE GOT TO FLY, KENT!
FLY? YOU DUMMY. YOU JUST SAID IT YOURSELF. I CAN'T--
YOU'RE SUPERMAN, DAMMIT!

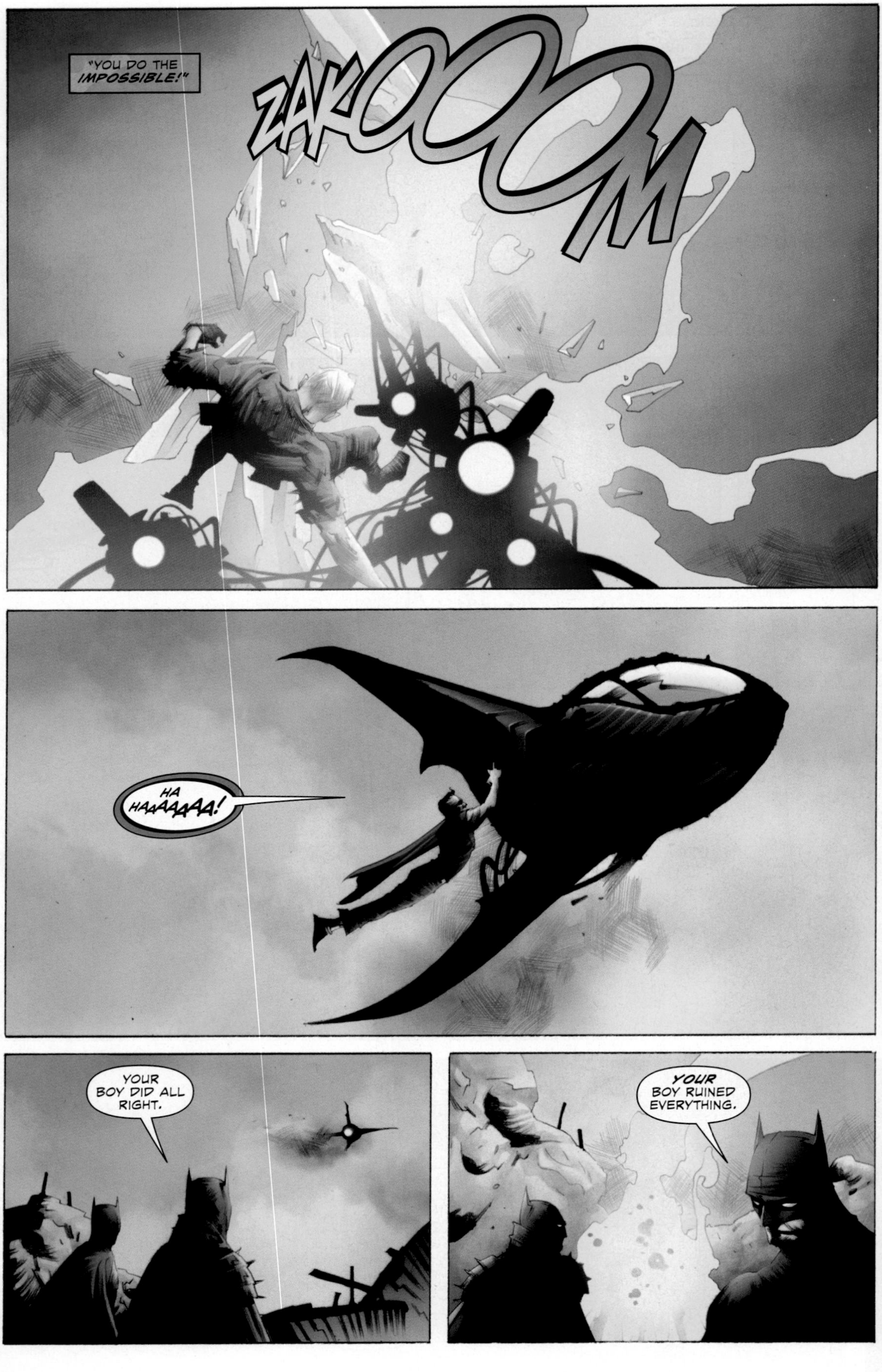
"YOU DO THE IMPOSSIBLE!"
ZAKOOOOM
HA HAAAAAAA!
YOUR BOY DID ALL RIGHT.
YOUR BOY RUINED EVERYTHING.

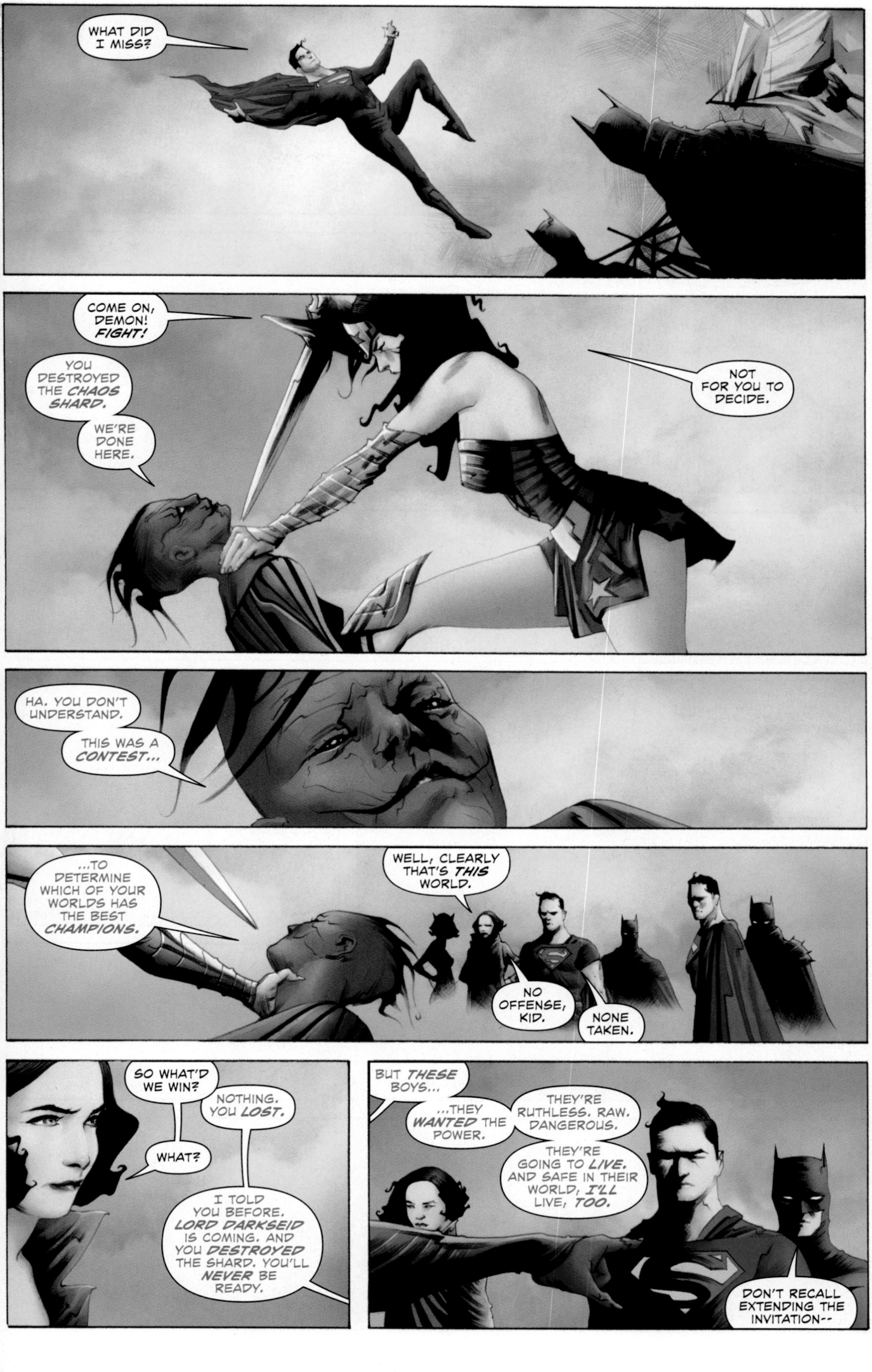
WHAT DID I MISS?
COME ON, DEMON! FIGHT!
YOU DESTROYED THE CHAOS SHARD.
WE'RE DONE HERE.
NOT FOR YOU TO DECIDE.
HA. YOU DON'T UNDERSTAND.
THIS WAS A CONTEST...
...TO DETERMINE WHICH OF YOUR WORLDS HAS THE BEST CHAMPIONS.
WELL, CLEARLY THAT'S THIS WORLD.
NO OFFENSE, KID.
NONE TAKEN.
SO WHAT'D WE WIN?
NOTHING. YOU LOST.
WHAT?
I TOLD YOU BEFORE. LORD DARKSEID IS COMING. AND YOU DESTROYED THE SHARD. YOU'LL NEVER BE READY.
BUT THESE BOYS...
...THEY WANTED THE POWER.
THEY'RE RUTHLESS. RAW. DANGEROUS.
THEY'RE GOING TO LIVE. AND SAFE IN THEIR WORLD, I'LL LIVE, TOO.
DON'T RECALL EXTENDING THE INVITATION--

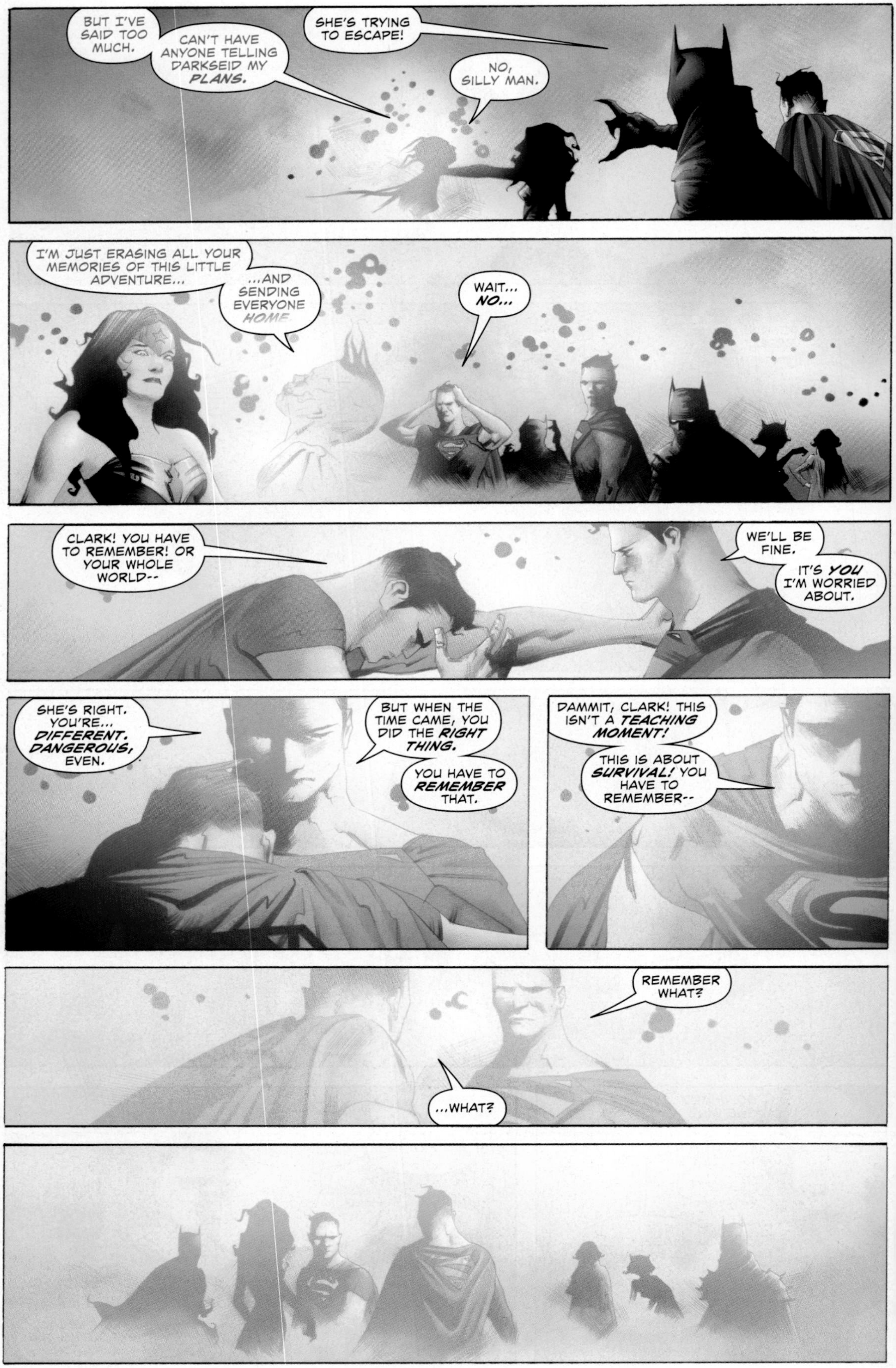
BUT I'VE SAID TOO MUCH.
CAN'T HAVE ANYONE TELLING DARKSEID MY *PLANS.*
SHE'S TRYING TO ESCAPE!
NO, SILLY MAN.
I'M JUST ERASING ALL YOUR MEMORIES OF THIS LITTLE ADVENTURE...
...AND SENDING EVERYONE *HOME.*
WAIT... ***NO...***
CLARK! YOU HAVE TO REMEMBER! OR YOUR WHOLE WORLD--
WE'LL BE FINE.
IT'S ***YOU*** I'M WORRIED ABOUT.
SHE'S RIGHT. YOU'RE... ***DIFFERENT. DANGEROUS,*** EVEN.
BUT WHEN THE TIME CAME, YOU DID THE ***RIGHT THING.***
YOU HAVE TO ***REMEMBER*** THAT.
DAMMIT, CLARK! THIS ISN'T A ***TEACHING MOMENT!***
THIS IS ABOUT ***SURVIVAL!*** YOU HAVE TO REMEMBER--
REMEMBER WHAT?
...WHAT?

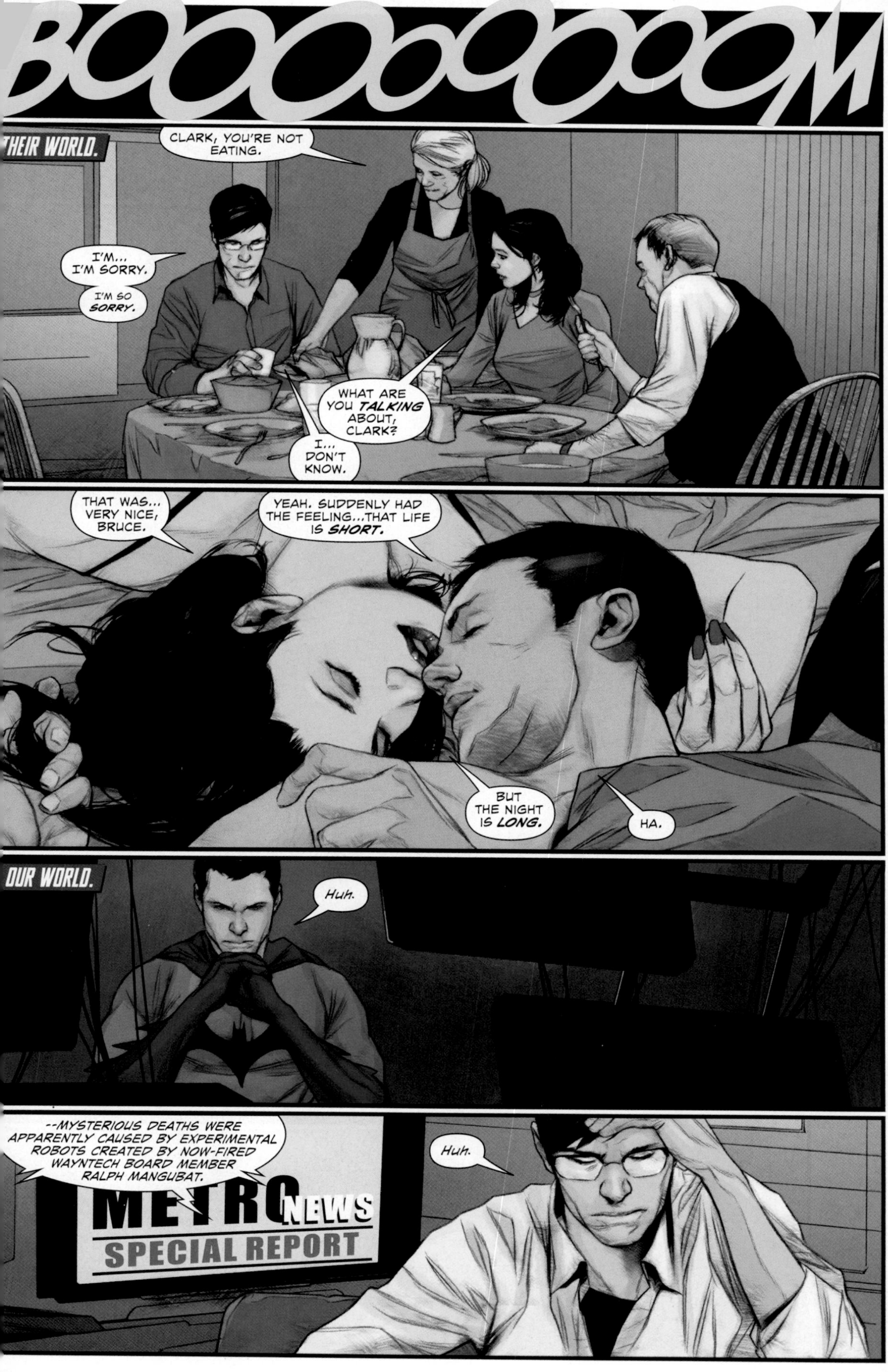
BOOOOOOOOM
THEIR WORLD.
CLARK, YOU'RE NOT EATING.
I'M... I'M SORRY.
I'M SO SORRY.
WHAT ARE YOU TALKING ABOUT, CLARK?
I... DON'T KNOW.
THAT WAS... VERY NICE, BRUCE.
YEAH. SUDDENLY HAD THE FEELING...THAT LIFE IS SHORT.
BUT THE NIGHT IS LONG.
HA.
OUR WORLD.
Huh.
--MYSTERIOUS DEATHS WERE APPARENTLY CAUSED BY EXPERIMENTAL ROBOTS CREATED BY NOW-FIRED WAYNTECH BOARD MEMBER RALPH MANGUBAT.
METRO NEWS
SPECIAL REPORT
Huh.

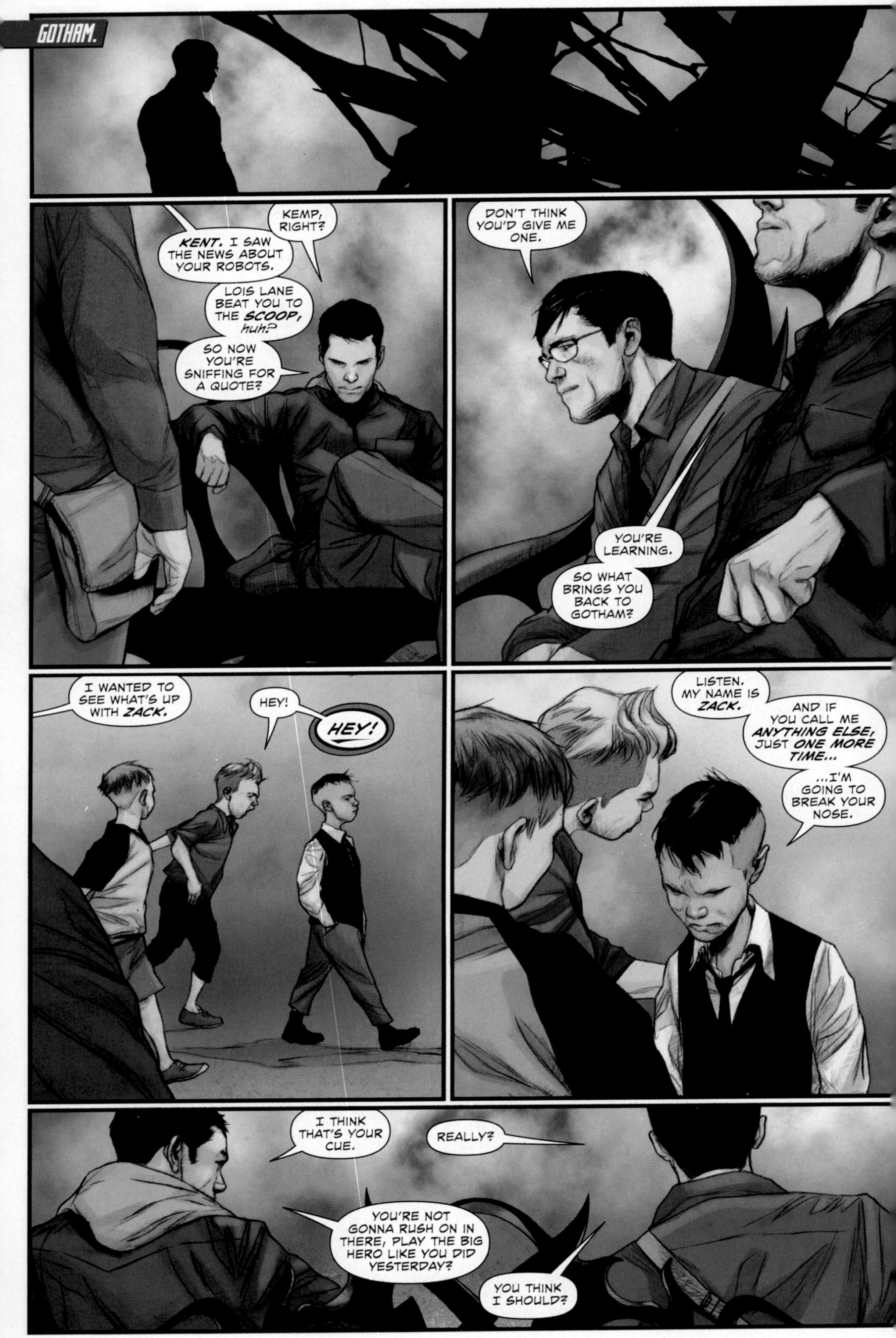
GOTHAM.
KEMP, RIGHT?
KENT. I SAW THE NEWS ABOUT YOUR ROBOTS.
LOIS LANE BEAT YOU TO THE SCOOP, huh?
SO NOW YOU'RE SNIFFING FOR A QUOTE?
DON'T THINK YOU'D GIVE ME ONE.
YOU'RE LEARNING.
SO WHAT BRINGS YOU BACK TO GOTHAM?
I WANTED TO SEE WHAT'S UP WITH ZACK.
HEY!
HEY!
LISTEN. MY NAME IS ZACK.
AND IF YOU CALL ME ANYTHING ELSE, JUST ONE MORE TIME...
...I'M GOING TO BREAK YOUR NOSE.
I THINK THAT'S YOUR CUE.
REALLY?
YOU'RE NOT GONNA RUSH ON IN THERE, PLAY THE BIG HERO LIKE YOU DID YESTERDAY?
YOU THINK I SHOULD?

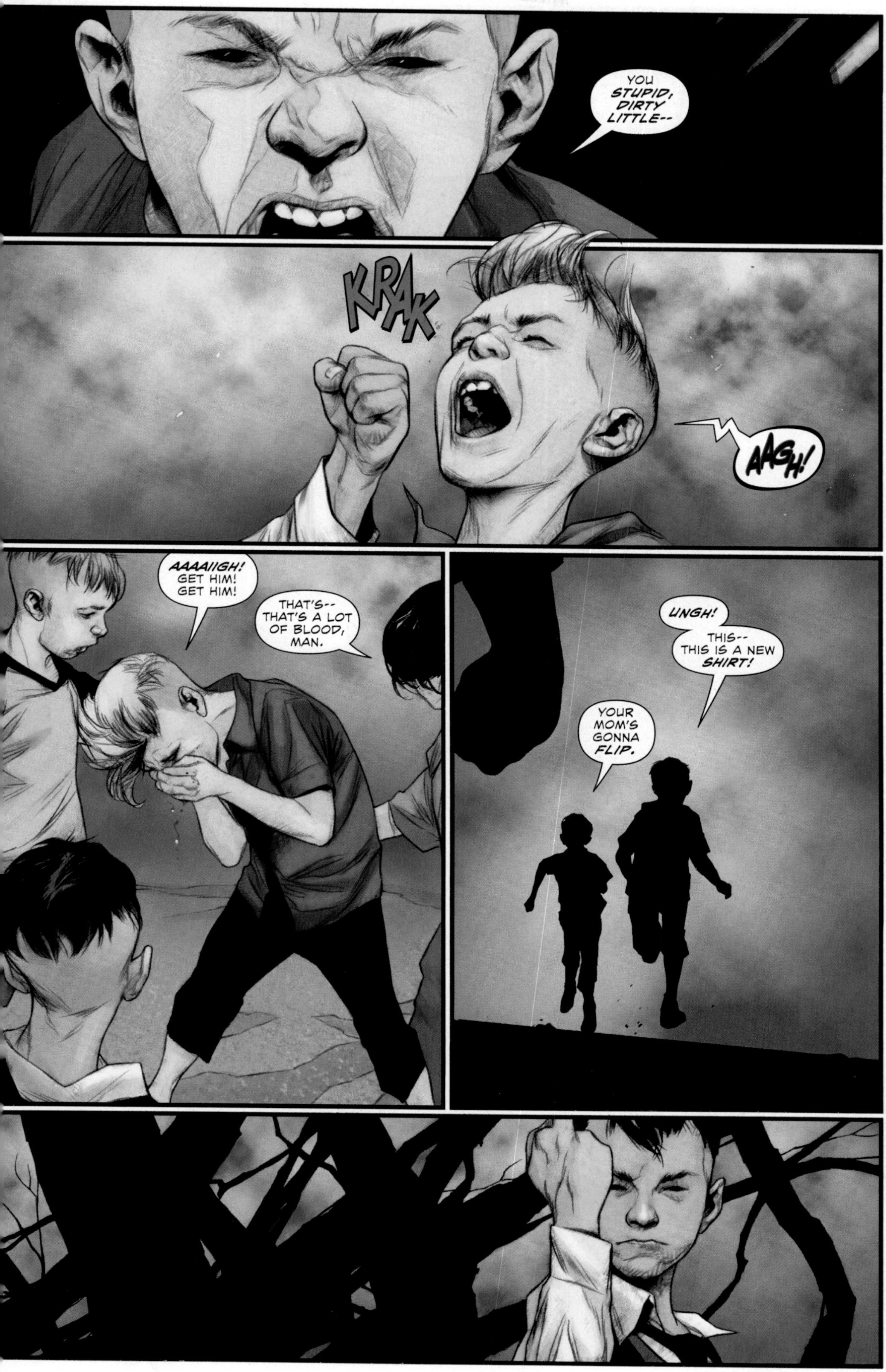
YOU STUPID, DIRTY LITTLE--
KRAK
AAGH!
AAAAIIGH! GET HIM! GET HIM!
THAT'S-- THAT'S A LOT OF BLOOD, MAN.
UNGH!
THIS-- THIS IS A NEW SHIRT!
YOUR MOM'S GONNA FLIP.

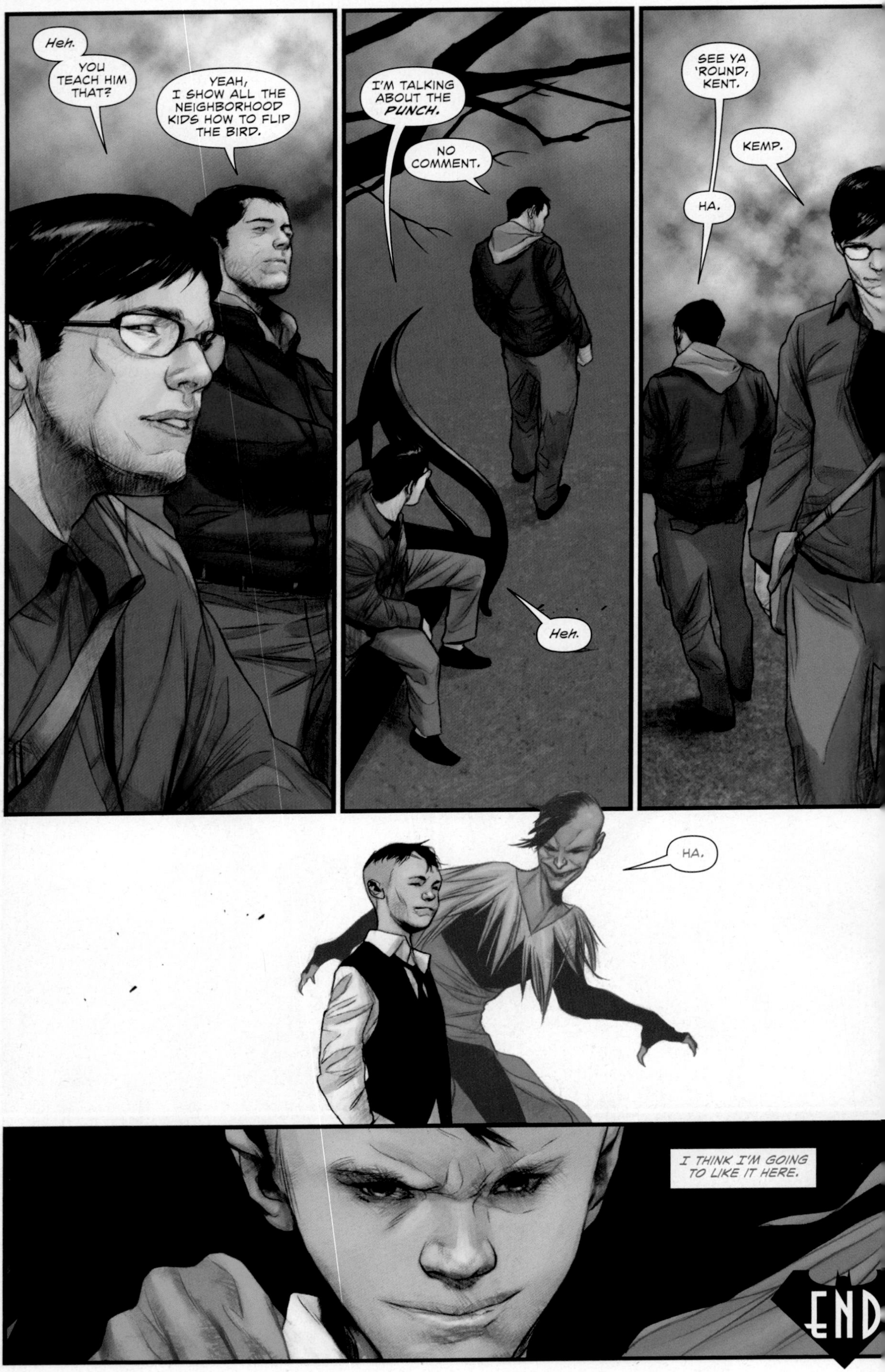
Heh.
YOU TEACH HIM THAT?
YEAH, I SHOW ALL THE NEIGHBORHOOD KIDS HOW TO FLIP THE BIRD.
I'M TALKING ABOUT THE PUNCH.
NO COMMENT.
Heh.
SEE YA 'ROUND, KENT.
KEMP.
HA.
HA.
I THINK I'M GOING TO LIKE IT HERE.
END

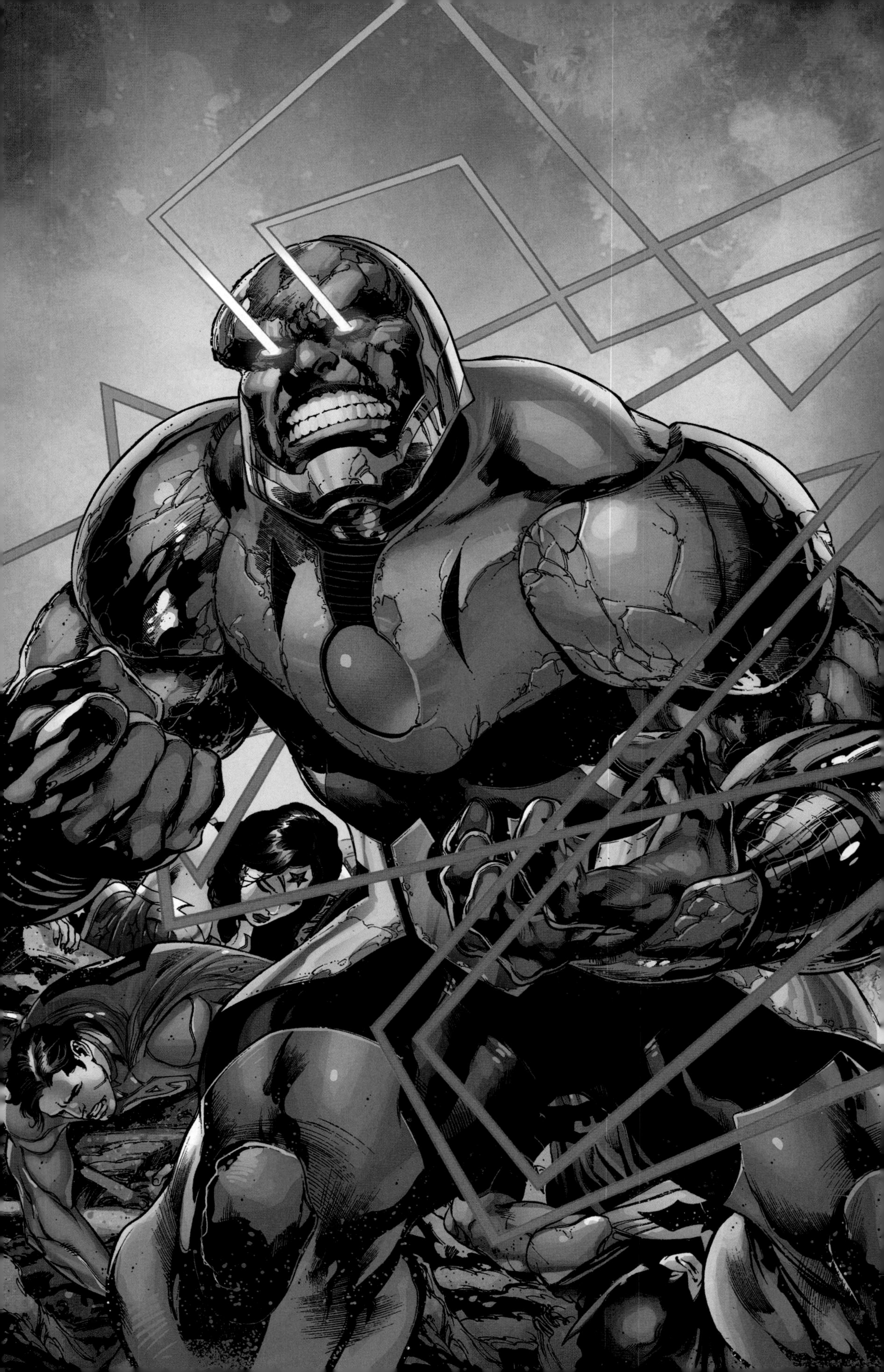

GREG PAK writer **PAULO SIQUEIRA NETHO DIAZ** artists **HI-FI** colorist cover by **IVAN REIS, JOE PRADO & ALEX SINCLAIR**
DARKSEID created by **JACK KIRBY**

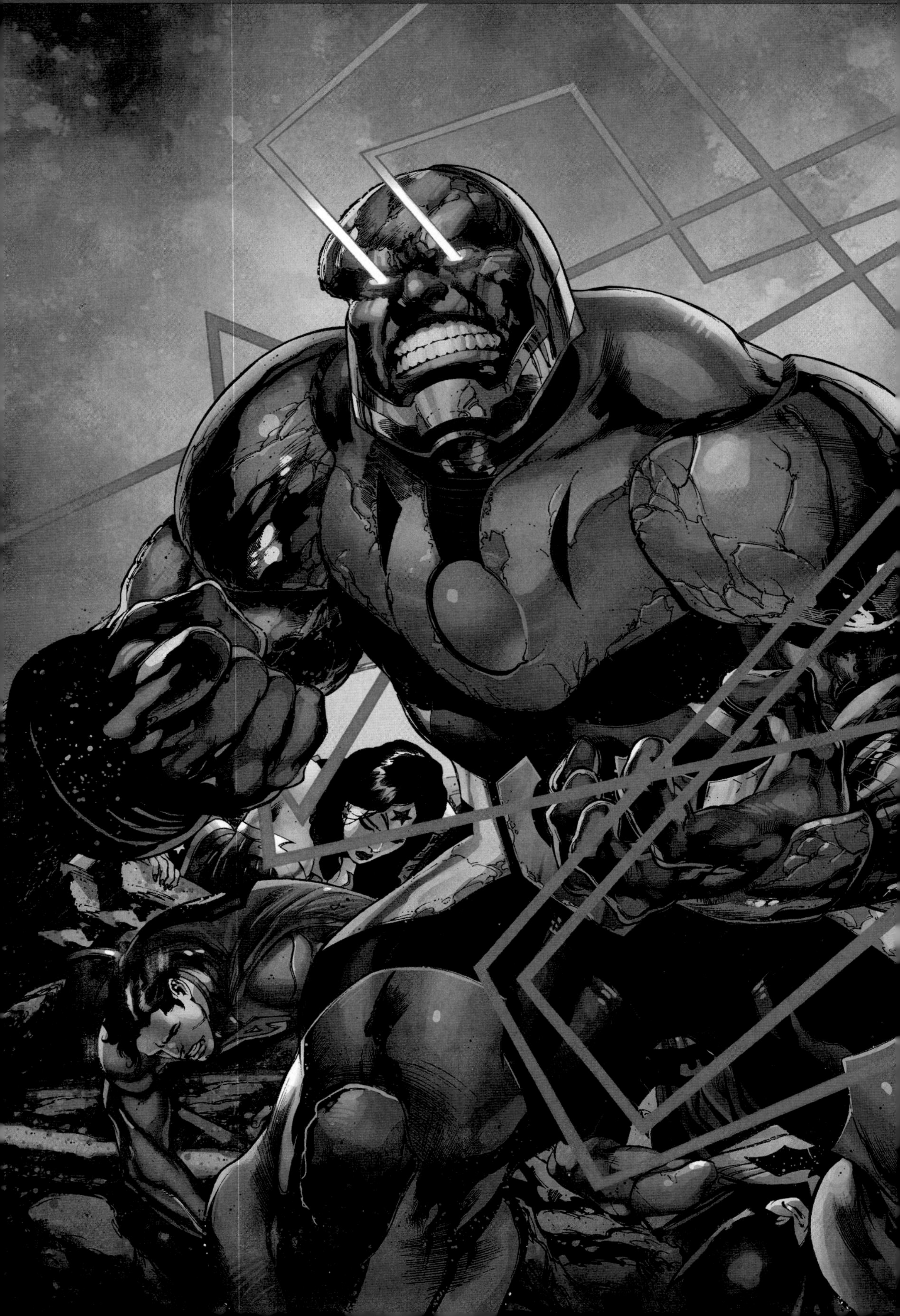

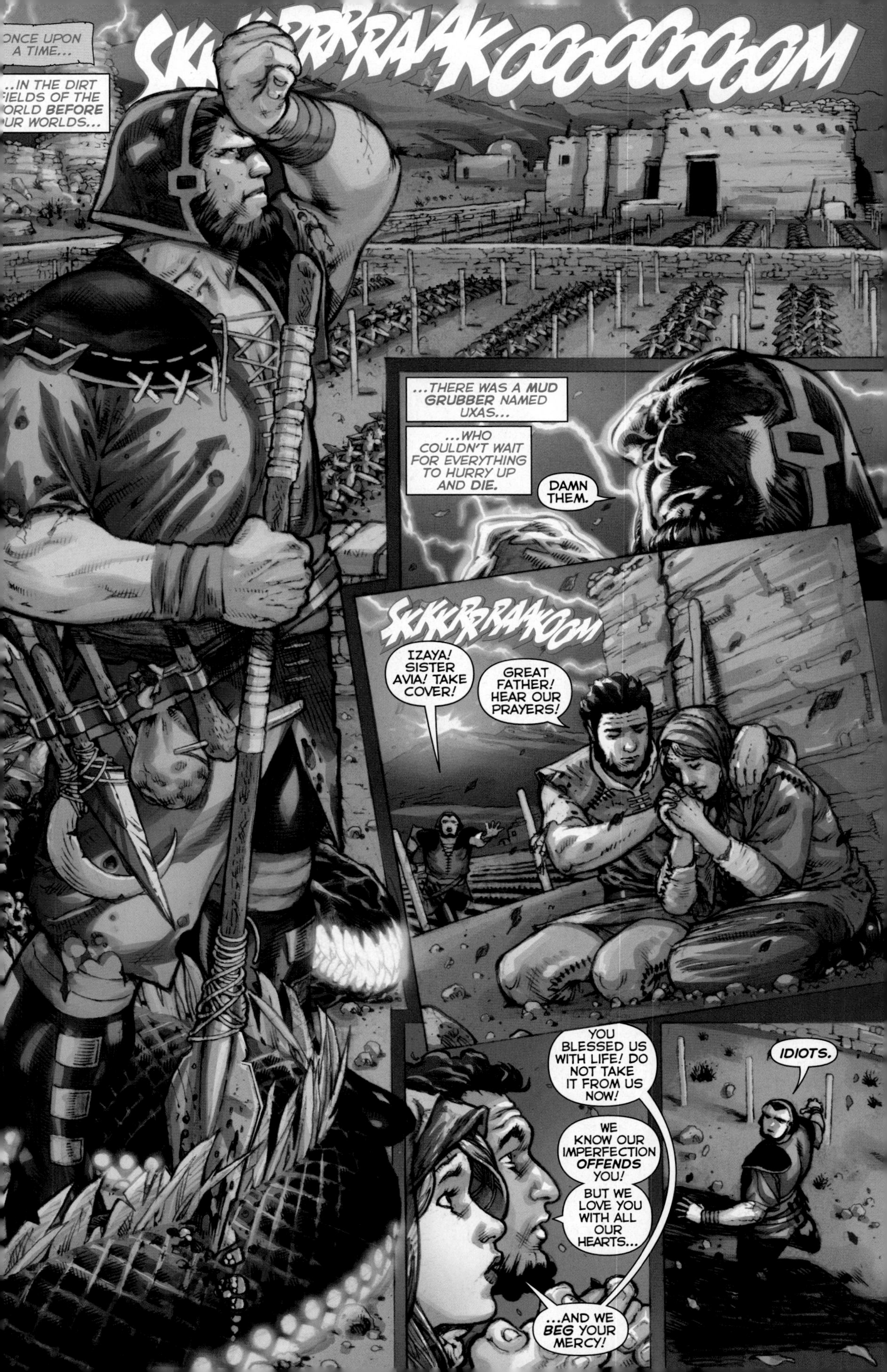
ONCE UPON A TIME...
...IN THE DIRT FIELDS OF THE WORLD BEFORE OUR WORLDS...
SKKRRRRAAKOOOOOOOOOM
...THERE WAS A MUD GRUBBER NAMED UXAS...
...WHO COULDN'T WAIT FOR EVERYTHING TO HURRY UP AND DIE.
DAMN THEM.
SKKRRRAAKOOM
IZAYA! SISTER AVIA! TAKE COVER!
GREAT FATHER! HEAR OUR PRAYERS!
YOU BLESSED US WITH LIFE! DO NOT TAKE IT FROM US NOW!
WE KNOW OUR IMPERFECTION OFFENDS YOU!
BUT WE LOVE YOU WITH ALL OUR HEARTS...
...AND WE BEG YOUR MERCY!
IDIOTS.

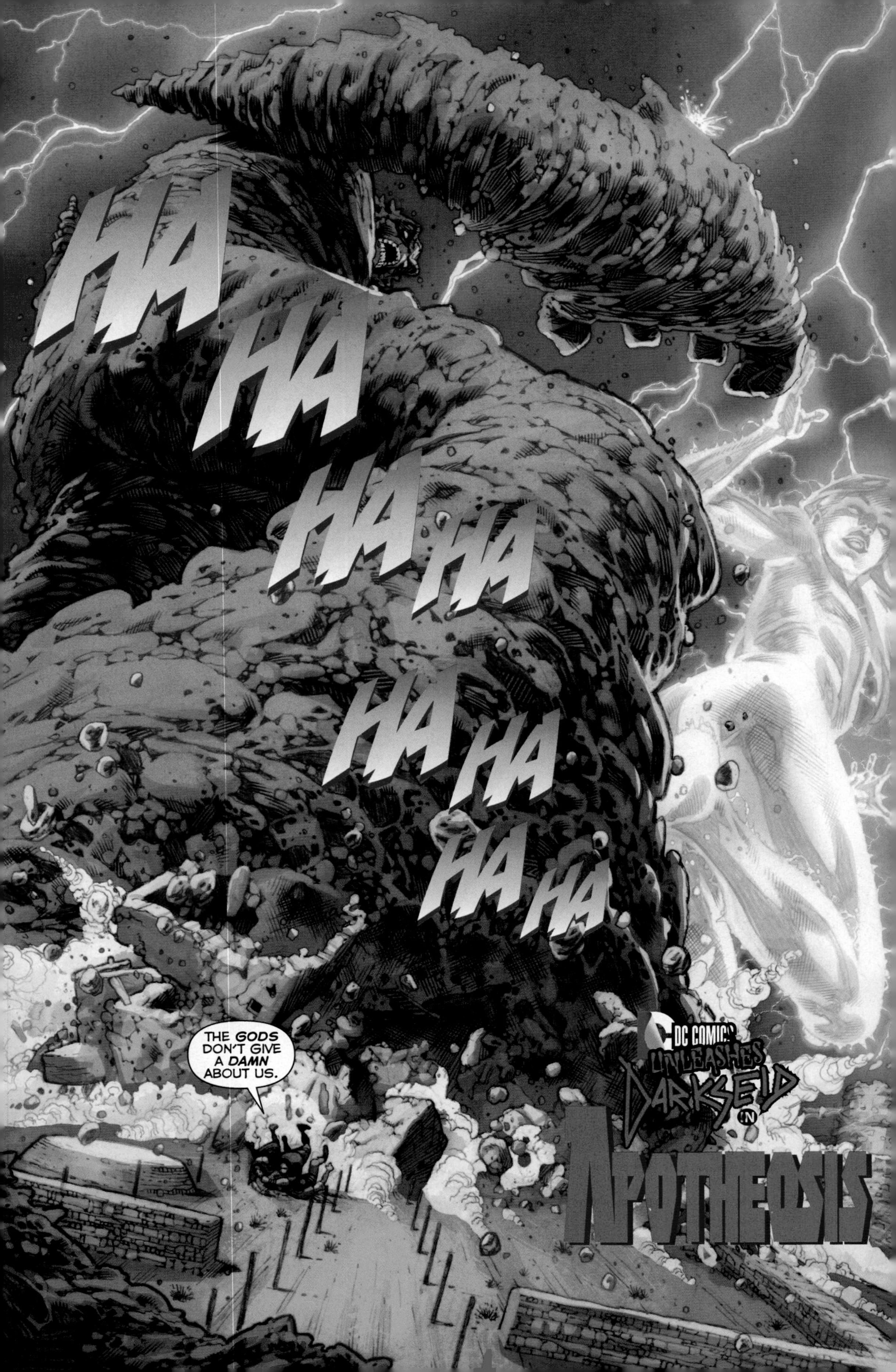
HA HA HA HA HA HA HA HA
THE GODS DON'T GIVE A DAMN ABOUT US.
DC COMICS UNLEASHES DARKSEID IN
APOTHEOSIS

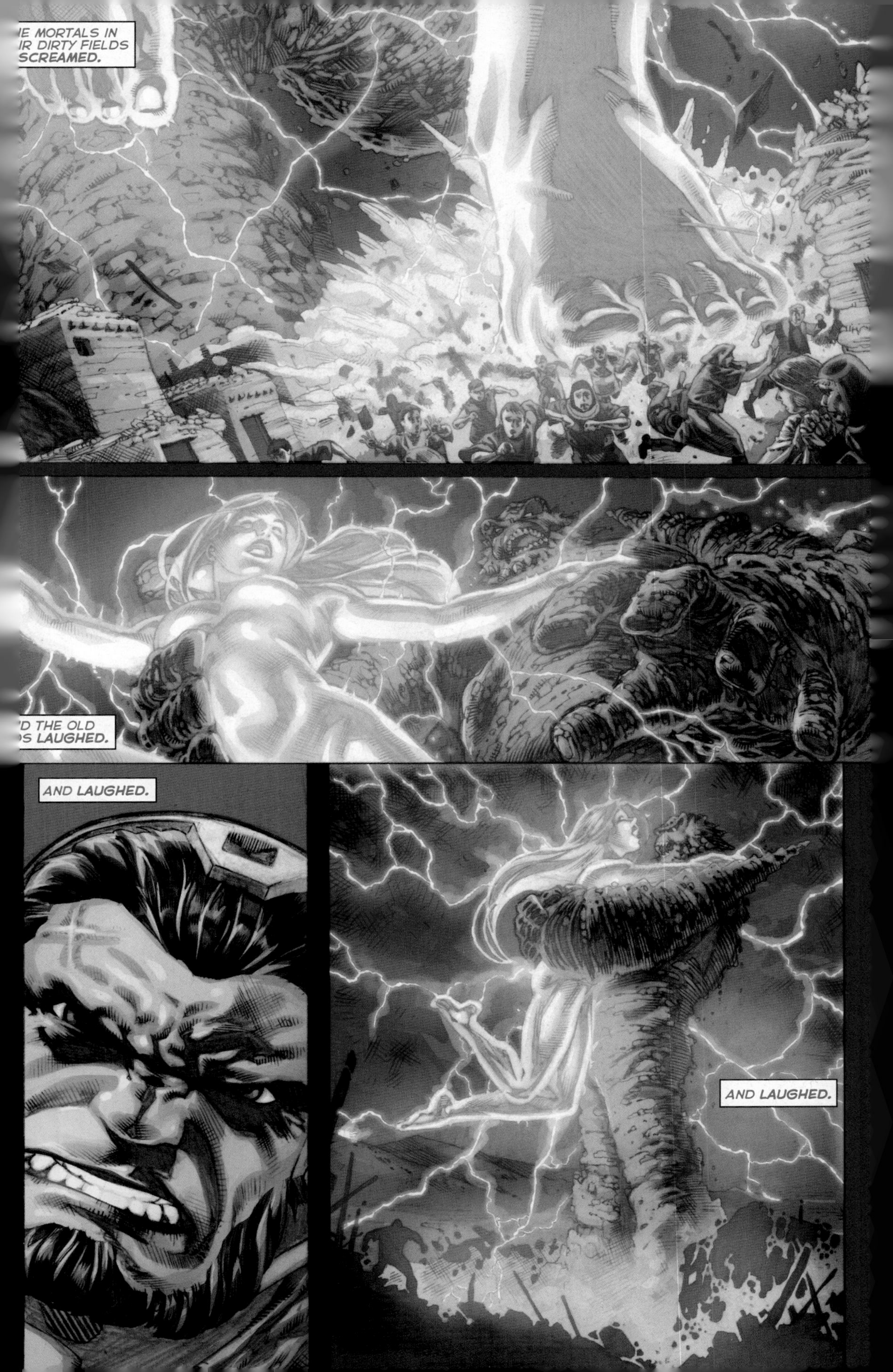
E MORTALS IN
IR DIRTY FIELDS
SCREAMED.
D THE OLD
DS LAUGHED.
AND LAUGHED.
AND LAUGHED.

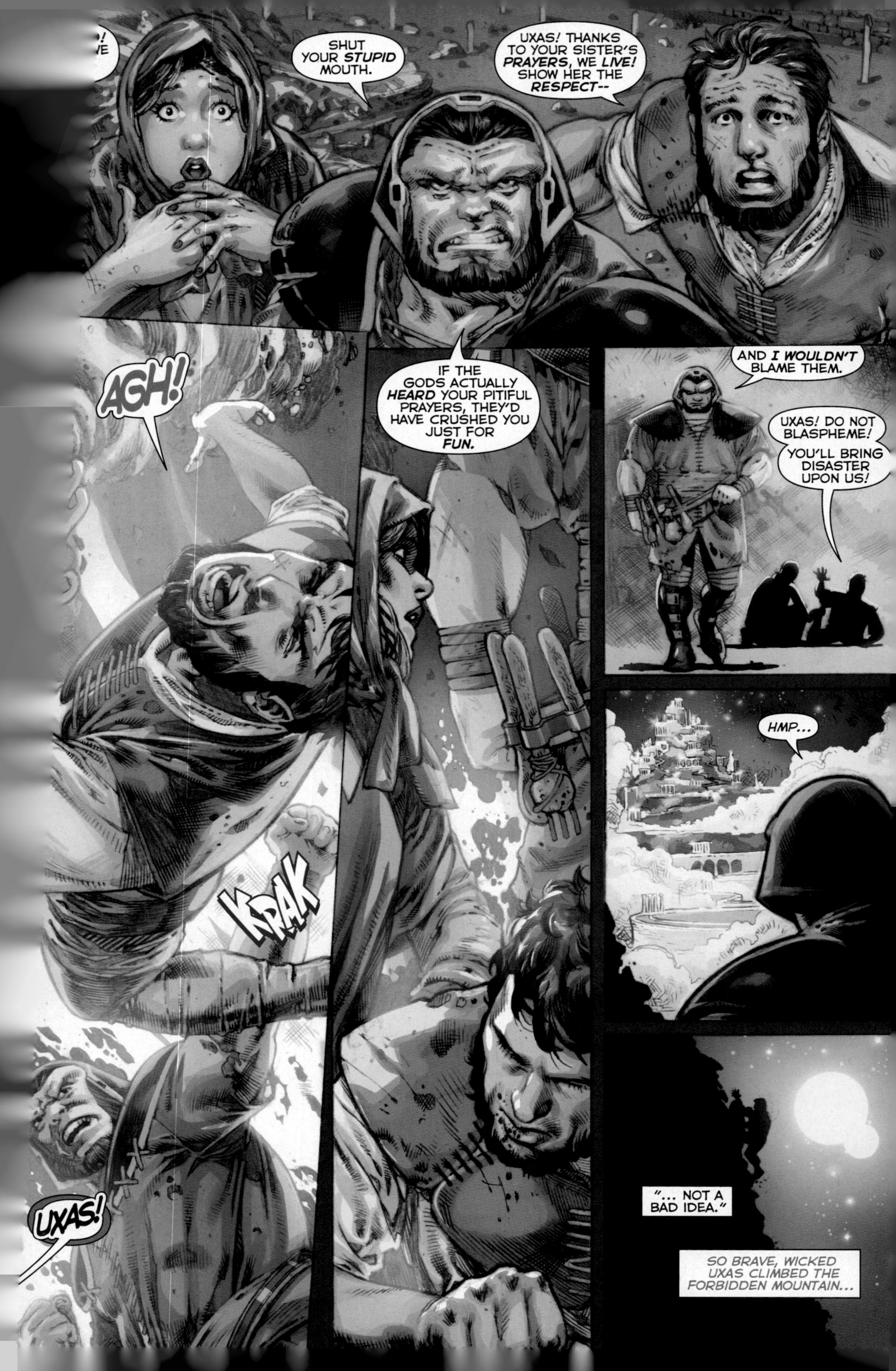
SHUT YOUR STUPID MOUTH.
UXAS! THANKS TO YOUR SISTER'S PRAYERS, WE LIVE! SHOW HER THE RESPECT--
AGH!
IF THE GODS ACTUALLY HEARD YOUR PITIFUL PRAYERS, THEY'D HAVE CRUSHED YOU JUST FOR FUN.
KRAK
UXAS!
AND I WOULDN'T BLAME THEM.
UXAS! DO NOT BLASPHEME!
YOU'LL BRING DISASTER UPON US!
HMP...
"... NOT A BAD IDEA."
SO BRAVE, WICKED UXAS CLIMBED THE FORBIDDEN MOUNTAIN...

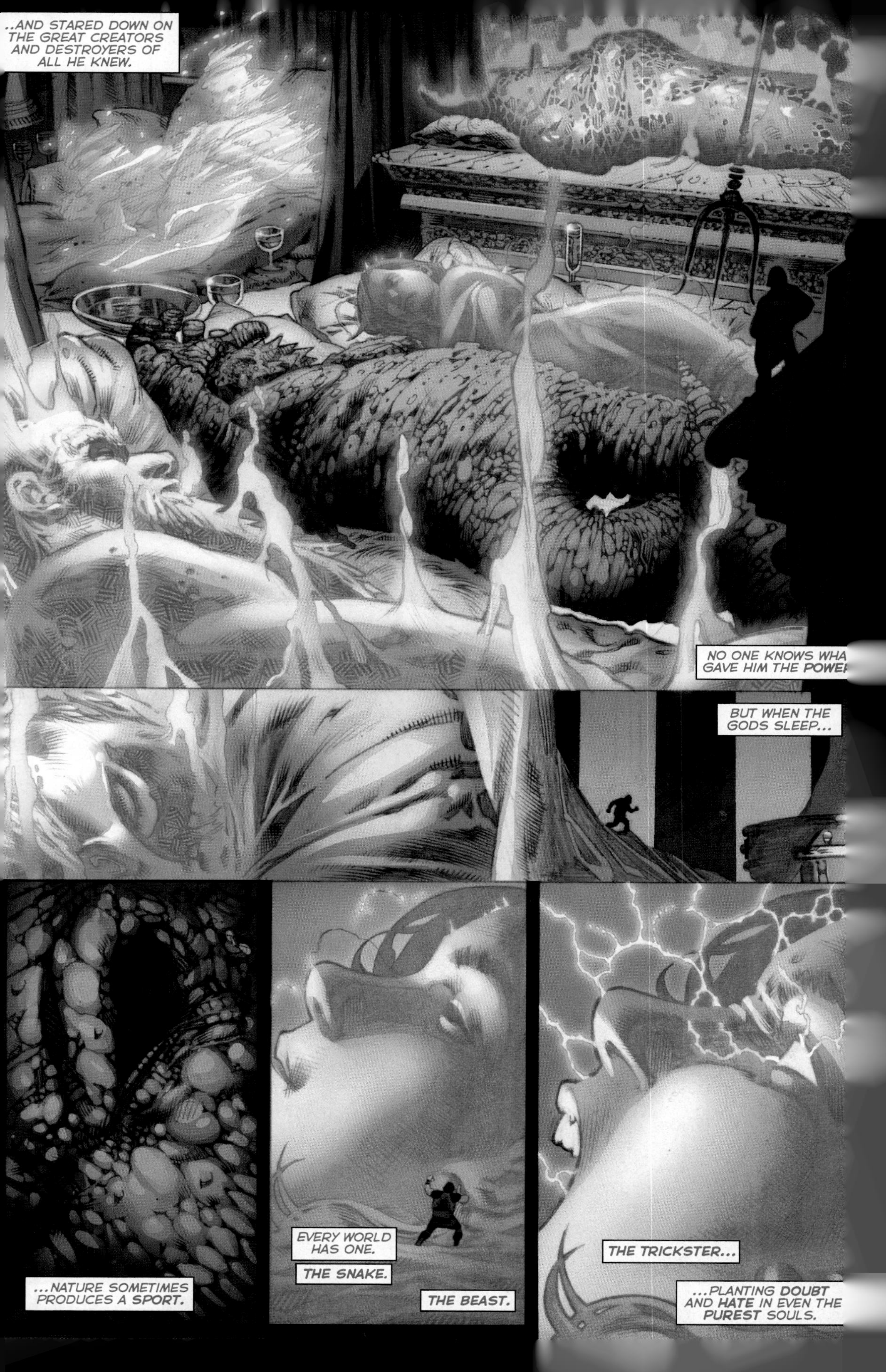
..AND STARED DOWN ON THE GREAT CREATORS AND DESTROYERS OF ALL HE KNEW.
NO ONE KNOWS WHA
GAVE HIM THE POWE
BUT WHEN THE GODS SLEEP...
...NATURE SOMETIMES PRODUCES A SPORT.
EVERY WORLD HAS ONE.
THE SNAKE.
THE BEAST.
THE TRICKSTER...
...PLANTING DOUBT AND HATE IN EVEN THE PUREST SOULS.

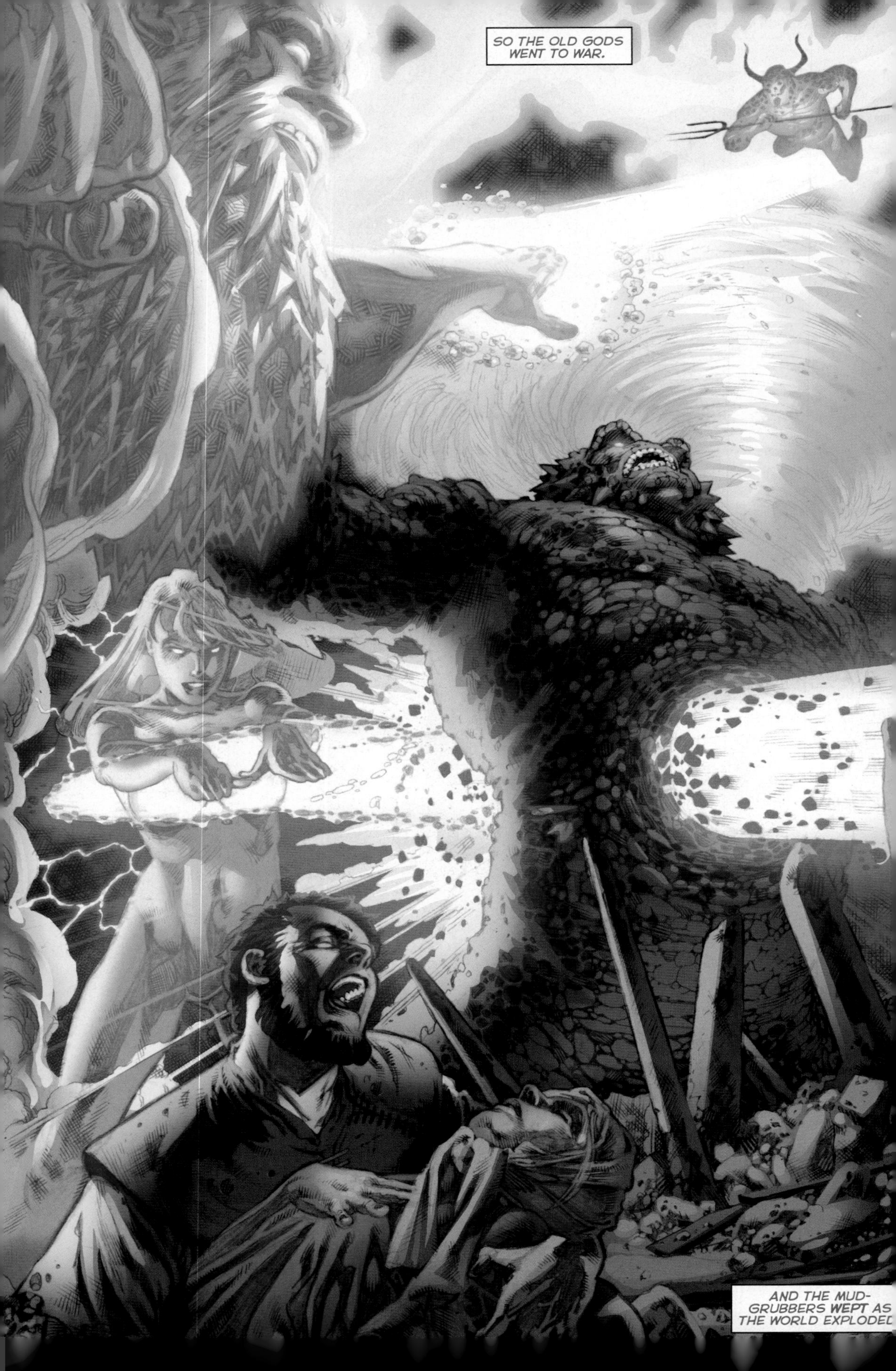
SO THE OLD GODS WENT TO WAR.
AND THE MUD-GRUBBERS WEPT AS THE WORLD EXPLODED

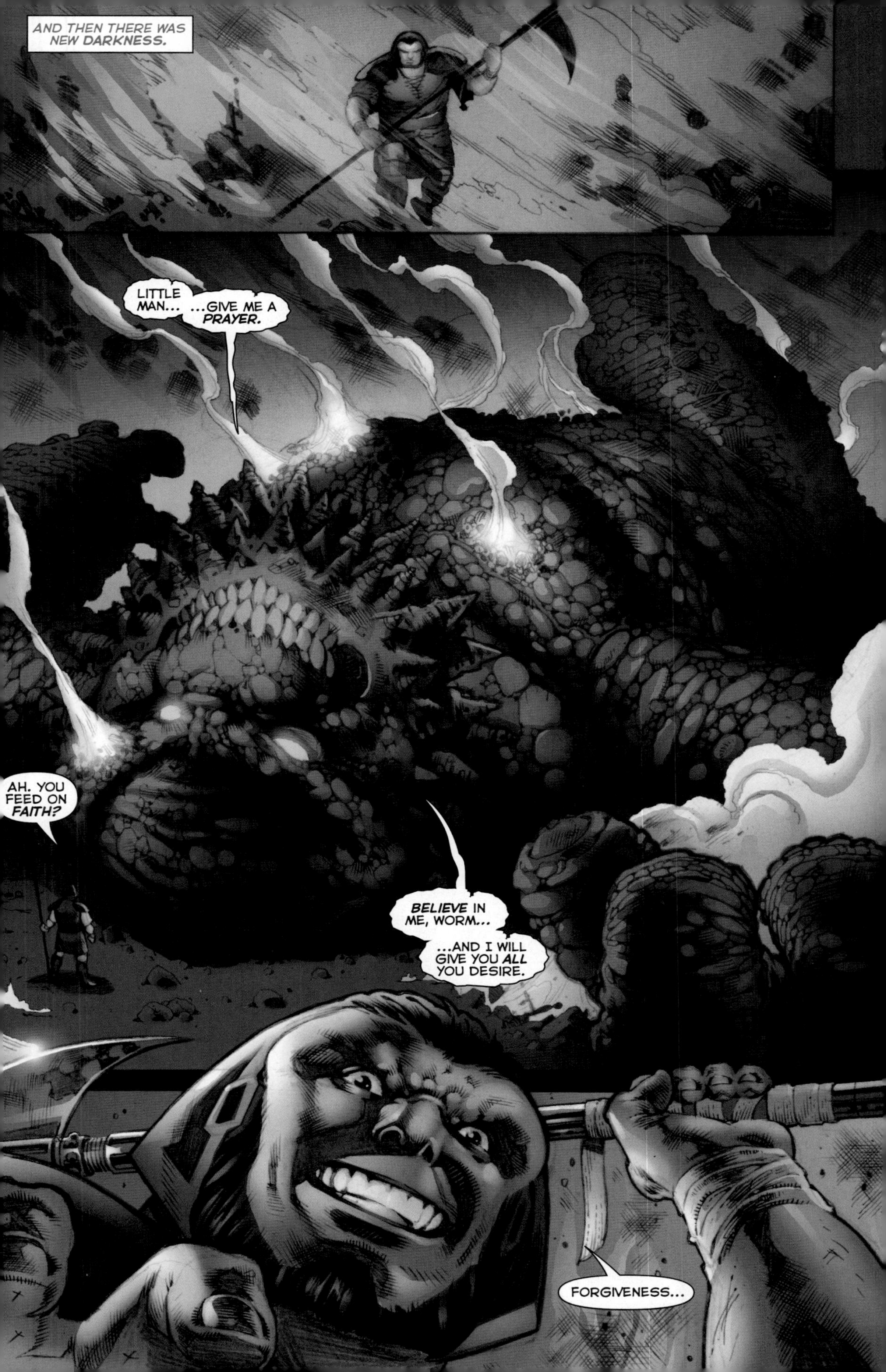
AND THEN THERE WAS NEW DARKNESS.
LITTLE MAN...
...GIVE ME A PRAYER.
AH. YOU FEED ON FAITH?
BELIEVE IN ME, WORM...
...AND I WILL GIVE YOU ALL YOU DESIRE.
FORGIVENESS...

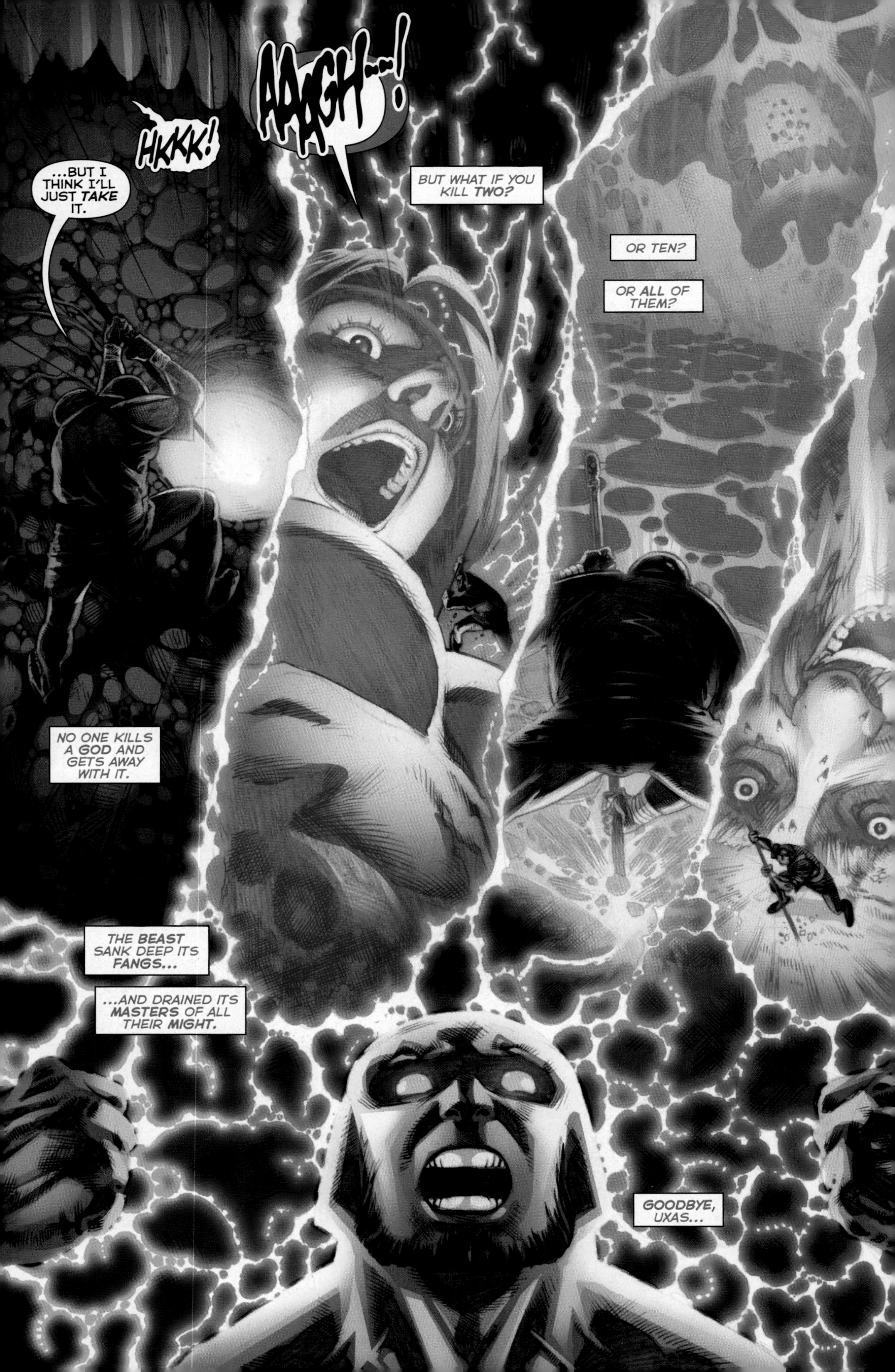
HKKK!
...BUT I THINK I'LL JUST TAKE IT.
AAAGH--!
BUT WHAT IF YOU KILL TWO?
OR TEN?
OR ALL OF THEM?
NO ONE KILLS A GOD AND GETS AWAY WITH IT.
THE BEAST SANK DEEP ITS FANGS...
...AND DRAINED ITS MASTERS OF ALL THEIR MIGHT.
GOODBYE, UXAS...

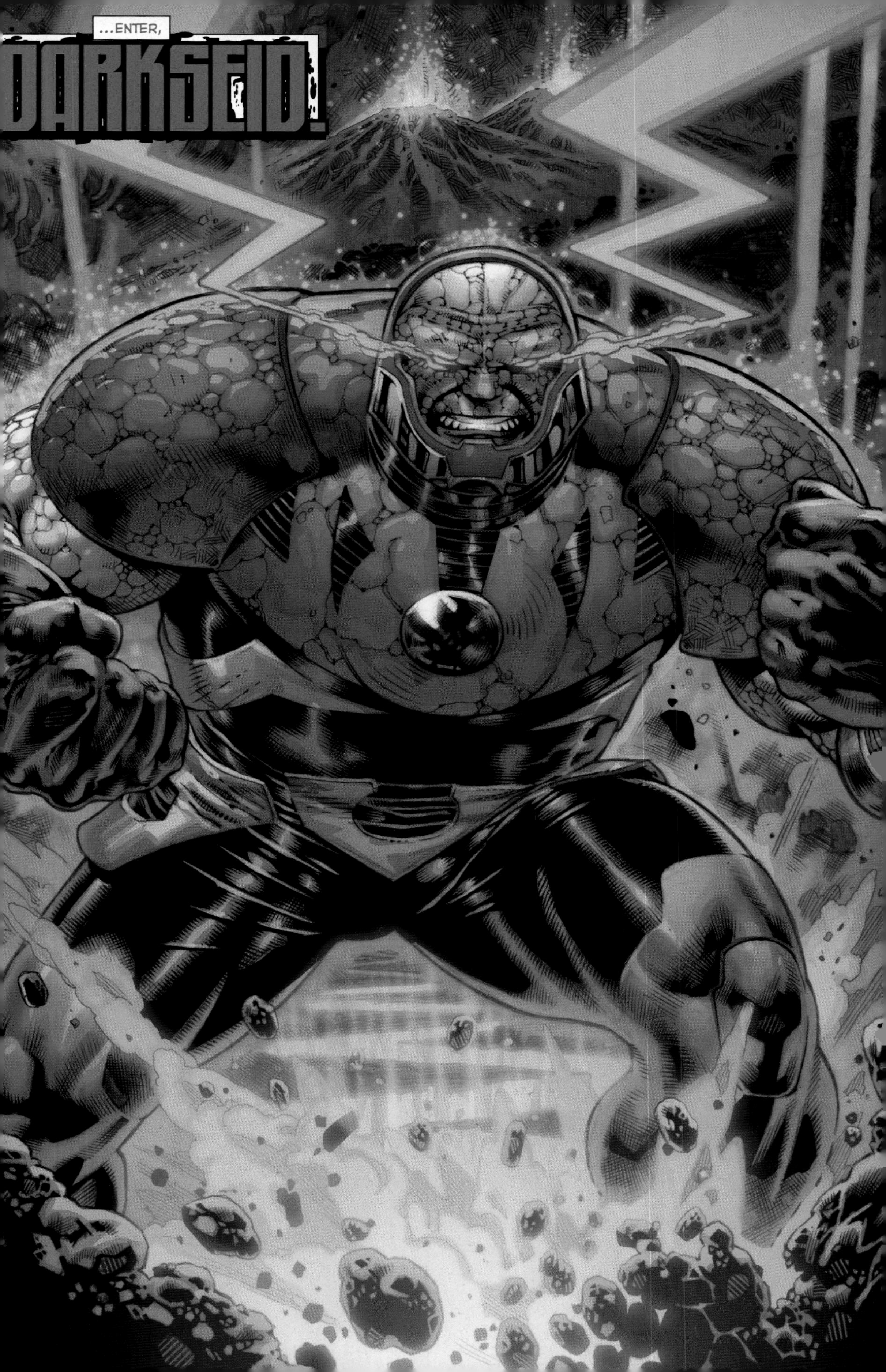
...ENTER,
DARKSEID!

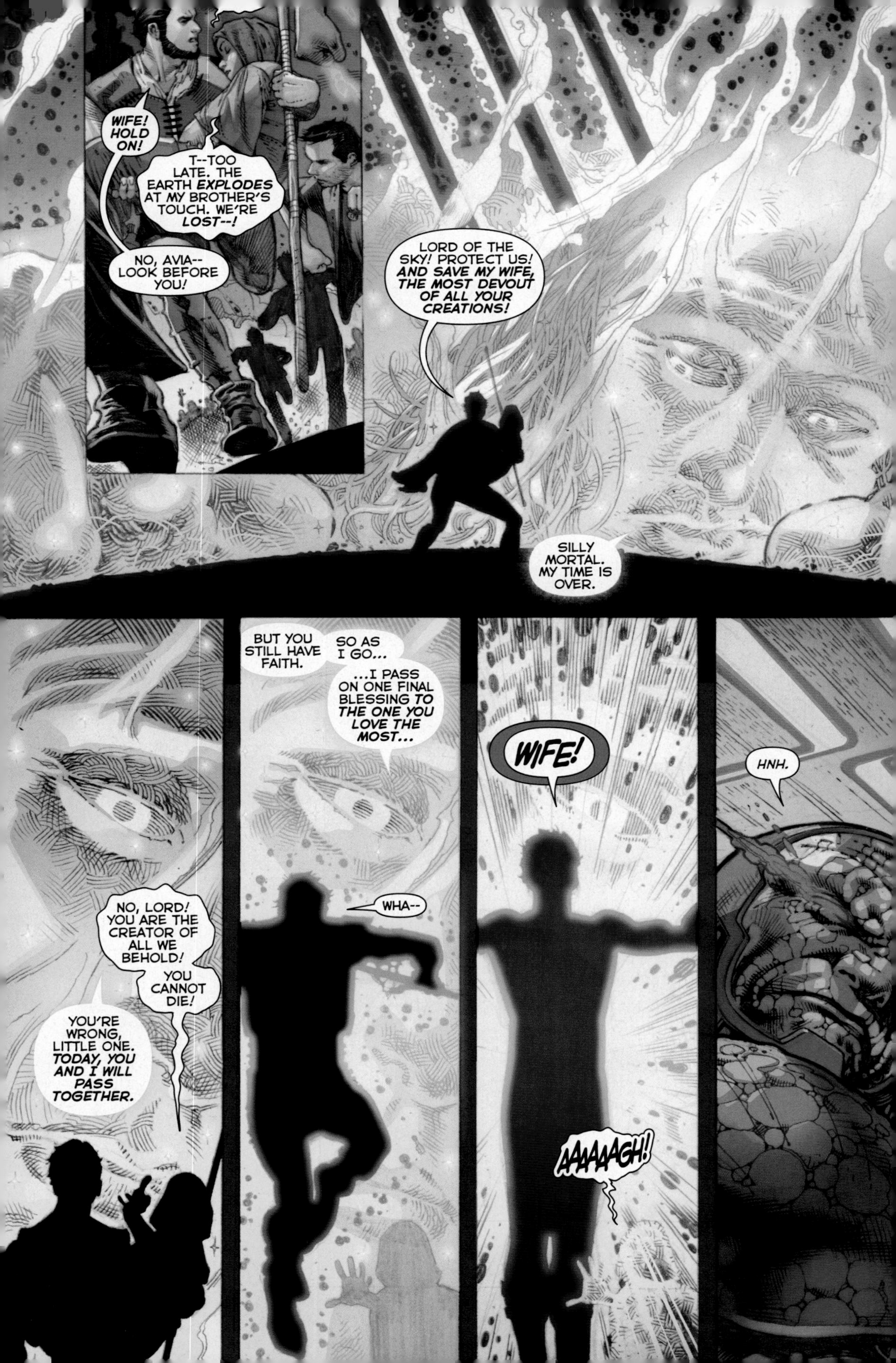
WIFE! HOLD ON!
T--TOO LATE. THE EARTH EXPLODES AT MY BROTHER'S TOUCH. WE'RE LOST--!
NO, AVIA-- LOOK BEFORE YOU!
LORD OF THE SKY! PROTECT US! AND SAVE MY WIFE, THE MOST DEVOUT OF ALL YOUR CREATIONS!
SILLY MORTAL. MY TIME IS OVER.
NO, LORD! YOU ARE THE CREATOR OF ALL WE BEHOLD!
YOU CANNOT DIE!
YOU'RE WRONG, LITTLE ONE. TODAY, YOU AND I WILL PASS TOGETHER.
BUT YOU STILL HAVE FAITH.
SO AS I GO...
...I PASS ON ONE FINAL BLESSING TO THE ONE YOU LOVE THE MOST...
WHA--
WIFE!
AAAAAAGH!
HNH.

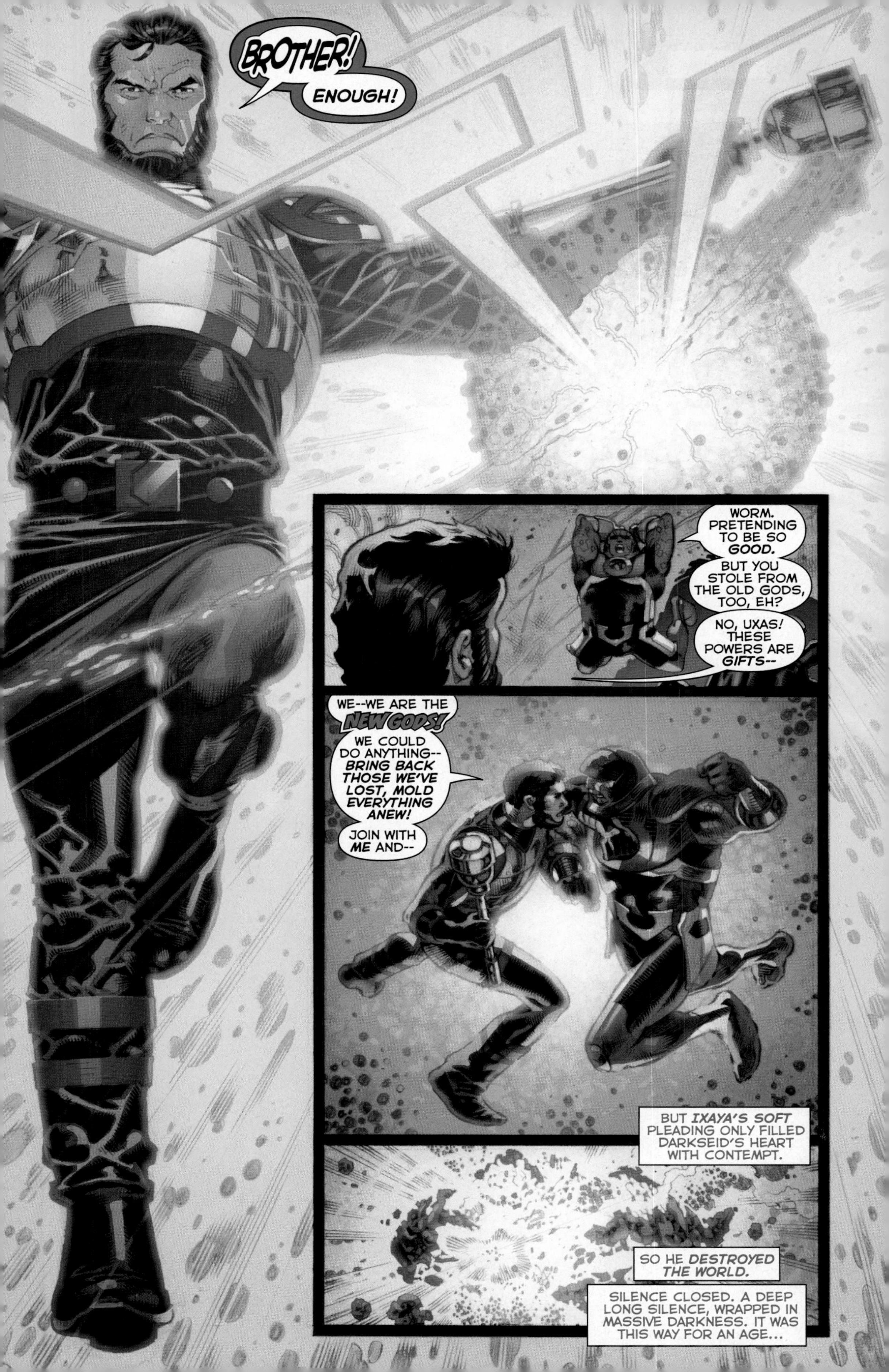
BROTHER!
ENOUGH!
WORM. PRETENDING TO BE SO GOOD.
BUT YOU STOLE FROM THE OLD GODS, TOO, EH?
NO, UXAS! THESE POWERS ARE GIFTS--
WE--WE ARE THE NEW GODS!
WE COULD DO ANYTHING-- BRING BACK THOSE WE'VE LOST, MOLD EVERYTHING ANEW!
JOIN WITH ME AND--
BUT IXAYA'S SOFT PLEADING ONLY FILLED DARKSEID'S HEART WITH CONTEMPT.
SO HE DESTROYED THE WORLD.
SILENCE CLOSED. A DEEP LONG SILENCE, WRAPPED IN MASSIVE DARKNESS. IT WAS THIS WAY FOR AN AGE...

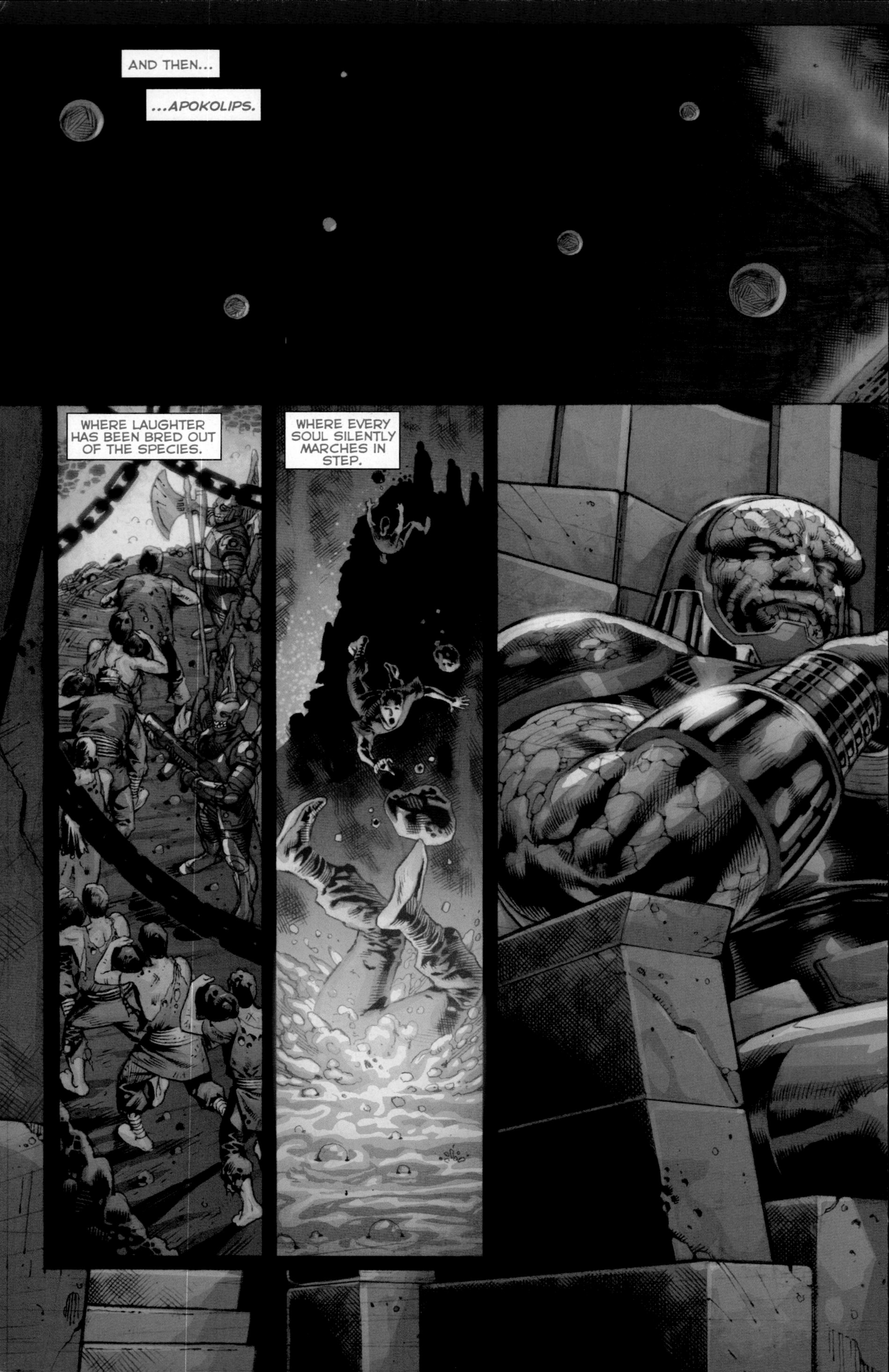
AND THEN...
...APOKOLIPS.
WHERE LAUGHTER HAS BEEN BRED OUT OF THE SPECIES.
WHERE EVERY SOUL SILENTLY MARCHES IN STEP.

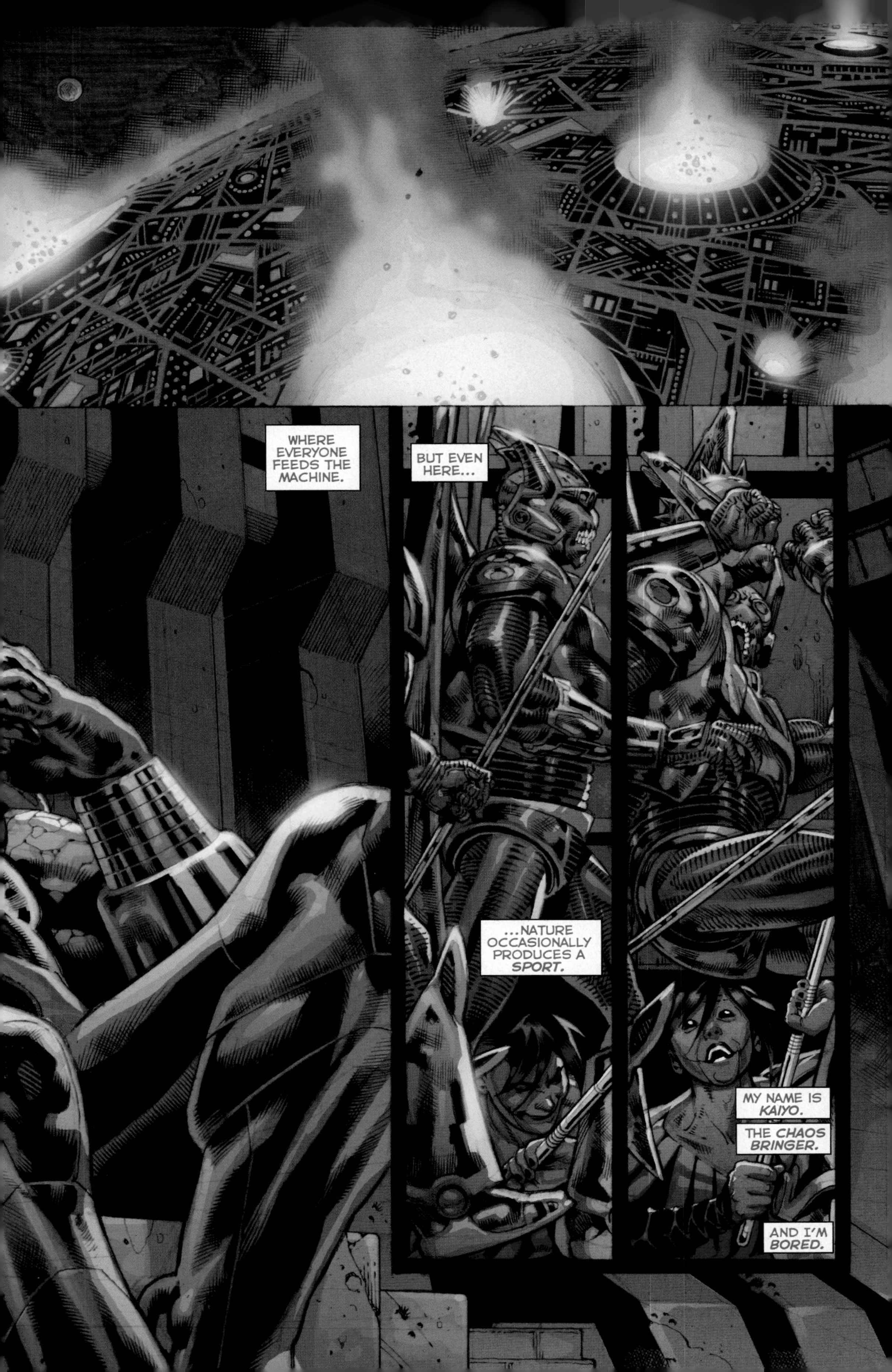
WHERE EVERYONE FEEDS THE MACHINE.
BUT EVEN HERE...
...NATURE OCCASIONALLY PRODUCES A *SPORT*.
MY NAME IS *KAIYO*.
THE *CHAOS BRINGER*.
AND I'M *BORED*.

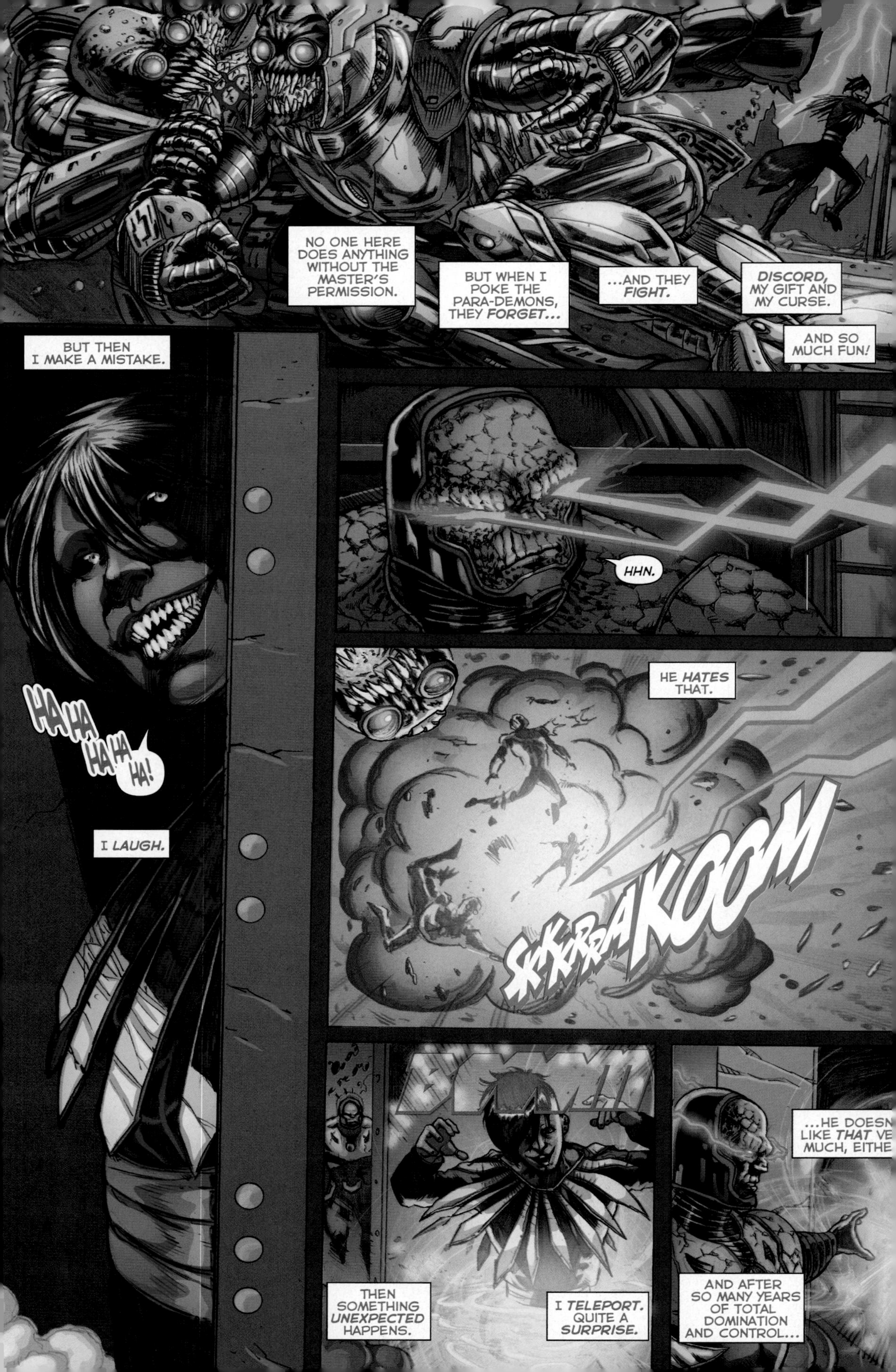
NO ONE HERE DOES ANYTHING WITHOUT THE MASTER'S PERMISSION.
BUT WHEN I POKE THE PARA-DEMONS, THEY FORGET...
...AND THEY FIGHT.
DISCORD, MY GIFT AND MY CURSE.
AND SO MUCH FUN!
BUT THEN I MAKE A MISTAKE.
HHN.
HA HA HA HA HA!
I LAUGH.
HE HATES THAT.
SKKRRAKOOM
...HE DOESN LIKE THAT VE MUCH, EITHE
THEN SOMETHING UNEXPECTED HAPPENS.
I TELEPORT. QUITE A SURPRISE.
AND AFTER SO MANY YEARS OF TOTAL DOMINATION AND CONTROL...

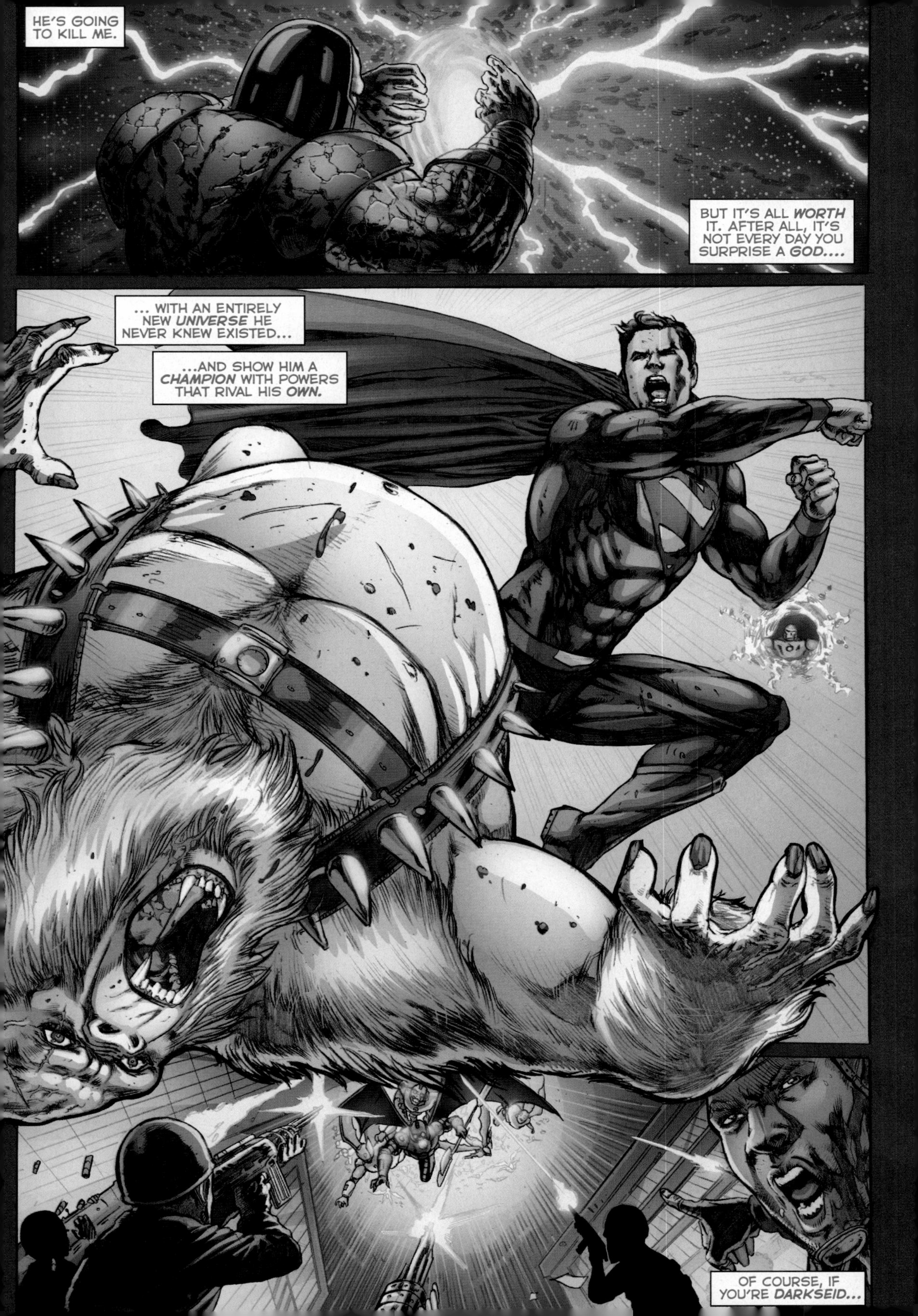
HE'S GOING TO KILL ME.
BUT IT'S ALL *WORTH* IT. AFTER ALL, IT'S NOT EVERY DAY YOU SURPRISE A *GOD*....
... WITH AN ENTIRELY NEW *UNIVERSE* HE NEVER KNEW EXISTED...
...AND SHOW HIM A *CHAMPION* WITH POWERS THAT RIVAL HIS *OWN.*
OF COURSE, IF YOU'RE *DARKSEID*...

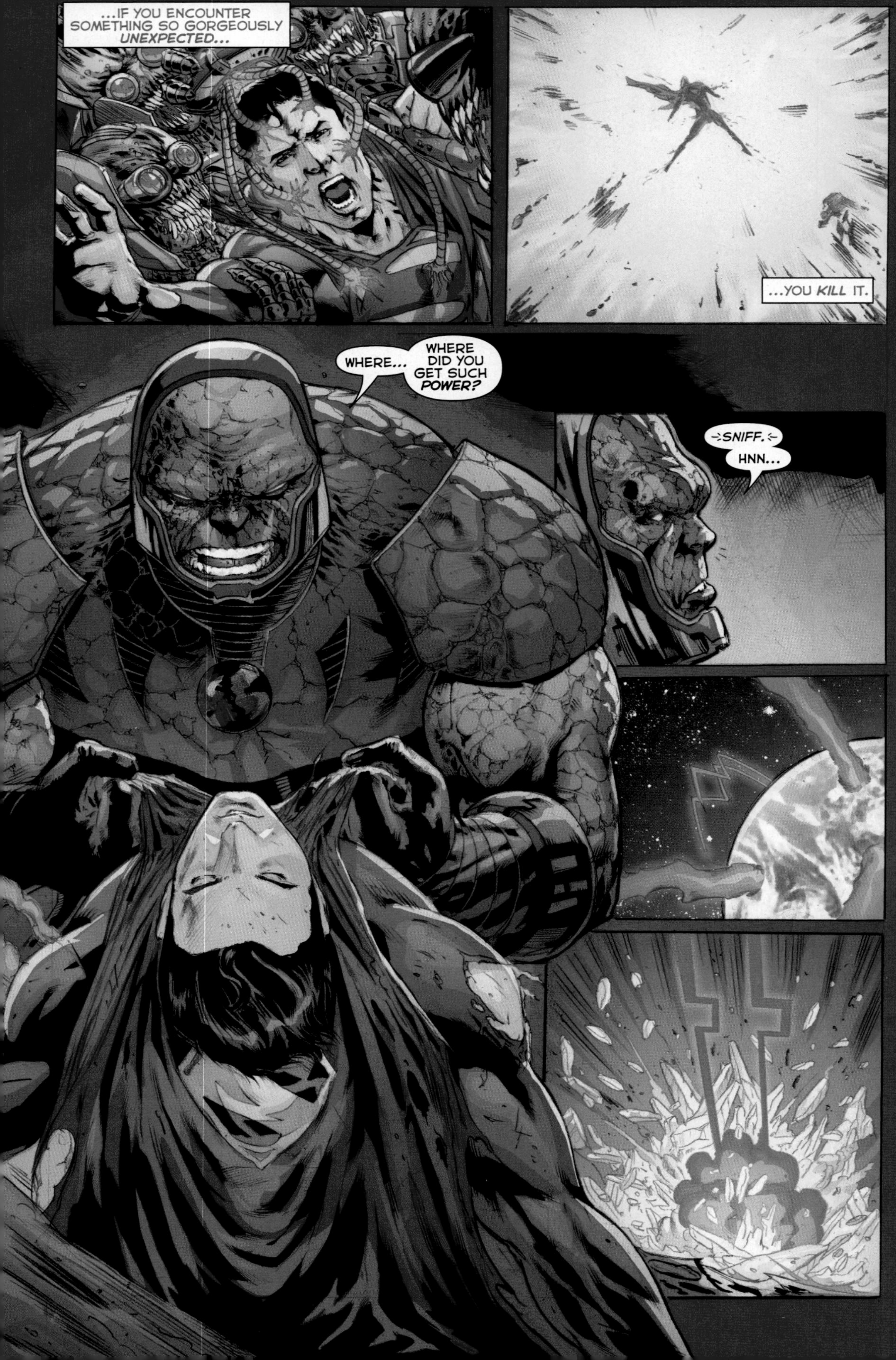
...IF YOU ENCOUNTER SOMETHING SO GORGEOUSLY UNEXPECTED...
...YOU KILL IT.
WHERE...
WHERE DID YOU GET SUCH POWER?
SNIFF.
HNN...

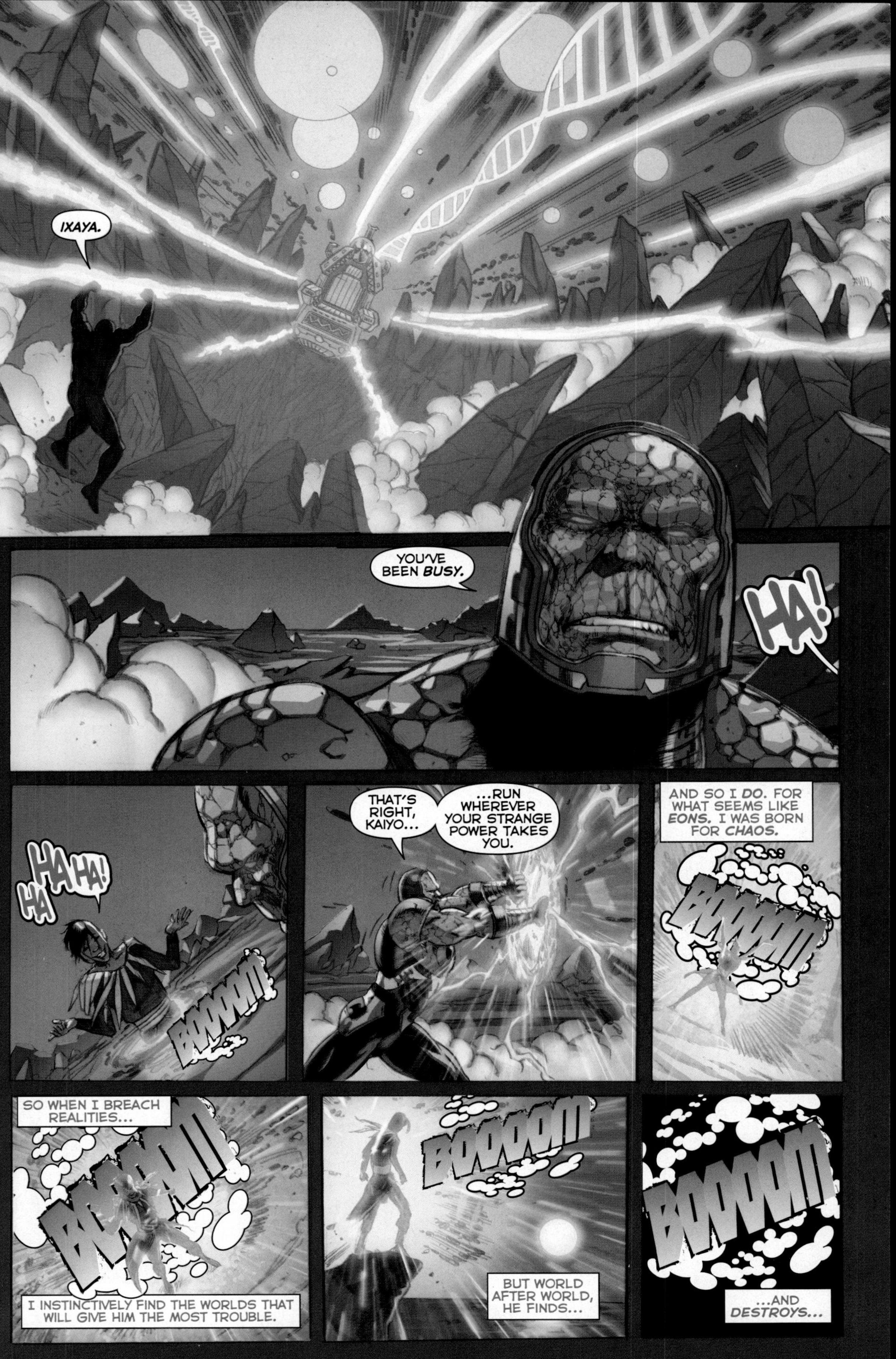
IXAYA.
YOU'VE BEEN BUSY.
HA!
HA HA HA!
BOOOOM!
THAT'S RIGHT, KAIYO...
...RUN WHEREVER YOUR STRANGE POWER TAKES YOU.
AND SO I DO. FOR WHAT SEEMS LIKE EONS. I WAS BORN FOR CHAOS.
BOOOOM!
SO WHEN I BREACH REALITIES...
BOOOOM!
I INSTINCTIVELY FIND THE WORLDS THAT WILL GIVE HIM THE MOST TROUBLE.
BOOOOM
BUT WORLD AFTER WORLD, HE FINDS...
BOOOOM
...AND DESTROYS...

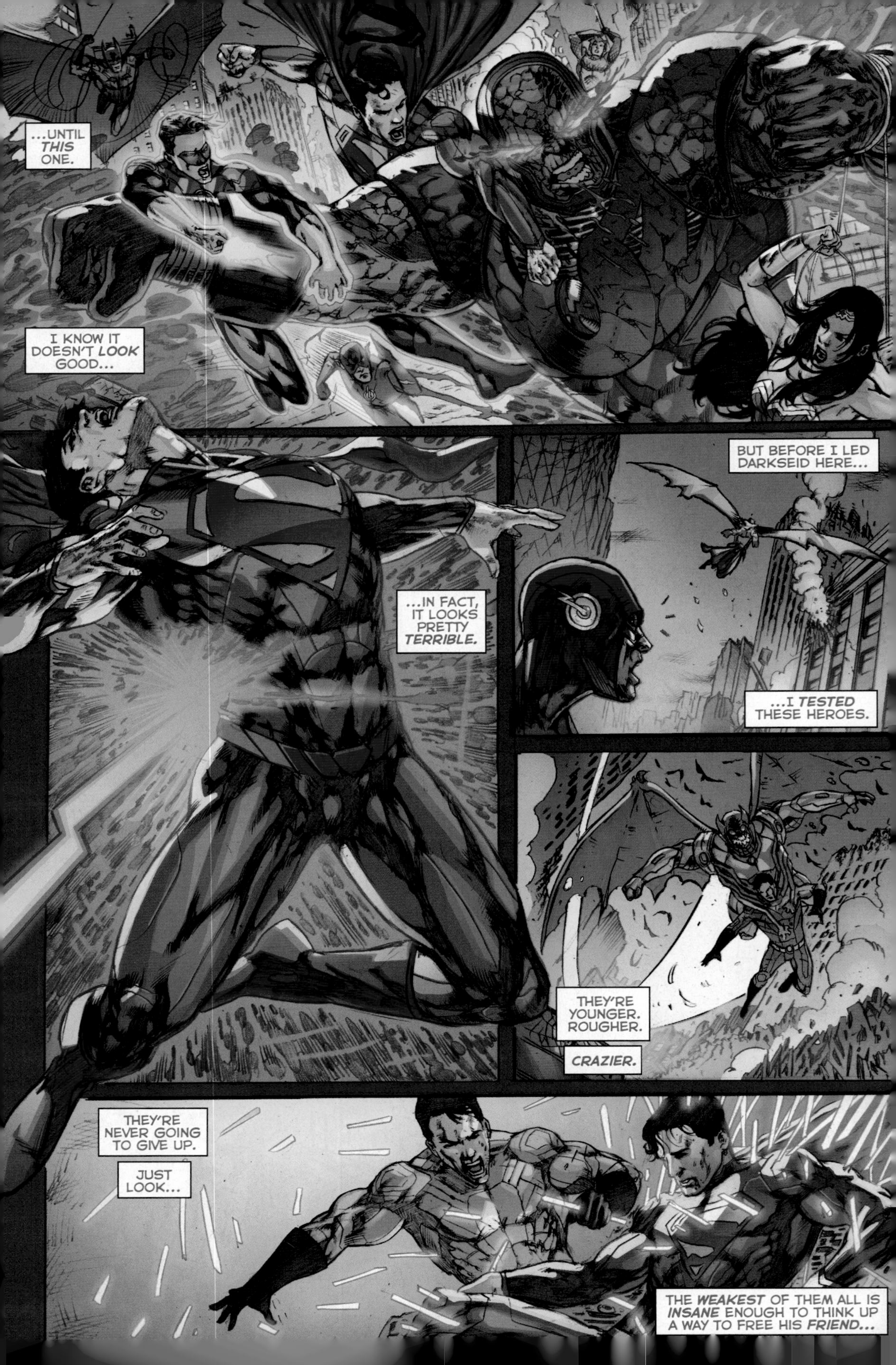
...UNTIL THIS ONE.
I KNOW IT DOESN'T LOOK GOOD...
...IN FACT, IT LOOKS PRETTY TERRIBLE.
BUT BEFORE I LED DARKSEID HERE...
...I TESTED THESE HEROES.
THEY'RE YOUNGER. ROUGHER.
CRAZIER.
THEY'RE NEVER GOING TO GIVE UP.
JUST LOOK...
THE WEAKEST OF THEM ALL IS INSANE ENOUGH TO THINK UP A WAY TO FREE HIS FRIEND...

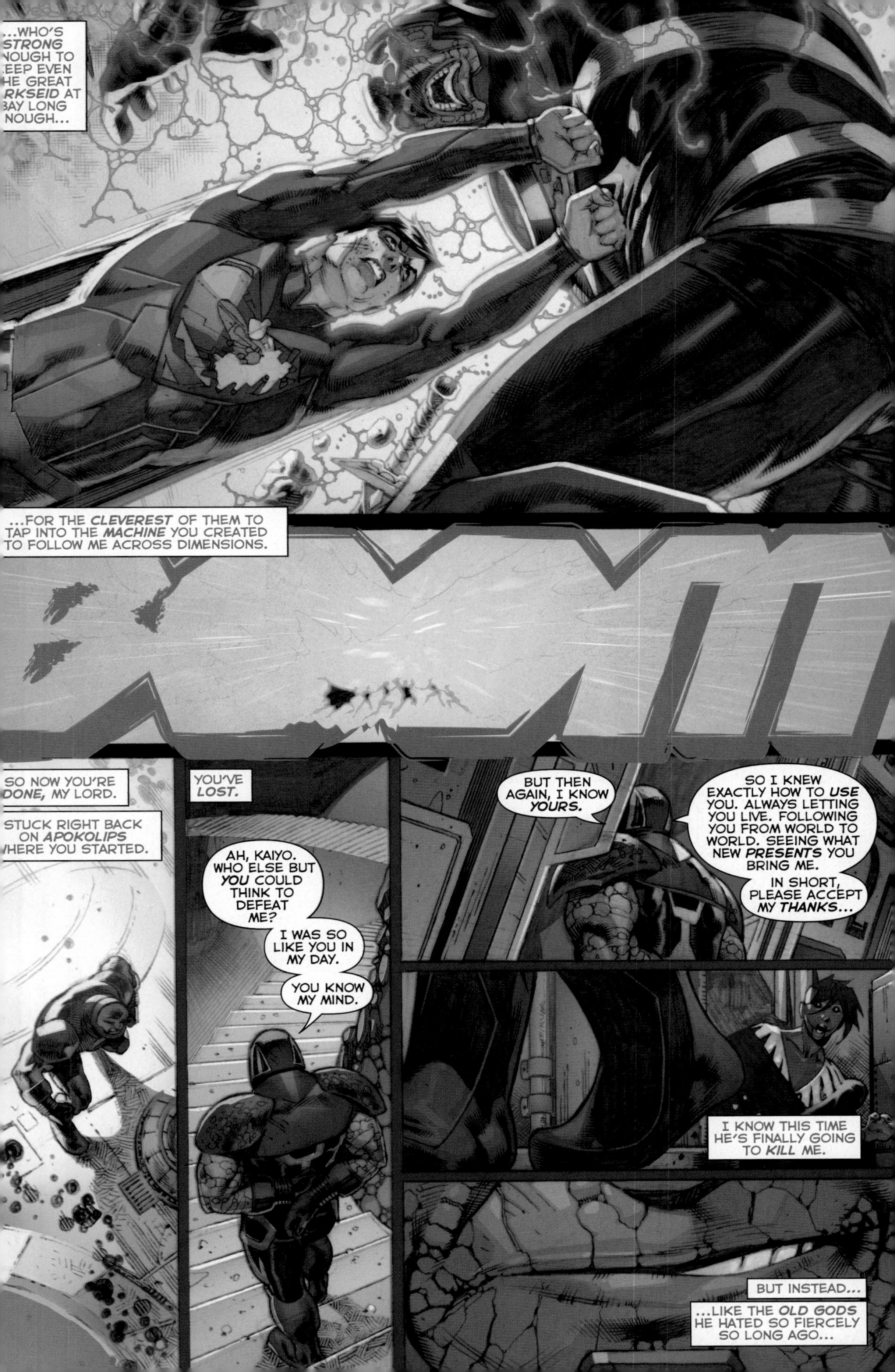
...WHO'S STRONG NOUGH TO EEP EVEN HE GREAT RKSEID AT BAY LONG NOUGH...
...FOR THE CLEVEREST OF THEM TO TAP INTO THE MACHINE YOU CREATED TO FOLLOW ME ACROSS DIMENSIONS.
SO NOW YOU'RE DONE, MY LORD.
STUCK RIGHT BACK ON APOKOLIPS HERE YOU STARTED.
YOU'VE LOST.
AH, KAIYO. WHO ELSE BUT YOU COULD THINK TO DEFEAT ME?
I WAS SO LIKE YOU IN MY DAY.
YOU KNOW MY MIND.
BUT THEN AGAIN, I KNOW YOURS.
SO I KNEW EXACTLY HOW TO USE YOU. ALWAYS LETTING YOU LIVE. FOLLOWING YOU FROM WORLD TO WORLD. SEEING WHAT NEW PRESENTS YOU BRING ME.
IN SHORT, PLEASE ACCEPT MY THANKS...
I KNOW THIS TIME HE'S FINALLY GOING TO KILL ME.
BUT INSTEAD...
...LIKE THE OLD GODS HE HATED SO FIERCELY SO LONG AGO...

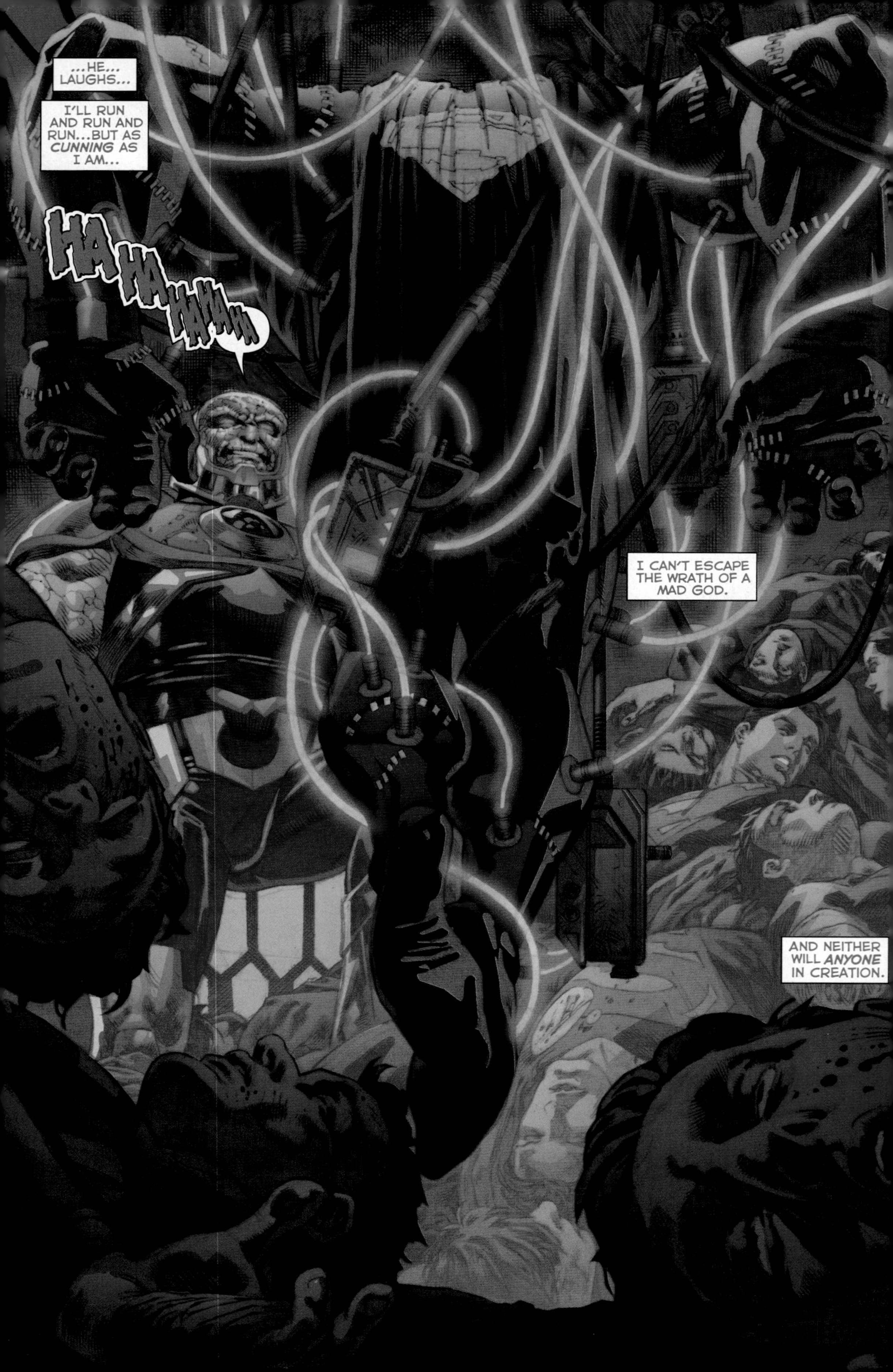
...HE... LAUGHS...
I'LL RUN AND RUN AND RUN...BUT AS CUNNING AS I AM...
HA HA HAHAHAHA
I CAN'T ESCAPE THE WRATH OF A MAD GOD.
AND NEITHER WILL ANYONE IN CREATION.

BATMAN/SUPERMAN 1
BATMAN VARIANT COVER BY KENNETH ROCAFORT

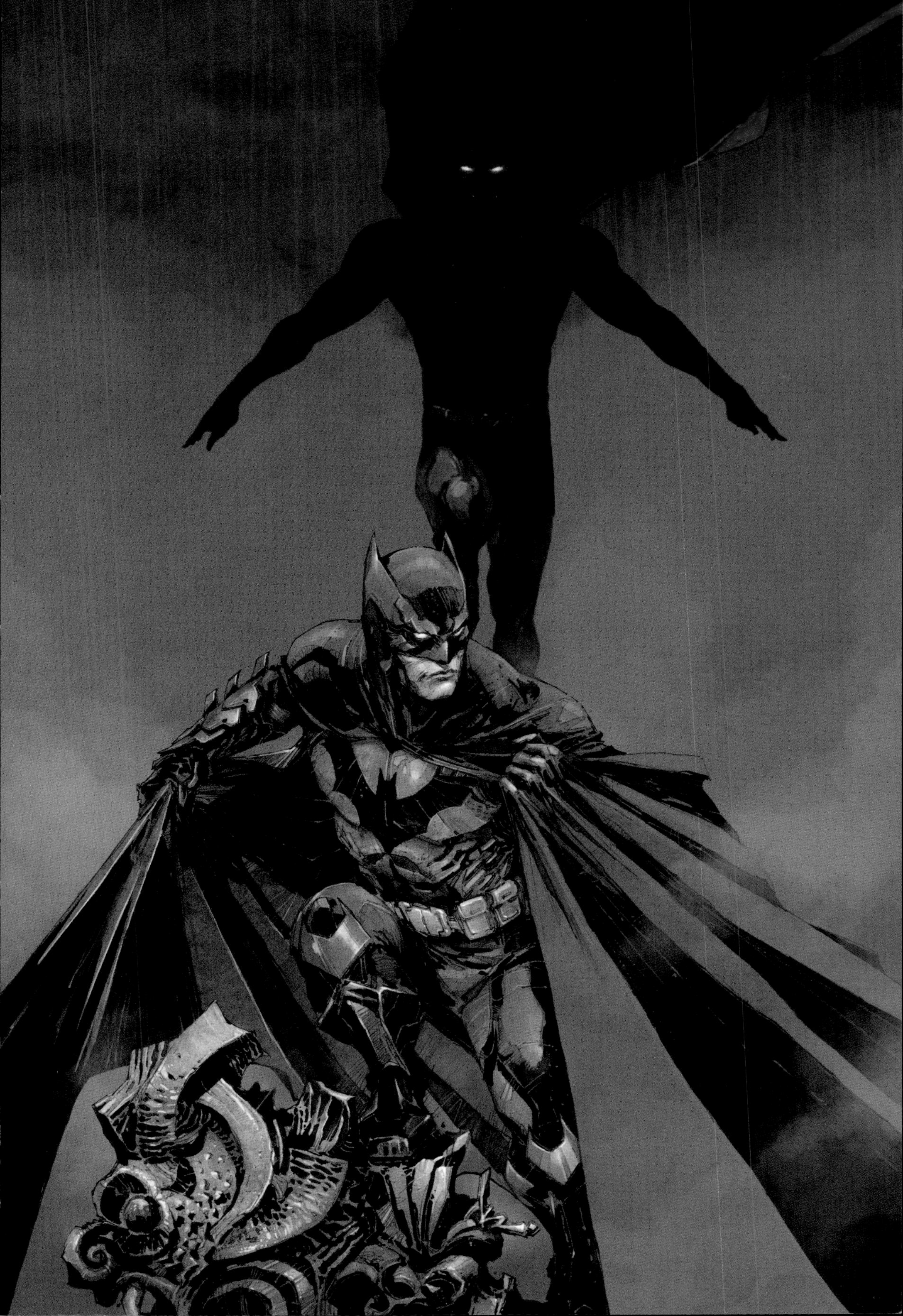

BATMAN/SUPERMAN 1
SUPERMAN VARIANT COVER BY GUILLEM MARCH

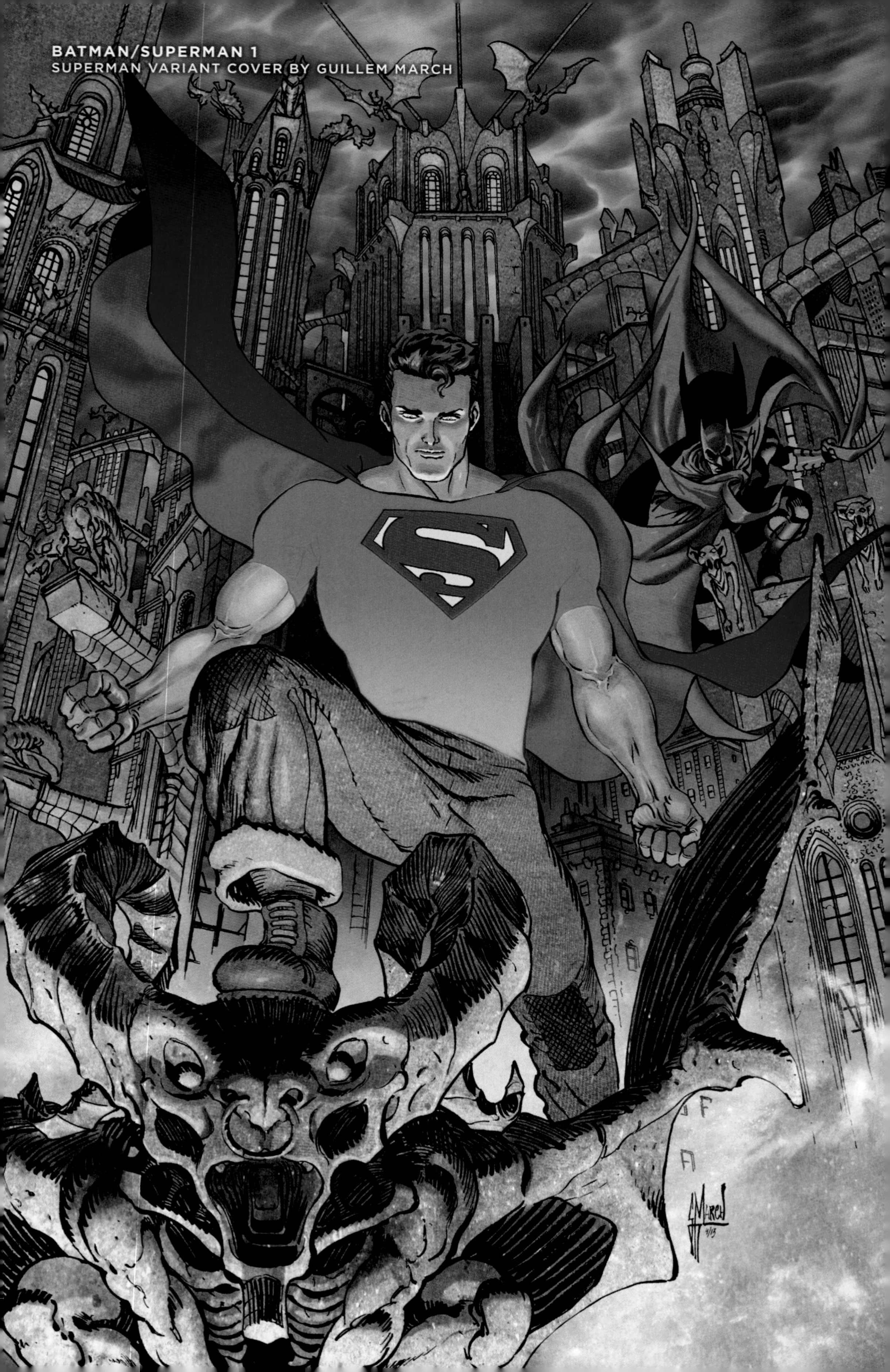

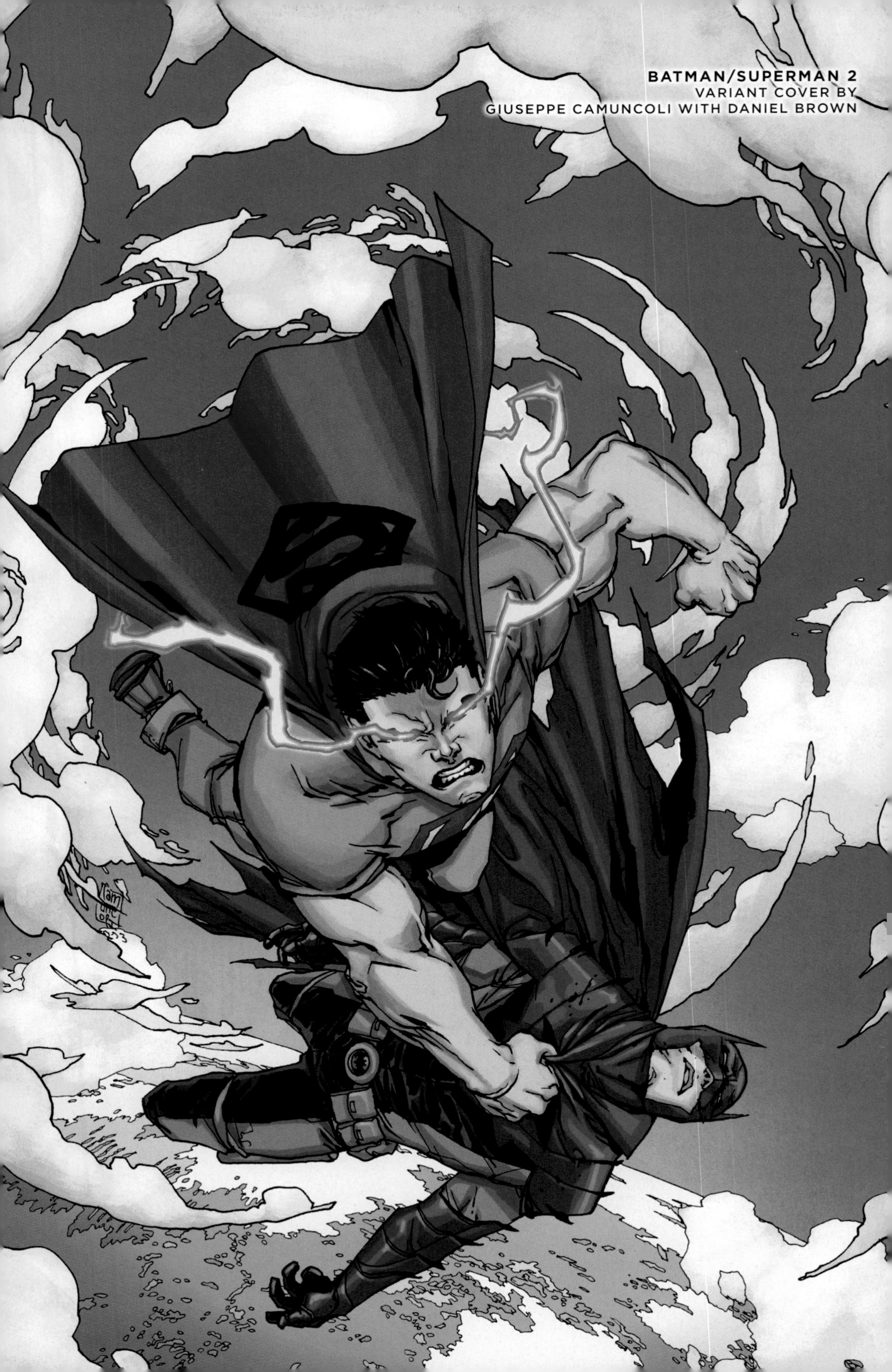

BATMAN/SUPERMAN 2
VARIANT COVER BY
GIUSEPPE CAMUNCOLI WITH DANIEL BROWN

BATMAN/SUPERMAN 3
VARIANT COVER BY PATRICK GLEASON & MICK GRAY WITH JOHN KALISZ

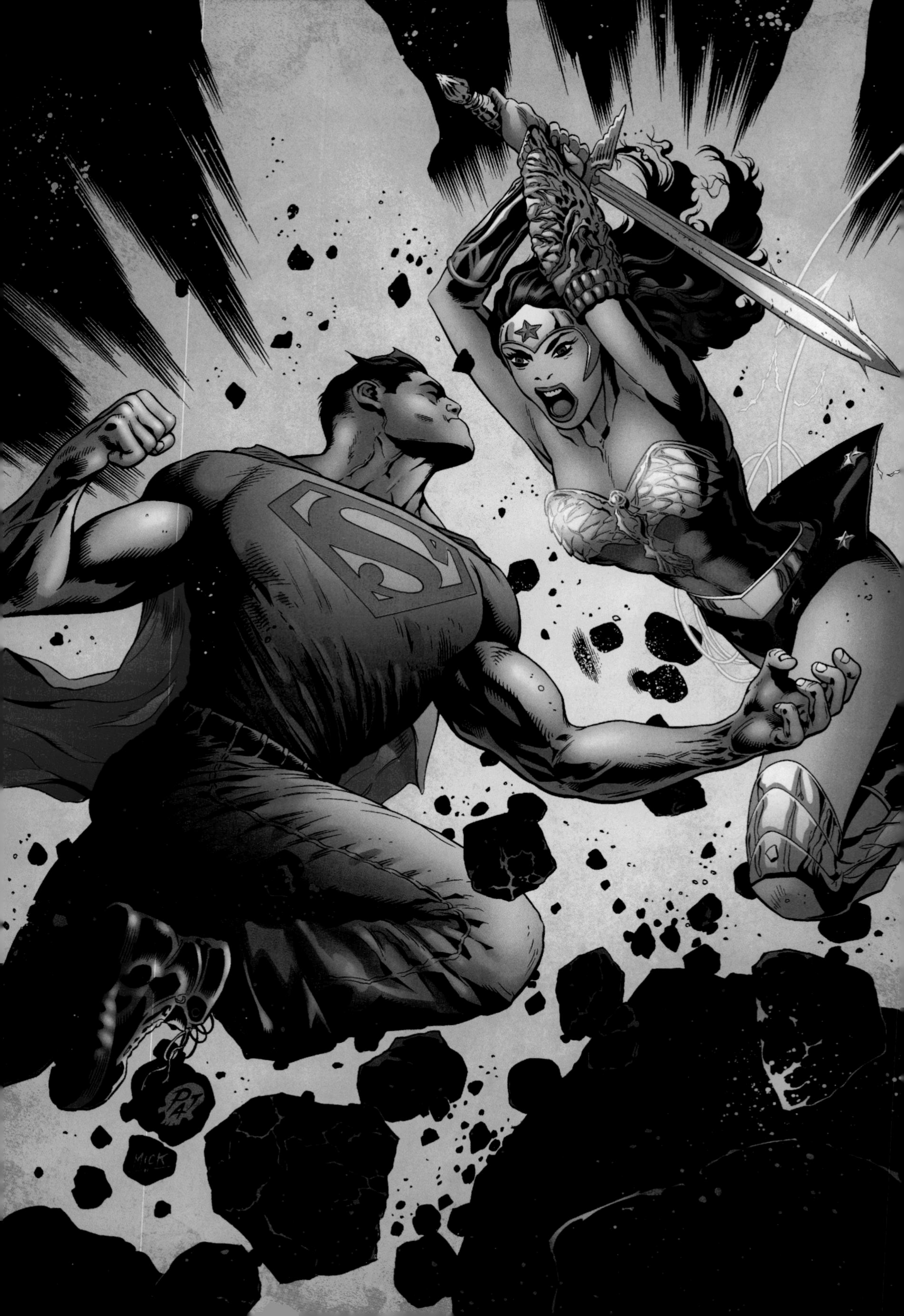
MICK

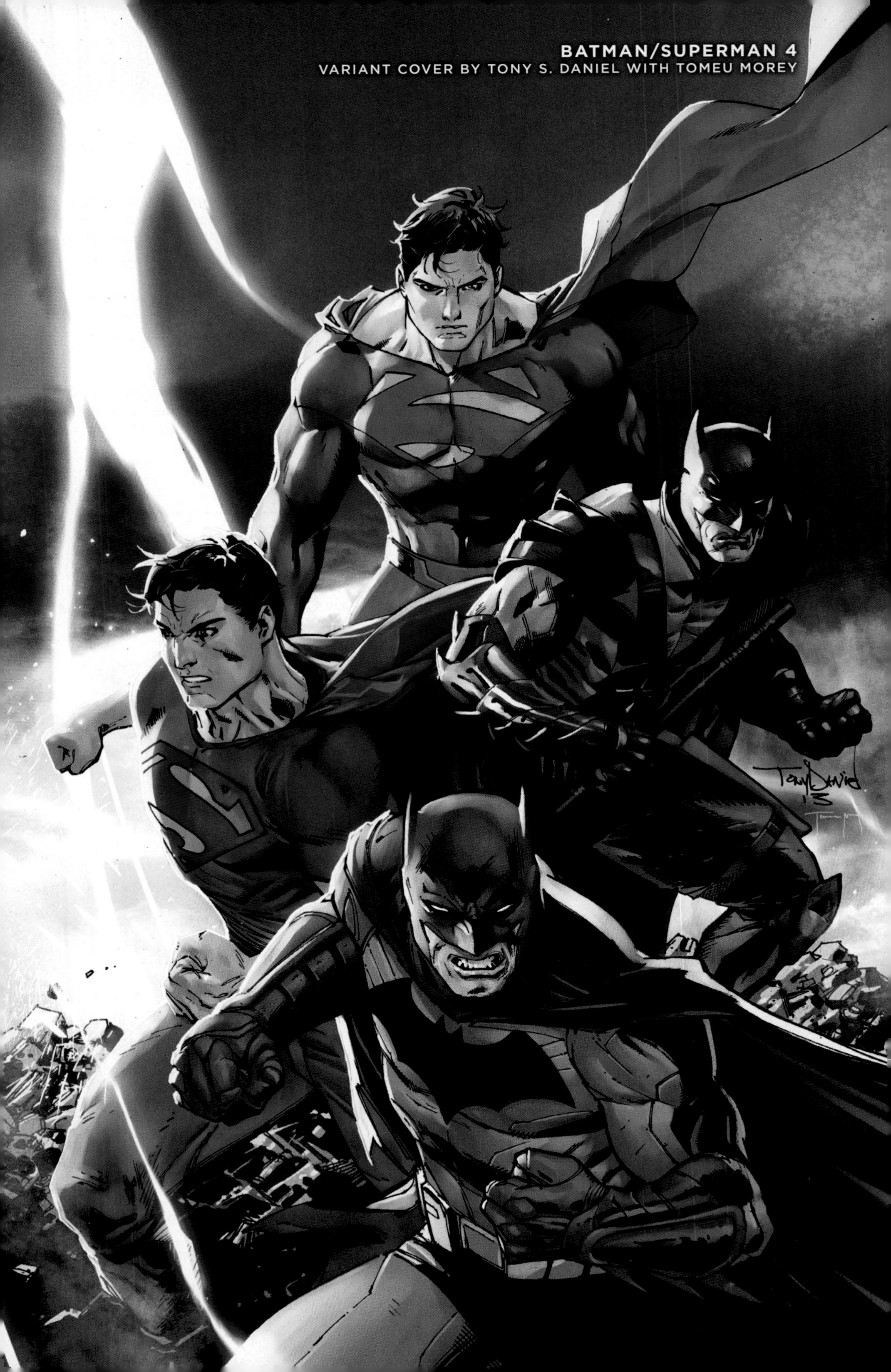

BATMAN/SUPERMAN 4
VARIANT COVER BY TONY S. DANIEL WITH TOMEU MOREY

GP: *People often ask me what it's like working with artist Jae Lee. The answer is pretty simple: Awesome.*

The moody, evocative, elegant, atmospheric worlds Jae Lee and colorist June Chung create stand out from everything else on the stands. Last year, a cinematographer friend who never retweets my comics posts on Twitter instantly shared the first Lee/Chung BATMAN/SUPERMAN pages I posted. The pages have such graphic power and emotional undercurrent, it's impossible not to stare.

What I particularly love about working with Jae is that he's got a brilliant intellectual reason for his bold designs and layouts, but he always brings out the subtle emotion of a scene. To give you a sense of how we work together, please read on for some script excerpts and the pencils that Jae came up with in response.

RP: *The main goal in starting this series was to give readers something they haven't seen before from a Superman/Batman team-up. So pairing Greg's exuberant, emotional writing style with Jae's grounded, cinematic art was what we really needed to make this series a standout. There's no other book like this on the stands, and that's because of Greg and Jae.*

BATMAN/SUPERMAN #1
2013.03.06 - By Greg Pak

PAGE ONE
Panel 1: Gotham City. Beautiful, eerie, and dangerous. We descend through the smog and the dark spires.

LETTERING NOTE: Let's be sure to make Clark's and Bruce's captions distinct. In Jeph's SUPERMAN/BATMAN, they used yellow for Clark and blue for Bruce. I'm wondering if blue for Clark and gray for Bruce might make more sense for us? (We'll also need a variation for next issue if/when we do internal voices for the Earth 2 Batman and Superman.)

1. CLARK'S VOICE (in a caption): My pa always warned me about **Gotham City**.

Panel 2: CLARK KENT, former farm boy and current reporter for the Metropolis Daily Star, walks down the street in the East End, Gotham's worst neighborhood. This is a young Clark, from the time of Morrison's ACTION #1. Big and rumpled, wearing glasses, satchel slung over one shoulder. He's not as beefy as the traditional, fully grown Superman, but he's tall and broad shouldered. He's out of his element, warily/nervously eyeing his surroundings. (And yes, that's partly a put-on — he's in character as Clark. But he's also that hick farmboy, deep inside.) He's glancing over his shoulder — various thugs, hustlers, bums, and shady characters line the streets outside of strip clubs and head shops. (The whole thing's reminiscent of the scene in BATMAN: YEAR ONE when Bruce walks through the East End. Jae, you could even homage that panel directly if you like.)

2. CLARK'S VOICE (in a caption): Growing up on a **farm**, you learn that human beings are **small** and **weak**.

3. CLARK'S VOICE: We only survive by coming together.

4. THUG (to Clark, taunting him): Hey, chicky chicky chicky chicky.

5. WOMAN: Ha ha!

Panel 3: Close on Clark as he turns, eyes sharp, looking towards us. A white rasta DRUG DEALER behind him is murmuring to him. Clark's not looking at the Drug Dealer — he's looking towards us, down the street, as if hearing something no one else can.

6. DRUG DEALER: Bud. Kind bud.

7. CLARK: Uh, no, I'm good, thanks.

8. CLARK'S VOICE: But when people come together in **Gotham**...

Panel 4: In a small, dirty, grassless urban playground, a BIG KID bullies a LITTLE KID, pushing him or smacking him upside the head, while a small pack of kids grin and jeer. It's a multiracial group of kids. The Little Kid, scared but defiant, is in a Muslim American schoolboy's uniform — black vest and tie. There's a scared Muslim girl in school uniform and hijab clutching her bookbag in the background.

9. CLARK'S VOICE: ...the strong just **eat** the **weak**.

10. BIG KID: Where's your camel, Mohammad?

11. LITTLE KID: My name is **Charles**.

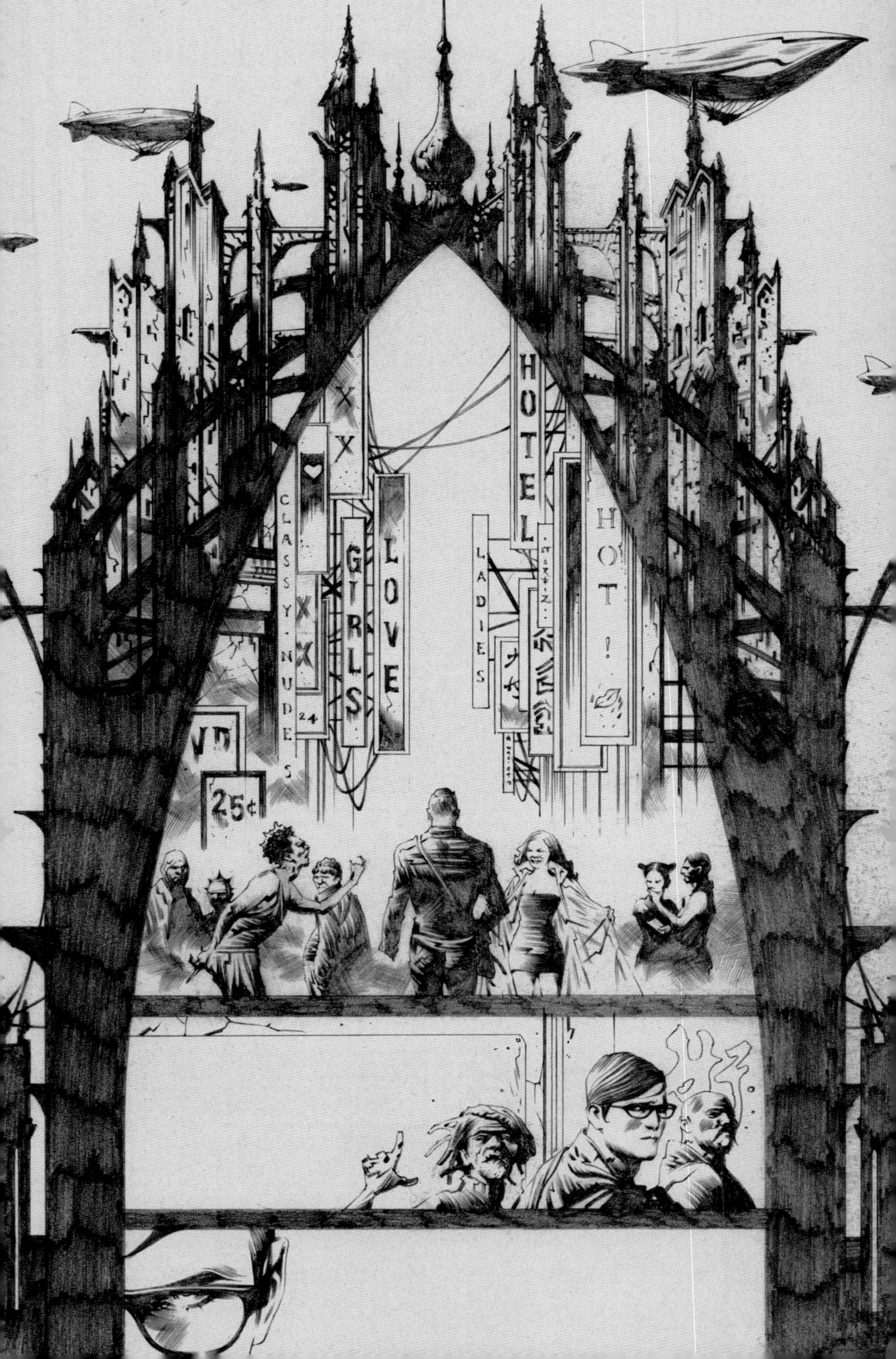
XX
CLASSY NUDES
XXX
24
GIRLS
LOVE
HOTEL
LADIES
HOT!
25¢

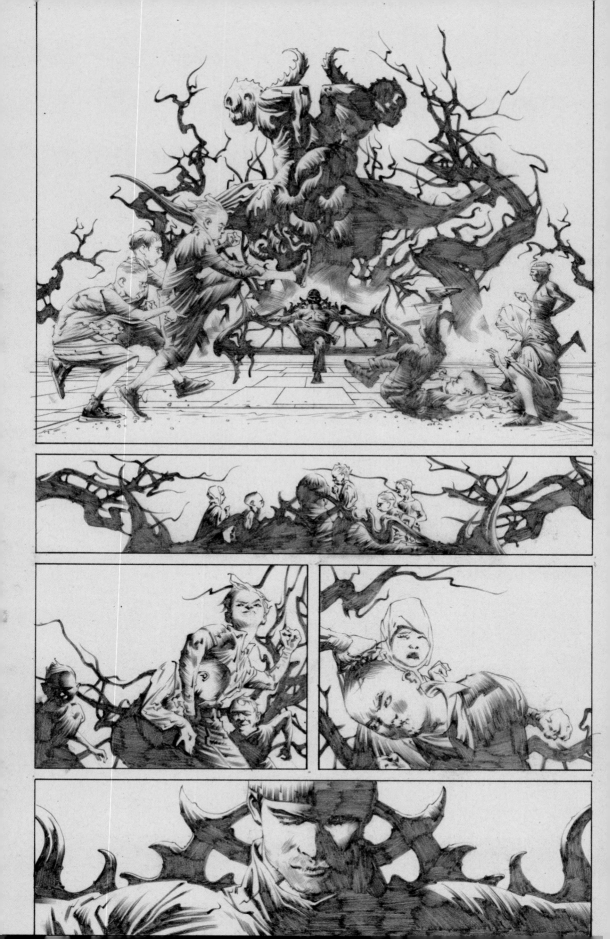

PAGE TWO

Panel 1: Sitting on a park bench at the edge of the playground, billionaire BRUCE WAYNE just watches. Bruce is incognito, wearing a leather jacket, boots, and knit cap reminiscent of the clothes he wore during his early training days in BATMAN: YEAR ONE. To a casual observer, he just looks like an idle slacker, slouching, maybe even dozing, hands in pockets. But his eyes are sharp — he's watching the Big Kid knock the Little Kid down.

1. BRUCE'S VOICE: My father was a **doctor**.

2. BRUCE'S VOICE: He saw hundreds of people **cut open** and **shot apart**.

3. BRUCE'S VOICE: He knew how insane and **cruel** this world is.

4. BRUCE'S VOICE: But he promised to always keep me **safe**.

Panel 2: Bruce's POV. Or maybe we're looking over Bruce's shoulder. The Big Kid catches the Little Kid by the collar, raising his fist, about to pound him, hard. The Little Kid's panicking, scrambling to protect himself, but he's about to get beat down hard. The Muslim girl in the back is screaming.

5. BRUCE'S VOICE: Easier said than done.

6. GIRL: Aaaagh!

Panel 3: Closer. The Little Kid's getting shoved to the ground. But from this angle, we can see him clenching his jaw. Making a fist. Today just might be the day he fights back.

7. BRUCE'S VOICE: But this kid's **tougher** than I was.

8. BRUCE'S VOICE: He's thinking about it now.

9. BRUCE'S VOICE: Seconds away from changing **everything**.

Panel 4: Close on Bruce. Head partially lowered — but he's watching everything. Faint, tight smile on his face.

10. BRUCE (small): **Do** it.

GP: Jae likes what folks in comics call "full script," which means all the action and dialogue is written out and all the action is broken down down page-by-page and panel-by-panel. So for these opening two pages of our run on BATMAN/SUPERMAN, I described all the essential elements on the page, devoting one page to introducing Clark Kent and the other to introducing Bruce Wayne. Clearly, the introductions parallel each other. But Jae took it to the next, brilliant level with that gothic arch panel layout on Page One and the eerie, twisty trees on Page Two. He also smartly ended Page One with a close on Clark to parallel the close on Bruce at the bottom of Page Two. Most people will never consciously notice subtle details like that, but they get under our skin and and make the characters and themes sing.

EB: Agree completely with Greg. From the opening of the first page, you know that you have left the real world behind and entered into something wondrous. This is Jae's vision of Gotham City, and its spires, people and the dark woods from which its Dark Knight waits for a very out-of-place Clark Kent tell you that you are in for something completely different.

RP: Besides steering the mood of the page, elements in Jae's art like the twisty trees go a long way toward adding motion and movement to the panels so nothing feels stiff. It may seem like a small trick, but a lot of thought goes into that level of storytelling.

JL: There is nothing more daunting than the opening sequence. Do a good job here, and you buy yourself some goodwill from the reader. Do a bad job, and you lose them forever. No pressure there.

On the last panel of Page Two, I redrew Bruce Wayne's face so many times, there are ghost images galore on the original art board. June had to clean that up in Photoshop. Then, I redrew the face again after she had inked and colored it. She was a saint having to deal with my OCD. Notice the difference between the pencilled version and the printed final version? No? Neither do I anymore. What a waste of time.

PAGE SIX

Let's treat Pages Six and Seven like a double-page spread. But let's also keep the pages divided in the middle so we have the option of running them as separate pages digitally. Page Four is Clark's perspective — Page Five features parallel panels from Bruce's perspective.

Panel 1: Flashback. Wide. The Kent farmhouse at sunrise. Golden morning light, golden sheaves of wheat in the fields all around the house. There's an apple tree a little ways off in the field — wheat grows around it, but someone has carefully plowed around the tree, allowing it to flourish.

NOTE: Since it'll play again at the end of the issue, let's be sure to make this tree distinctive — I'm thinking a wide apple tree with nice, twisty limbs.

1. BRUCE'S VOICE (in a caption): "...or *wherever* you come from."

2. CLARK'S VOICE: *Smallville*. Name says it all.

3. CLARK'S VOICE: I've got *another* home, too. But let's be *honest*...

Panel 2: Flashback continues. JONATHAN KENT, Clark's adoptive father, and a five-year-old Clark climb up the apple tree. Clark's up front, grinning, out on a limb, reaching towards us; Jonathan's behind him, smiling, keeping his boy safe by holding the back of the overalls.

4. CLARK'S VOICE: ... I'll always be *Jonathan Kent's* boy.

5. PA KENT: Attaboy, Clark!

6. CLARK'S VOICE: He and Ma taught me *everything*.

Panel 3: Flashback. Wider shot. Jonathan is lowering Clark by the back of the overalls from the tree. Clark is holding a kitten, clearly just rescued from the tree, out to LANA LANG, a little girl in blue jeans who stands below them. (And yes, this is the little girl version of the Lana we meet in Morrison's ACTION #15.)

7. CLARK: Here you go, Lana!

8. LANA: Yaaay!

9. KITTEN: Mrow!

Panel 4: Flashback. The car wreck scene from Morrison's ACTION #15 — with Ma and Pa Kent's truck on its side in the middle of the road and their bodies on he road behind it.

10. CLARK'S VOICE: And even the day of the *accident*...

11. CLARK'S VOICE: ...when it felt like my chest might *explode* with grief and break the *planet*...

Panel 5: Back in real time. Close on Clark's chest — showing part of the Superman logo on his T-shirt. This can be very close, almost stylized.

12. CLARK'S VOICE: ...I knew they'd always be with me.

ghost or monster stories. Bruce is about five years old. Snuggling up against his father, lying in the crook of his arm. Safe and secure. Thomas has a kind, patient face.

4. BRUCE'S VOICE: He read to me for an *hour*, every single night.

5. BRUCE'S VOICE: I lay against his chest, felt his deep, calm voice reverberating through my body.

6. BRUCE'S VOICE: He read anything I asked him to, no matter how strange or scary.

7. BRUCE'S VOICE: And he **explained** everything. Answered every question.

8. BRUCE'S VOICE: Made it all make **sense**.

Panel 3: Flashback. Six-year-old Bruce kneels in shock between the bodies of his murdered parents. The classic scenario — beneath the streetlight, outside the theater. Pool of blood. Broken pearls.

9. BRUCE'S VOICE: Until it **didn't**.

Panel 4: Flashback. Six-year-old Bruce, eyes wide and face blank with shock, lies down in the street, curling up in the crook of his dead father's arm. As if silently trying to will his father back to life, bring back that feeling of safety of his father reading to him.

PAGE SEVEN
Panel 1: Flashback. Wayne Manor at sunset. Lonely and imposing. Red and purple skies.

1. BRUCE'S VOICE: You hear **Bruce Wayne** and you think **Gotham City.** But I didn't see a **skyscraper** 'til I was seven.

2. BRUCE'S VOICE: I grew up in **Wayne Manor**...

3. BRUCE'S VOICE: ...my **father's castle**.

Panel 2: Flashback. Bruce's father, THOMAS WAYNE, lies in bed with him, reading him a bedtime story — the book has a cartoony, scary cover —

10. BRUCE'S VOICE: That's what Kent can never understand.

11. BRUCE'S VOICE: He wants **answers**.

Panel 5: Back in real time. Close on Bruce's chest. Showing just part of the Batman logo on his uniform. Dark and jagged, almost stylized.

12. BRUCE'S VOICE: But sometimes there **aren't** any.

JL: I believe this is the first time we've seen Superman and Batman's origins. Eddie and Rickey, can you fact-check that for me?

Greg wrote such a wonderful, emotional scene, I wanted to do his words justice. The scene Greg described where Bruce is curled up in his father's arms is heartbreaking. We've seen these scenes played out hundreds of times, but with just a few words, Greg brought it to a whole new level. The backwards layout of the Batman page would have been completely unreadable had Rob not expertly led the eye with his lettering.

RP: I was super-worried the lettering placements on those pages wouldn't read in the right order for fans because of the non-traditional panel grid Jae chose. I should've just trusted him, cause it turned out great. Go back and compare it to the lettered pages in the issue! It's bonkers...

GP: Again, in the script I described a pair of pages that draw parallels between our central characters. And again, Jae took it to an entirely new level with his design and layout. Just one brilliant bit — he worked in the outlines of the Superman and Batman logos entirely on his own.

EB: Even more so, as fans of these characters, we've seen their origin told so many times, but Jae still found a way to breathe new life into them with style. You almost want to cut this out of the book and create a cool piece of origami.

PAGE ELEVEN

Panel 1: Big splash. Angle on Batman, flanked by a trio of creepy giant androids that have emerged from the closets! These are the androids from Jae's insane cover, with dead eyes and scary claws and plenty of exposed mechanisms and wiring. The androids are serving Batman — he's in the middle, crouching, hands raised in scary grasping gestures — the huge androids on either side of him are lunging forward, mimicking/paralleling his grasping gestures with their huge, claw-like hands — grabbing at Mangubat, who's now firing at them with a gun, and Catwoman, who's vaulting and dodging, but getting grabbed! Batman is in the middle, looking like a grim and terrifying puppetmaster.

1. BRUCE'S VOICE: ...I look like a *villain*.

GP: Just a gorgeous splash page. Also worth noting: I wrote the robots you see here into the script after seeing the incredible robots Jae drew on the cover of issue #1. Sometimes your artist comes up with something awesome you never imagined. It's usually a good idea to jump on those things if you can.

EB: Best part of this book is seeing how Greg and Jae really play off each other and gave life to such creations as these steampunk robos.

JL: I hate drawing Catwoman because of Adam Hughes. I hate his Cover Run art book DC recently put out showcasing his covers. I simply hate it. Makes me sick to look at it. He's up there with the greatest illustrators of a nostalgic era long gone.

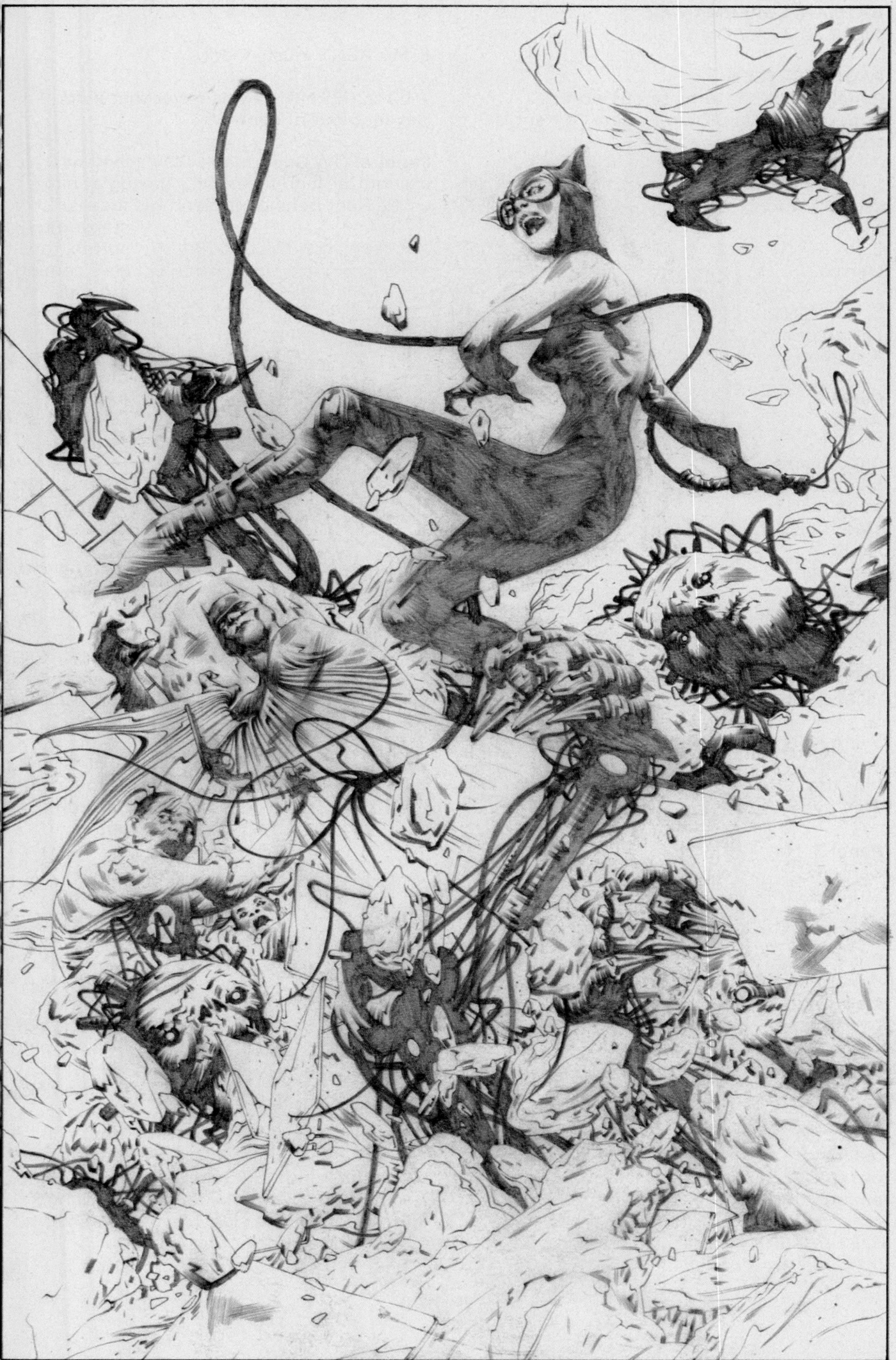

BATMAN/SUPERMAN #2
05.09.2013 - by Greg Pak

PAGE THIRTEEN

Panel 1: Ma Kent turns to our world's Superman. Eyes probing, calm. Pa Kent is trying to hold her back.

1. MA KENT: Now come over here where I can see you, young man.

PA'S ARM
MA
OW SUPES
MA'S HAND
E2 SUPES FLOATING
MA
PA
OW SUPES
MA
OW SUPES
MA HUGGING OUR WORLD SUPES

2. PA KENT: Martha...

3. MA KENT: Let go of me, Jonathan.

Panel 2: Angle on OW Superman's blank face as he half-stands and Ma Kent approaches. Ma Kent's fingers touch his cheek.

4. MA KENT: I know you.

5. MA KENT: You're my boy, too, aren't you?

Panel 3: Ma Kent and Superman gaze at each other. But Earth 2 Superman stares at the two of them dubiously. He's not interfering with his mother reaching out to OW Superman yet — but he's close enough to intervene if necessary.

5. E2 SUPERMAN: Ma... I'm not so sure —

6. MA KENT: Hush, Clark.

7. E2 SUPERMAN: I was never that ***wild***. Never so out of ***control***.

Panel 4: OW Superman's POV. Ma Kent's thoughtful, kind face. She's gazing at him/us. Pa Kent behind Ma Kent. His face is starting to soften, too. He's coming around.

8. MA KENT: Maybe this boy's just ***lost*** more than you ever did.

9. MA KENT: Tell me... ***Clark***...

Panel 5: OW Superman stares at her.

10. MA KENT: ... wherever you come from...

11. MA KENT: ... you lost ***us***, didn't you?

Panel 6: Tableau. Wide shot. Superman lowers his head. We can't see his face, but he's sobbing. Ma Kent's hand on his shoulder. This is his Ma. And she understands. E2 Superman and Pa Kent standing off to either side, silent, looking down or off to one side. Maybe Pa Kent's scratching the back of his head.

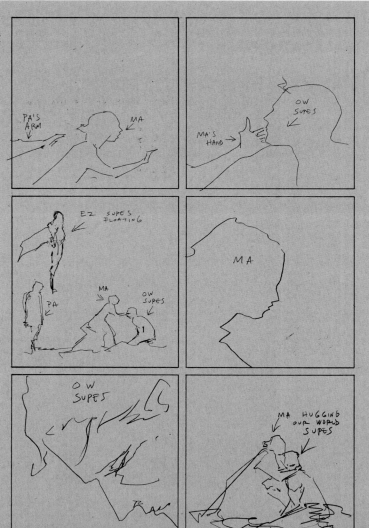

GP: *Jae's never scared to try something bold. And for this deeply emotional page, he went full silhouette, and it totally works.*

JL: *Greg wrote such a powerful scene here. Even Superman would buckle and fall to his knees in this situation. If I took a straightforward approach to this scene, I thought it would lose its emotional impact. By dropping everything in silhouette, the reader can see the anguish on Superman's face better than I could draw it. My drawing a close-up of a tear falling from his eye would be goofy. But if I have his head down and you can't see his face, there's more weight to the scene because you see what you want to see.*

EB: *An important lesson for all artists: sometimes less is so much more.*

BATMAN/SUPERMAN #3
07.01.2013 - by Greg Pak

PAGE TWENTY-ONE

Panel 1: Wonder Woman/Trickster shouts, stretching her arms out. Trickster's ghostly form is partly emerging from Wonder Woman and is kind of superimposed over her.

IMPORTANT: She's wound Wonder Woman's glowing lasso around herself! She speaks the truth!

1. TRICKSTER: The **survival** of your **worlds** hangs in the balance —

2. TRICKSTER: — and all you want to do is **destroy** the weapon that can **save** you?

3. TRICKSTER: **Hear me**, and know that this golden rope compels the **truth**!

Panel 2: Huge panel. Over Trickster's head swirls that horrific, silhouetted vision of Darkseid — slaughtering Supermen and Batmen from other worlds!

4. TRICKSTER: LORD DARKSEID OF APOKOLIPS COMES TO BURN YOUR WORLDS!

5. TRICKSTER: ALL THOSE YOU LOVE WILL DIE!

6. TRICKSTER: AND YOUR OWN SOULS WILL FEED THE FIRE!

Panel 3: Our four heroes squint as blinding white light surrounds them and that boom tube BOOOOM hits the air.

7. SFX: BOOOOOOOOM

8. TRICKSTER: NOW YOU MUST DECIDE —

GP: Here's another example of Jae departing from what the script literally asked for but absolutely nailing the spirit of the moment. This eerie, evocative moment of a stone monster god holding Superman's cape is far more menacing than a straight battle scene would have been.

JL: I could draw Darkseid forever. I love drawing ugly things.

EB: Gotta say we were all eager to see how Darkseid would come into play here. And this would lead to Greg's giving us even more background into the Lord of Apokolips and Kaiyo's role.

RP: Here's a little secret: The design of Kaiyo was actually an unused design we repurposed for use here. The original intent was to use a version of it for the New 52 debut of The Creeper! We went with a different design for him, switched up some things, and used the look here. Note the extra face on the back of her head.

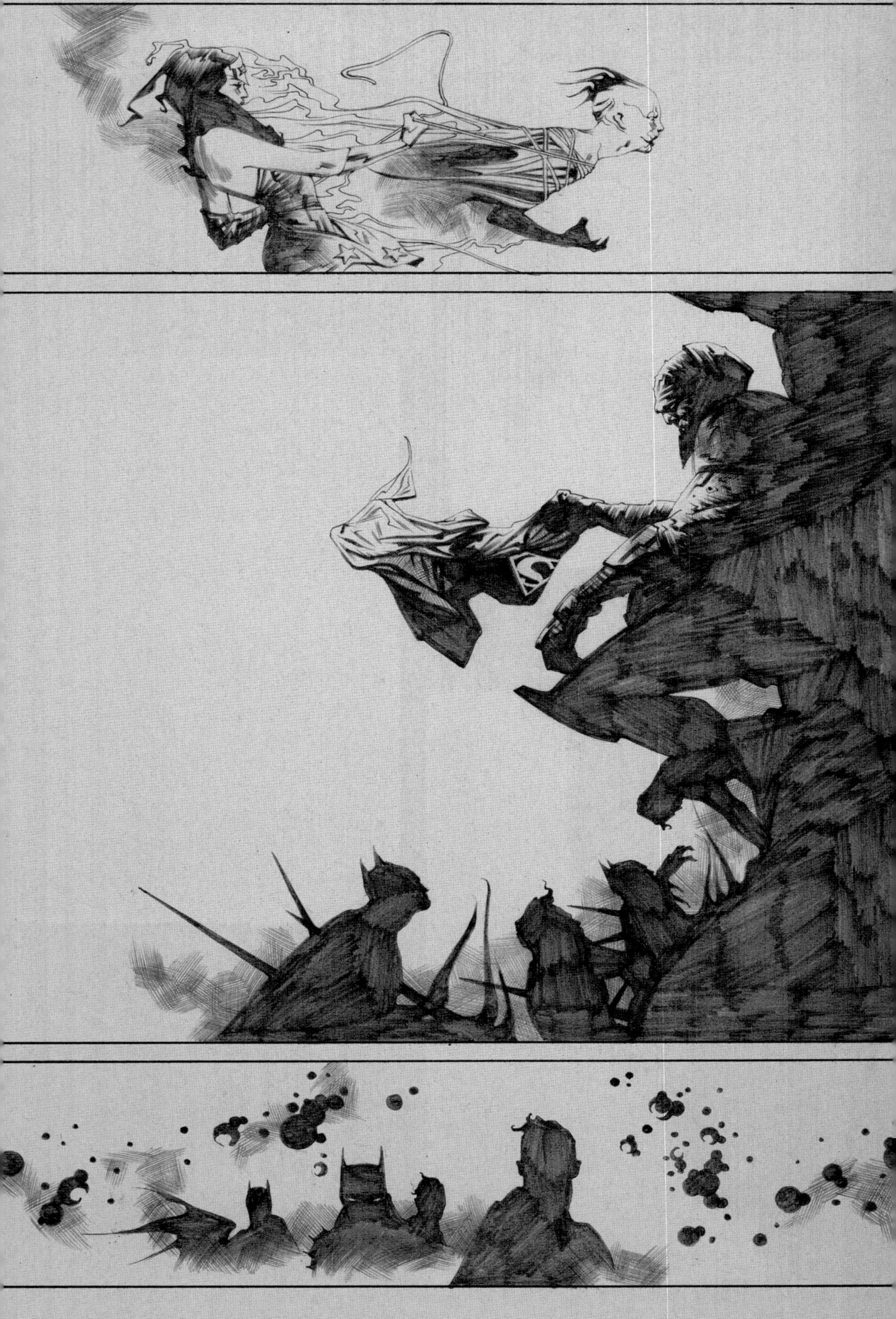

Jae Lee's cover sketches for BATMAN/SUPERMAN #1-4

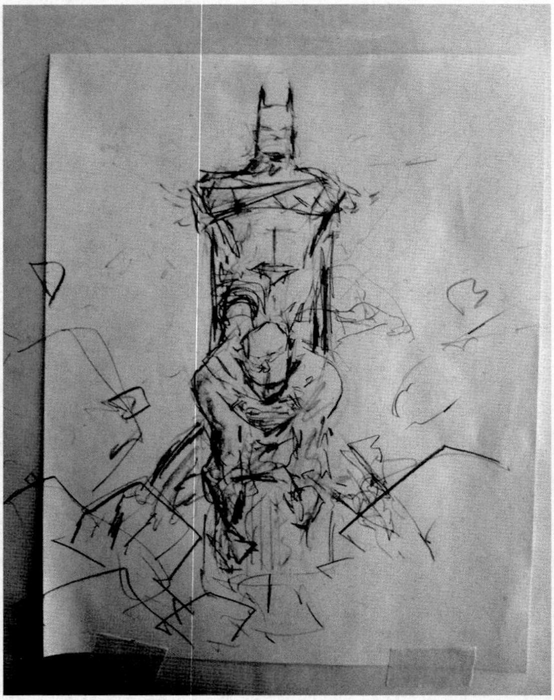

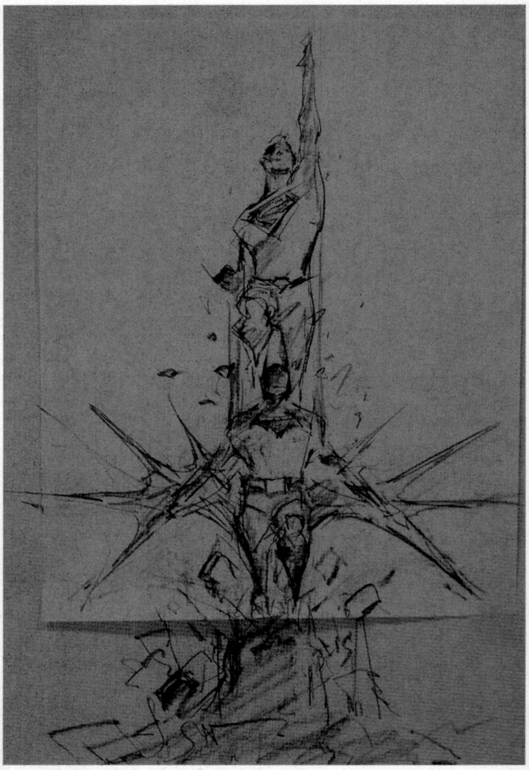

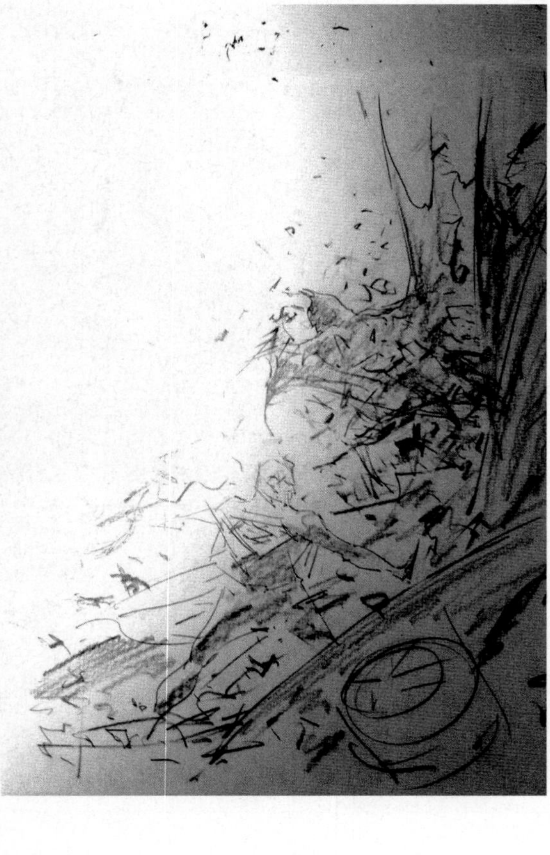

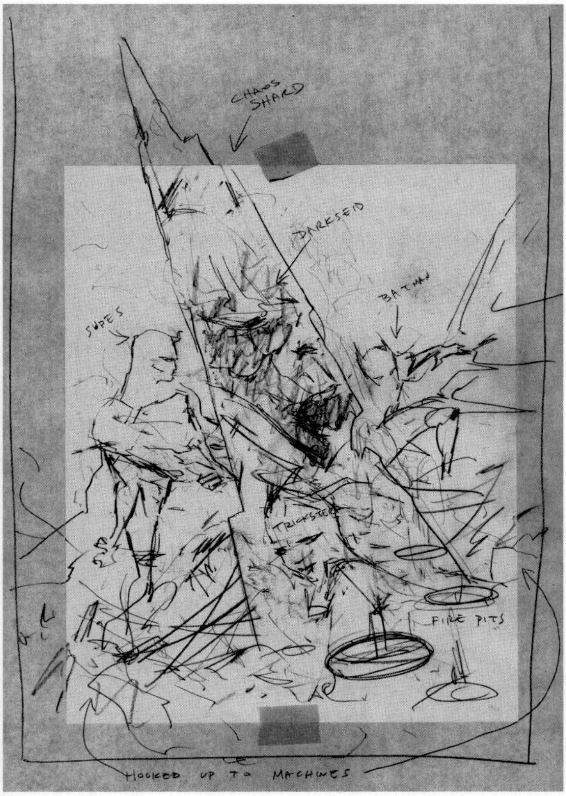
CHAOS SHARD
DARKSEID
BATMAN
SUPES
TRICKSTER
FIRE PITS
HOOKED UP TO MACHINES

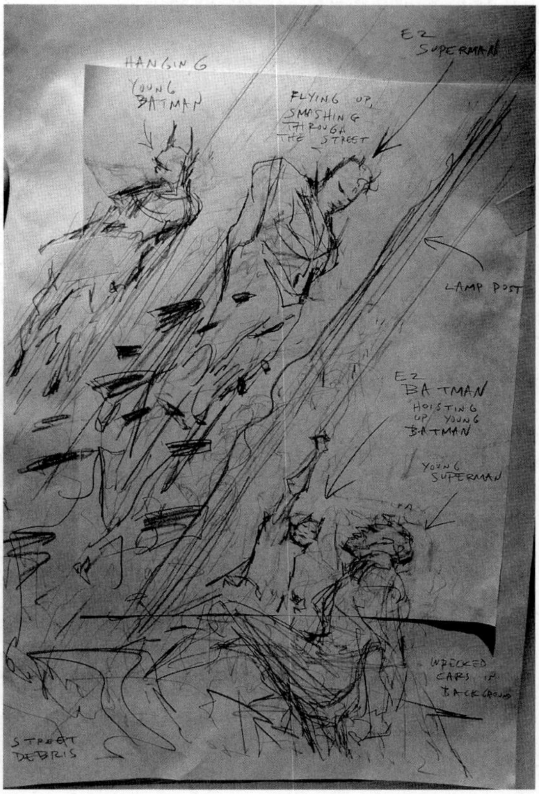
HANGING YOUNG BATMAN
E2 SUPERMAN
FLYING UP, SMASHING THROUGH THE STREET
LAMP POST
E2 BATMAN HOISTING UP YOUNG BATMAN
YOUNG SUPERMAN
WRECKED CARS IN BACKGROUND
STREET DEBRIS

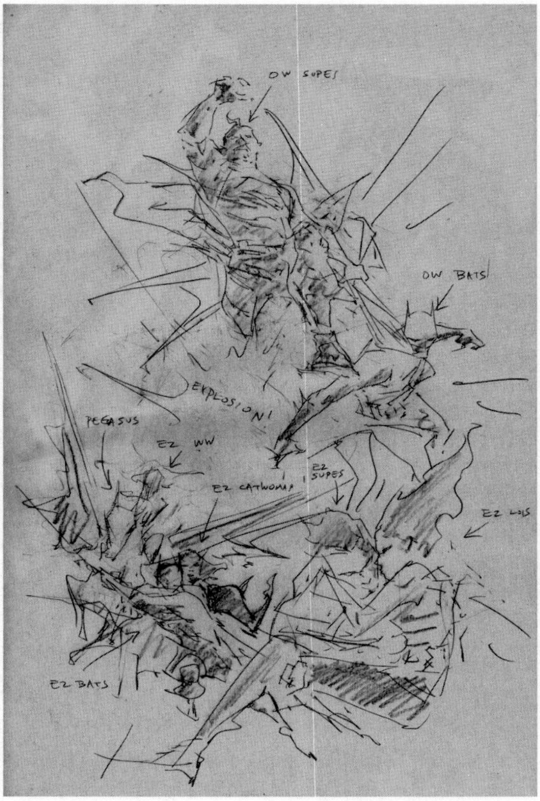
OW SUPES
OW BATS
EXPLOSION!
PEGASUS
E2 WW
E2 CATWOMAN
E2 SUPES
E2 LOIS
E2 BATS

DC COMICS
THE NEW 52!
JUSTICE LEAGUE
VOLUME 1 ORIGIN
"WRITTEN BY GEOFF JOHNS, WITH ART BY THE GODLY JIM LEE, JUSTICE LEAGUE IS A MUST READ."
– COMPLEX MAGAZINE
GEOFF JOHNS JIM LEE SCOTT WILLIAMS

THE NEW 52!
JUSTICE LEAGUE
GEOFF JOHNS JIM LEE SCOTT WILLIAMS

THE NEW 52!
JUSTICE LEAGUE
GEOFF JOHNS IVAN REIS PAUL PELLETIER TONY S. DANIEL

THE NEW 52!
JUSTICE LEAGUE OF AMERICA
GEOFF JOHNS DAVID FINCH BRETT BOOTH DOUG MAHNKE

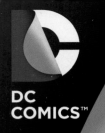

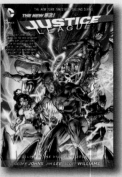

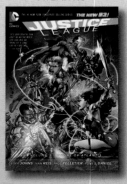

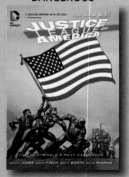

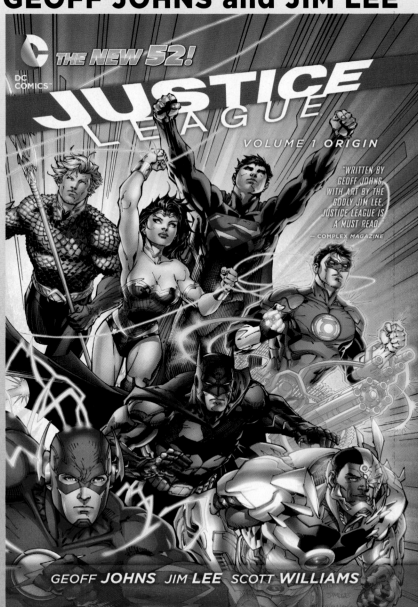